CHANGING CLASSROOM BEHAVIOR

Changing
Classroom Behavior

Second Edition

MERLE L. MEACHAM   *University of Washington*

ALLEN E. WIESEN   *Issaquah Professional Center, Washington*

Intext Educational Publishers   New York and London

Library of Congress Cataloging in Publication Data

Meacham, Merle L.
  Changing classroom behavior.

  Includes bibliographies.
    1. Teaching—Handbooks, manuals, etc.
2. Educational tests and measurements. I. Wiesen,
Allen E., joint author. II. Title.
LB1025.2.M4 1974   371.1'02   73-18431
ISBN 0-7002-2450-5

Intext Educational Publishers
257 Park Avenue South
New York, New York 10010

Contents

Preface to the Second Edition

An objective attitude toward one's own ideas is a prerequisite for progress. In the years since the publication of the first edition, our contacts with students, teachers, and parents, both in school and out, have been the primary criteria against which we have measured the validity of our premises. We are pleased that our theses have, with few exceptions, stood the rigorous test of confrontation with direct experience. But we must face these exceptions as well if we hope to make progress.

In this revision we have attempted to strengthen the role of humanism in our concept of humanistic behaviorism. Because the term *precision teaching* has become associated with a somewhat narrower and more rigid approach than we had in mind, we have decided to eliminate it from our discussion. We maintain that it is crucial to obtain objective measurements of student responses in many areas, and to rely on methods and concepts which have consistently proven themselves effective. Among these are positive reinforcement, programming, imitative learning, and now expectancy of outcome.

We have renamed our revised method *objective teaching*. This term reflects our basic assumption that it is our responsibility as educators to employ objectively tested methods and objective criteria of educational progress rather than relying on the essentially subjective methods that have proven themselves so inadequate in the past.

Objective teaching, then, subsumes the concepts of precision teaching and positive reinforcement, but includes as well the essential attitude of objectivity in regard to all teaching methods that are selected. The importance of an objective response rate as a criterion of classroom progress has not diminished in our thinking, but duration and intensity of behavior also deserves consideration. Our direct experience has further shown us that all behaviors are not equally amenable to empirical analysis.

Central to our thinking at this time is the idea that an educational system requires a view of man to guide it. This is not to suggest that we are proposing a rigidly defined educational "product," but rather a discernible direction toward which we feel the educational process must move if it is not to flounder haphazardly upon the rocky shores of faddish and fanciful assertions. We believe that a primary purpose of education ought to be the development of a self-directed person. In the school years, much of a child's behavior is directly or indirectly determined by others. He has little or no control over his environment. But education, as we perceive it, involves a gradual movement from an externally controlled environment to one in which the person himself has much greater relative control. The self-directed person has acquired the necessary communicative tools with which to express his choices and assume responsibility for them. But his options are broadened by his acquisition of skills which enable him to have a greater role in determining the shape his life will take. Without necessary educational skills, the person is more greatly limited by the whims of his environment; with them he can act to alter his environment with more success. Thus, we suggest that the primary rationale for a structured and programmed classroom is to facilitate the learning of skills which permit self-direction and increasing freedom from the control of the environment.

As in the first edition, *Changing Classroom Behavior* is divided into two parts. Part I, A Manual for Objective Teaching, outlines the specific principles of learning which can be applied by the classroom teacher to enhance learning and reduce or eliminate disruption. As before, we have supported our principles whenever practical with relevant findings reported in the psychoeducational literature. This is intended to give the reader further understanding of the derivation and application of the essential elements of objective teaching.

Part II, Additional Applications of Objective Teaching and Behavior Modification, brings together recent developments in retardation, social deprivation, and severely deviant behavior. In addition, this section provides further applications of objective teaching in the normal classroom.

We wish to give special acknowledgment to our wives who provided valuable editorial criticism throughout the preparation of the revised edition and who steadfastly stood by their sometimes tired and grumpy husbands without once resorting to physical violence.

Preface to the First Edition

An author does not merely write a book, he lives with it and it consumes most of his attention during the period in which it is written. This volume closely reflects our thinking at this time, and we feel it also reflects much of the thinking in contemporary education as well.

One of the most difficult problems we had was in keeping pace with our own philosophies of education. Some of the things we were certain about one month, we had some doubts about the next and, by the completion of the manuscript, we revised several of our earlier notions about education. The thought, "how could I have possibly said that," occurred more than a few times as we reread material written some months earlier.

The integration of what appear at first glance to be opposing philosophies—humanism and behaviorism—is an enormously humbling task. We feel, however, that a *humanistic behaviorism* offers the greatest promise for the education of students who will have to run a complex technological society but who must understand also that basic human needs should dictate the course of technological development.

Precision Teaching, as set forth in this volume, blends what we know as educators with what we know as behavioral scientists. We have attempted to provide rather specific guidelines for teachers regarding positive behavior change in the classroom, but have also included general directions in which education must go if it is to be relevant to the lives of people in these changing times.

Part I, A Manual for Precision Teaching, outlines the specific principles of learning which can be applied by the classroom teacher to enhance learning and improve behavior. We have backed the instructional material with research findings so as to give the reader a further understanding of the derivation and application of the principles of Precision Teaching.

Many of the studies reported in Part I have been carried out in classroom settings, but even if conducted elsewhere, the research has immediate relevance for the classroom teacher. We have chosen to include a chapter on ethical considerations and advise the reader to read it before applying the principles.

Part II, Additional Applications of Precision Teaching and Behavior Modification, brings together recent educational developments in retardation, social deprivation and severely deviant behavior as well as providing further applications of Precision Teaching in the normal classroom. This section is meant to round out the teacher's knowledge in areas closely related to classroom teaching. We hope that it will enable the teacher to communicate better with his colleagues in the mental health professions through mutual understanding and similar terminology.

Thanks are due to the hard working graduate students who contributed case material through class assignments and individual projects. While it is not possible to name them all we do wish to mention Mary Pneuman, Karen Musser, and Fred Vaughn whose experiences are detailed in the text. And we are grateful to our wives who mopped our weary brows and helped in many other ways during the preparation of the manuscript.

CHANGING CLASSROOM BEHAVIOR

Part I

A Manual
for Objective Teaching

1
The Challenge
of Objective Teaching

The classroom teacher is entrusted with the major responsibility of making the classroom an effective learning environment. Teaching and learning are interdependent terms: one can hardly regard something as having been *taught* if it has not been *learned*. Only objective measures of student learning are certain evidence of effective teaching.

Objective teaching is not merely a method, but an attitude as well. The objective teacher attempts to verify the effectiveness of his or her teaching skills, not in the shadow of subjectivity but in the light of objectivity. The objective teacher is not afraid to experiment with new teaching methods, but tends to choose those which have produced substantial evidence of their success. He is not afraid to innovate or modify existing methods, but he accepts responsibility for collecting sufficient data concerning his students' learning to assess the validity of his methods. He uses those methods which objectively promote the greatest degree of learning and rejects those which, while perhaps traditional, are less effective.

This attitude has gained surprising momentum in the last few years and is being endorsed by a rapidly growing number of teachers. Each day, new refinements occur which offer great opportunity for the teacher who is genuinely interested in making the classroom a successful learning environment.

Objective teaching has adopted many of the concepts of modern learning theory, particularly the use of precise terminology and careful observation of behavior. It is a system of education which evaluates its own methods and results from an objective viewpoint. The objective teacher makes adjustments in curricula, classroom procedures, and the manner in which he relates with students on the basis of information rather than guesswork.

But objective teaching, rather than being a totally new theory, is really a refinement of what many good and experienced teachers already practice. It is new in the sense that it calls for the revision of those practices that have no objective merits in terms of results. It does not place more demands on a teacher's most precious commodity—time—but it actually gives a teacher more time to do things which he must now pass over. Objective teaching is a tested and logical method of increasing the learning and motivation of all students. At the same time, it takes full account of the individuality of each student and provides an atmosphere in which creativity can flourish.

THE LANGUAGE OF OBJECTIVE TEACHING

The terms we have employed have been selected because they are easily understood and permit a more exact comprehension of the learning process. By becoming familiar with some of the terms, you will be able to communicate more clearly with school administrators and fellow teachers. Let us now look at some of the basic concepts and language of objective teaching.

Behavior

Objective teaching is concerned primarily with those activities that are observable. If the activity can be observed directly or even indirectly through instruments, then it is behavior. When a student is reading, you are observing "reading behavior." When he is talking, we speak of his "verbal behavior." The emphasis here is on what is known as public data. Behavior is public in the sense that it can be seen with general agreement as to what it is that is being observed. This permits far better description of student performance and allows for objective assessment of ability.

While objective teaching is based upon the precise study of classroom behavior, we are by no means denying the existence of a wide range of personal experiences, including thoughts and emotions. These subjective phenomena are attracting greater attention as subjects of study as we become increasingly aware of the role that our family and culture play in shaping the way we perceive ourselves, our fellow man, and the nature of society. It is important that the teacher recognize the degree to which he himself has been affected by the society in which he lives so that he does not interpret his students' behavior solely through his own frame of reference. Thus, the teacher is well advised to maintain the highest possible degree of objectivity in observing his students' behavior. Lack of bias, after all, promotes clear understanding which lies at the heart of great teaching and successful learning.

Behavior is often too complex to be observed accurately; to facilitate measurement, the *response*[1] is used. A response is a single completed action which has a clearly observable beginning and end. The response, as it is used in objective teaching, is voluntary. The student, therefore, is regarded as capable of emitting behavior on his own without it necessarily having to be triggered by a prior event, though certain stimuli can certainly prompt responses. Behavior, then, is broken down into smaller units—responses—which can be recorded. In the classroom, a student's spelling behavior might be broken down into the number of correct spelling responses. His class participation behavior could be measured by recording his hand-raising responses. The response may be considered a building block of behavior. Upon close examination, even many highly complicated behaviors are capable of being broken down into individual responses.

In later chapters you will be introduced to additional terms used in objective teaching. It should be quite easy for you to gain mastery of these, and you will find that your ability to communicate via these terms will be greatly facilitated.

UNDERSTANDING EACH STUDENT

New methods tend to create critics as well as advocates, and objective teaching is no exception. Critics of objective teaching usually attack the approach as being too cold and not allowing for the emotional growth of the individual student. They feel that an approach that is too scientific creates robotlike beings rather than human beings.

Quite contrary to these beliefs, objective teaching provides an atmosphere in which the individuality of each student—his uniqueness as a human being—can be truly actualized. The reason for this is quite simple. The approach requires that the teacher have some understanding of the particular likes and dislikes of each student, his present behavior in the classroom (academic and nonacademic), and his specific preferred activities. The teacher cannot make assumptions about the student but must actually observe him in action to obtain accurate information concerning his performance. Furthermore, he should learn what a student is likely to do in various school situations so that he can alter his environment for maximal learning. Above all, objective teaching emphasizes a student's present performance without excessively dwelling upon his past. This is not to say that the past has no influence on present behavior, but merely that only certain past events are really meaningful in understanding a student's present behavior. By bringing into question many of the unfounded ideas about how students are supposed to behave, objective teaching sets the stage for a truly creative atmosphere conducive to meeting the educational needs of all students.

[1]While the original use of the term in Pavlovian conditioning was reserved for a reaction to a stimulus, here we use response in an *operant conditioning context* in which it means a unit of emitted behavior not necessarily preceded by a stimulus.

THE CHALLENGE IS OURS

Traditional teaching methods are often based on the assumption that children have a sort of built-in mechanism which, given an average environment, will magically enable a child to learn as soon as he is "ready." If a child does not learn, the mechanism, and indirectly the child, is held to be faulty or deficient and incapable of future learning. Thus, if a child does not learn in a given school situation, it may be assumed that he cannot learn in any classroom. This, of course, you will recognize as faulty logic.

Objective teaching does not favor the assumption that built-in processes dictate the quality and quantity of a child's learning. If a child fails to learn, barring significant brain damage or a profound physical handicap, it suggests that the environment is responsible and not merely the child. Objective teaching involves establishing an environment in which optimal learning occurs, one in which there is a consistent relationship between a student's classroom performance and its consequences. Such a relationship is said to be *contingent*. What happens to a student in objective teaching is contingent upon what he does. Should a student fail to learn or should he misbehave, the classroom environment is explored to determine those ways in which it can be modified to promote learning. Objective teaching is based on the idea that *faulty learning is the product of a faulty environment rather than of a faulty student.* It provides specific ways to change the environment for the purpose of increasing a student's motivation to learn.

RESPONSIBILITY

While traditional philosophies of education have tended to view a sense of responsibility as a positive attribute, it is doubtful whether they have contributed much to its development. A student may be told repeatedly that he is responsible for a particular assignment or level of performance, but he will not act responsibly until he is motivated to do so. Unfortunately, attempts to motivate students frequently take a negative form: students who do not function at the level required by the teacher face disciplinary measures or poor grades. Such punishment is notoriously ineffective on large numbers of students who have easily surmised that while they are held nominally responsible for their behavior, they do not experience consequences directly related to it. They avoid punishment through evasive actions or by failing to attend school.

Objective teaching, on the other hand, adheres to the principle of contingent outcomes in which the student directly experiences the consequences of his behavior. The student is not merely told that he is responsible, but is actually held accountable by the outcomes his behavior produces. The student is rewarded for objective gains in academic and related classroom activities, not for the mere illusion of progress.

THE SKY'S THE LIMIT

Time and time again man has broken records thought to be unbreakable. He has exceeded limitations imposed by earlier men and shattered obstacles which have withstood all previous efforts. One would imagine that man would gradually come to realize that he cannot be certain of the limits he sets on progress, yet he continues to erect imaginary ultimates, dead-end streets of progress.

Unfortunately, teachers, too, may set imaginary limits on students. If they consider a child bright, they may spare no effort to ensure that he is provided an enriched classroom environment. On the other hand, if they consider a child dull, they assume that he is incapable of progressing much despite the environment, and they expect only minimal learning. Wherever it is used, objective teaching is demonstrating that we are not yet capable of predicting how much children are able to learn, and certainly not yet ready to pinpoint the limits of the individual child. Even psychological tests, long viewed as providing a measure of intellectual ability, are being pushed aside daily as children overcome the limitations of their supposed IQ's. Objective teaching is enabling us to stop the self-fulfilling prophecy which results when a child is provided an environment which coincides with his expected potential. Obviously, if a child is presumed to be "slow" and is consequently placed in a low-level environment, he will very likely learn at a low level. To then assume that it is the child's native inability to learn that is responsible is overlooking the obvious.

It is presumptuous of us to assume that we can predict an individual's ultimate potential. The changes in the learning environment possible through objective teaching offer vast promise. As teachers, the burden of developing an environment in which maximal learning can occur rests squarely on our shoulders.

THE CLASSROOM-LABORATORY

It has been said that a good teacher learns from his students. Objective teaching borrows heavily from this concept in treating the classroom not only as a room in which academic subjects are taught, but as a living educational laboratory in which new and creative teaching techniques are sought and evaluated without bias. The teacher is not merely a conveyor of information, but a trained observer whose area of study is the behavior of students in school. From his students' behavior, the teacher can learn those principles of teaching which are fundamental to rapid, efficient, and profound education.

Objective teaching, then, really involves a teacher-observer working in a classroom-laboratory. This provides an ideal opportunity to test the principles of behavior which have been firmly established and which will be presented in the chapters to follow. This method enables continuous evaluation of presented educational materials and teaching techniques. If a certain type of material does not result in successful learning, it may be modified or even rejected. If a particular student does not respond correctly to given material, material more appropriate for that student might be tried or other factors may be examined. What is important is that objective teaching emphasizes the unbiased review of classroom data rather than simply relying on the conventional use of curricula and techniques which may not result in adequate learning.

In this way, the teacher receives immediate feedback and is in a far better position to react appropriately to the actual educational needs and performance of his students. In the classroom-laboratory, the teacher must be prepared to assume the basic attitude of the unbiased observer and be ready to abandon his method, however attached he is to it, if it does not prove effective. In other words, in objective teaching it is the student's rate of progress which determines the next move. And, if one can assume that objective definitions of progress are approachable through democratic or philosophical methods, then there is additional credibility for objective teaching as a humanistic process which is sensitive to the immediate educational needs of students.

TEACHING AND PSYCHOLOGY

Objective teaching is very closely aligned with the current trends in psychology. As a matter of fact, the language of objective teaching and psychology overlap in so many areas that it is becoming increasingly difficult to differentiate the two professions as they meet in the educational area. This alliance, however, is particularly useful to the classroom teacher as it has resulted in specific applications of psychological principles to behavior and learning problems in the classroom. Since many academic problems are really those of disruptive classroom activities by students, the methodology of objective teaching, which makes provisions for these disruptive behaviors, proves especially fruitful. Through the concept of "interfering behavior" (Chapter 5), the classroom teacher can help the disruptive student overcome his behavior problem far more knowledgeably.

THE POSITIVE SIDE OF EDUCATION

For too many years children have entered school with hope and enthusiasm only to leave with pessimism and despair. There is no reason for this to continue. Objective teaching enables us to look at education from a perspective which has been obscured for too long—as a series of positive and successful learning experiences contributing to knowledge, personal satisfaction, and motivation to learn still more.

The emphasis on a contingent environment promotes the kind of consistent climate in which students can gain confidence as their correct responses bring about positive outcomes. Rather than squelching initiative and originality, objective teaching provides a child with a positive approach to problem solving. In the hands of a concerned teacher it becomes the soil in which an attitude of learning for learning's sake can take root and grow.

A contingent environment encourages a trusting relationship between teacher and student. This is also fertile ground in which a child's trust of his fellow man can flourish. Furthermore, this contingent, consistent environment permits the teacher to observe more clearly the esthetic qualities of human learning—the truly subtle patterns of learning which are a source of so much satisfaction to both student and teacher.

THE ETHICAL QUESTION

Far too often people become so impressed with new scientific and technological developments that they do not look closely enough into the ethical questions that surround their use. The authors have been highly impressed with the integrity of those who employ objective teaching techniques. Though neither author has ever witnessed flagrant or intentional misuse of the approach, it is still vital to explore the ethical implications of its use. We believe that objective teaching can only attain its goals when it operates within an environment in which human concerns predominate. Consequently, the reader is urged to read Chapter 8 with particular attention.

SUMMARY

In this introductory chapter we pointed out the change that is occurring in classroom teaching today and introduced the concept of objective teaching. Recent scientific developments in our understanding of human learning can now be directly applied in the classroom. The basic terms, *behavior* and *response*, were presented, and the concept of a *contingent* environment, in which the outcomes a student experiences are directly influenced by his behavior, was introduced.

We emphasized the teacher's ability to influence and improve student progress by modifying the classroom environment, and underlined the importance of objectivity.

Objective teaching fosters a sense of responsibility in students by exposing them to the logical consequences of their actions. Improvement in academic and related social behavior receives deserved recognition.

The teacher may actually be regarded as a teacher-observer working in a classroom-laboratory, modifying his own actions in accordance with his data—the performance of his students.

Objective teaching derives many of its concepts from current knowledge of learning principles in psychology, and the two fields blend in the classroom.

While precise use of these new principles in teaching are encouraged, we also recognize the individuality and human integrity of each student. Objective teaching establishes an environment in which creativity and warm personal relations between teacher and student flourish. We emphasize the teacher's need to be objective without diminishing his need to be human.

SUGGESTED READINGS

Brown, D. G. *Behavior modification in child, school and family mental health: an annotated bibliography.* Champaign, Illinois: Research Press, 1972.

Goodall, K. Who's who and where in behavior shaping. *Psychology Today,* 1972, **6** (6), 58.

Krishnamurti, J. *Life ahead.* New York: Harper and Row, 1966.

London, P. The end of ideology in behavior modification. *American Psychologist,* 1972, **27** (10), 913–920.

Meacham, M. L. Reinforcement theory as a basis for clinical school psychology. *Psychology in the Schools,* 1968, **5**, 114–117.

Michael, J., & Meyerson, L. A behavioral approach to counseling and guidance. *Harvard Educational Review,* 1962, **32**, 382–402.

Skinner, B. F. Humanistic behaviorism. *The Humanist,* 1971, 31, 35.

Ullmann, L. P., & Krasner, L., *Case studies in behavior modification.* New York: Holt, Rinehart & Winston, 1966 (especially pp. 1–63).

Woody, R. H. Behavior therapy and school psychology. *Journal of School Psychology,* 1966, **4**, 1–14.

2
Measuring Behavior
in the Classroom

WHY MEASUREMENT?

We conceive of the classroom as a laboratory in which there is a continuous complex of experiments. The teacher is the manager of the laboratory with the task of so arranging the learning environment as to maximize the desired changes in the behavior of the students. In experimental terms, the teacher's behavior is the *independent variable* and the student's behavior the *dependent variable*, i.e., the teacher makes changes in the classroom environment which are intended to effect changes in the behavior of students; thus the behavior of students is dependent on the behavior of the teacher. This is true for academic as well as nonacademic behaviors. It is also true, as we will see later, that many student behaviors influence the teacher and to some extent control him. For our purposes, however, we will concentrate on the role of the teacher as one who can systematically arrange the major classroom variables which he changes in order to get specific learning outcomes. All of this takes precise measurement.

There are three major kinds of teacher behaviors. The first consists of those which are designed to elicit some response from the student. These are instructional in nature and include such activities as asking questions, demonstrating processes, presenting materials, listening to recitations, etc. There are innumerable instances of these, and they often fall in the category of behaviors that are taught in "methods" courses. However, they all have a similar purpose and that is to get the student to make a substantial contribution to the learning process.

If the teacher asks, "What number, when multiplied by five, will give twenty?" he hopes to elicit the response "four." All of this careful delineation of the subject matter is called *programming* (see Chapter 7) and is a systematic way to describe the presentation of eliciting stimuli with the intent of producing specific student behavior. Much of a teacher's time is taken with this kind of activity both in and out of the classroom. A great deal of effort is given, and rightly, to planning activities which will make it possible for children to learn or respond.

The second major kind of teacher behavior is responding to what the student does. This may include some favorable or unfavorable comment, a smile, a frown, a mark on a paper, physical contact, or any number of things. It is some indication to the student that his behavior has been noted and is being evaluated in some way. This area of teacher behavior is one of the most neglected and yet one of the most important (see Chapters 4 and 5). For how we respond to children is closely related to how and what they learn. We can inhibit learning or enhance it by our responses.

The third major kind of teacher behavior is setting goals for children or helping them set their own goals. We discuss this in detail in Chapter 3. These involve both academic and nonacademic goals and depend very much on a thorough understanding of the student: where he "is" at the moment, what he is capable of achieving, and what steps will be necessary to help him towards these goals. This is not a static process but one which must constantly be revised in the face of new data. Ideally the goals are so selected that the youngster can achieve them with reasonable effort and experience success, and so stated that they are clearly recognizable by both the student and the teacher.

These three kinds of teacher behaviors, then, are broad categories from which we can select independent variables which we hope will effect changes in student behaviors. Generally we wish to increase the speed and accuracy of learning and to decrease errors and disruptive behaviors. To do this we make systematic changes in what the teacher does and observe if this affects what the child does.

We can classify the learner's behavior in two broad categories—academic and nonacademic. If we think of academic behavior as anything related to the goals of the curriculum, then we can include even such things as good social relations, ability to share, etc. Whatever the categorization, there are generally those behaviors that the teacher wishes to maintain or obtain and those he wishes to diminish or eliminate. The former, those to be maintained, may include such activities as studying, reciting, asking questions, and attending to the teacher. The latter, those to be eliminated, may include fighting, talking, inattention, and anything that interferes with learning. All of these are dependent variables for they are related to the environmental stimuli of the classroom. They "depend on" the conditions of the classroom. Since the teacher is in a position to largely control the events in the classroom, it is an important thesis of this book that there is a close relationship between what the teacher does and what students do, that to a very significant extent the behavior of the students depends on the behavior of the teacher. Thus a wild, disrupted classroom is just as much a function of teacher behavior as a quiet, studious one; one child's lack of progress is just as much a function of teacher behavior as another's rapid progress. This requires considerable sensitivity on the part of the teacher in regard to his own behavior and, at the same time, makes it vitally necessary to find those independent variables which produce the desired student behaviors. It also necessitates careful definition and objective measurement.

It is in the definition or description of these behaviors that the teacher may encounter some difficulty. As a general rule, there is little or no precision in describing the behavior of either the teacher or the student, and without this precision it is exceedingly difficult to determine (a) what the teacher is doing, (b) what the students are doing, and (c) if "a" is influencing "b" or if something other than "a" is influencing "b." The question we must ask again and again is *what effect, if any, does our behavior have on our students' behavior?*

If this sort of question seems esoteric or even silly let us look at the following example. Most teachers want good discipline. They may use various techniques to achieve this, but a common one recommended in many books and by many principals is "firm kindness." If the reader examines this phrase closely, he will soon realize that it allows for considerable breadth of interpretation, for it is a convenient abstraction rather than a precise term. For one teacher, good discipline may mean quiet, orderly children who remain seated unless specifically directed to do otherwise and who do not initiate contact with other children without first contacting the teacher. The evidence for good discipline would be a quiet orderly classroom.

To another teacher good discipline may involve reasonably orderly, though often enthusiastic, children moving around pretty much at will but involved in problem-solving tasks, frequently asking questions and getting into debates—in short, children excited and talkative about learning. Both of these instances of good discipline could be more specifically defined by measures such as the rates of academic behavior and disruptive behavior. However, the desired rates would vary significantly from teacher to teacher.

In our example, both teachers may see themselves as responding to children with "firm kindness," but we could predict that there would be different emphases on the "firm" and the "kindness." We might get closer to the real situation if we classified the behaviors of the teachers as "approving" and "disapproving" and obtained adequate measures of each. Then we would at least have a ratio of some fairly specific measures. The point is obvious: if we are to know what it is in the teacher behavior that is affecting changes in student behavior, we must deal with specifics and not abstractions. It is convenient and worthwhile to classify behaviors if we carefully define the specifics that go into the classification. For example, there could be various verbal and nonverbal behaviors that we label "approving." Verbal could include such statements as "fine," "good," "correct," and nonverbal could include nods, smiles, and pats on the back. Then we could treat these as a group and relate them to student behaviors. The more we can reduce ambiguity and the more we can describe objectively what it is that teachers and students do, the closer we can come to knowing what it is that makes a difference in the behavior of children. As we achieve greater precision in describing behavior, we are in a far better position to make specific changes in our own classroom behavior and to observe changes in student behaviors. Then the next step is to effect predictable changes in student behavior, and this is the essence of good teaching.

Good classroom management and good learning management depend, then, on precise, observable, behavioral measurements. Data gathering of this sort may require a good deal of ingenuity on the part of the teacher. Defining precisely what it is that one is interested in and how to go about measuring it is not always easy. However, the rewards are great. The teacher can make predictable changes in student behavior and exercise sufficient knowledge of important classroom variables to make this come about. In this chapter and the rest of the book, we shall give many examples of various ways in which teachers and psychologists have selected and measured behaviors. While these are not exhaustive, we hope that they are varied enough to suggest many approaches to the interested teacher who can then go on to create new and more ingenious ways of describing and measuring behavior.

While *rate*, the number of occurrences of a behavior per a selected period of time, and *frequency*, the actual number of times a selected behavior occurs, are the most commonly used measures of behavior, there are other dimensions that are frequently important if less subject to precise measurement. One of these is *duration*, which is often converted to a frequency or rate measurement by taking time samples. For example: out-of-seat behavior may have a very low frequency because it has a very long duration! A child may simply wander around the class for most of the hour and rate or frequency would not be a very meaningful measure unless, as is frequently done, his behavior was sampled every 10 or 15 seconds. Then each sample could be treated as a separate instance with the teacher obtaining a frequency count and establishing a rate. Another very useful measure of duration is simply to accumulate the time on a stopwatch; this is probably much easier for the teacher or teacher aide.

Saslow and Kanfer (1969) suggest two other dimensions that we tend to use subjectively but which are important in our judgments about behavior. These are *intensity* and *appropriateness*. We observed a youngster recently hitting a male teacher. However, the blows to the shoulder were very light and were received as they were intended as a show of affection. They were accompanied by much laughter and mock ferocity, much different than blows struck in anger. Yet both could be labeled "hitting behavior" differing greatly in intensity and meaning. Although some behaviorists would have us not ascribe meaning to behavior, since this is a subjective process, we feel that each time we select a behavior for attention it is partly on the basis of the meaning we ascribe to that behavior. We feel that since we are making subjective judgments based on intensity of response and its contextual meaning we should do this openly, then others can check us if we err.

Identical responses may be quite acceptable in one situation and not in another, thus appropriateness of behavior is a criterion we use in making judgments about a child. "Talk-outs" may be expected during a discussion period and completely unacceptable during a spelling lesson. It seems clear that the most objectively oriented teacher must also be subjective if he is to deal honestly with the situations he finds in his classroom. However, he will endeavor to be aware of those times in which subjective impressions are influencing him and he will try to obtain as much objective data as he can. At this state of the art and science it is impossible to measure everything that goes on in the classroom. We get what data we can and use it within the context of what we know to be important. The objectively oriented teacher, however, continually seeks ways to become more objective. In the following section we will look at some of the ways of gathering data and measuring behavior.

GETTING BASERATES

In order to know if we have made a change in the behavior of students or in our own behavior, we need a reference point from which to measure that change. Therefore, the first step in changing behavior is to get a measure of the amount or rate of the behavior that is occurring naturally in the classroom. We call this measure the *baserate* or *baseline,* and this becomes our reference point. Any change we note in the occurrence of the behavior after we change some classroom variable is a change from the baseline.

It is essential in getting adequate measures of the initial rate of any behavior to take measures of it over a reasonable period of time in the setting in which it is to be changed. The behavior of children, and adults for that matter, is often rather "stimulus specific," i.e., it appears in one situation and not another. Note the differential responses of most girls to a mathematics class as compared to a language arts class. A common example for counselors and school psychologists is that the child who is quite disruptive in class is not disruptive or even surly while being tested and counseled. This leads many of them to seek to provide changes in the classroom where the behavior is occurring "naturally" rather than in the different setting of the private office. Behavioral psychologists have found that it is more efficient to change behavior where it occurs than where it does not.

To get baserates we count clearly defined responses within a given period of time or over a period of timed samples. Let us look at the baserate of both an academic response and a nonacademic response in order to get a clearer picture of just what is done.

As an integral part of good classroom management, most teachers keep records of various aspects of their students' academic behavior. This is frequently percentage correct in such things as spelling and arithmetic or assigned grades in reading or theme writing. The latter (grades) do not really tell us very much about the child's academic behavior unless we know the specifics underlying the abstract grade. All too often it is a qualitative judgment that has little reliability. What does tell us something about the child's academic behavior is how much he accomplishes in a given period of time.

One of the authors recently taught a class for a group of experienced teachers in which they were to keep data on a student's behavior as well as on their own. This was accomplished by having the teachers work in pairs, one keeping data while the other taught. This was something of a "micro-teaching" situation since they were teaching only one student. However, these youngsters had been selected because they needed special help in various subject-matter areas. The teaching teams were instructed to obtain baserates for various academic behaviors and then institute changes and record the youngster's behavior.

One team, working with a ten year old girl, was interested in helping her with simple multiplication facts. The teachers established a baserate for "twos and threes" by testing her for 10-minute periods and found that she did about 17 correct multiplications in that time. Then they established baserates on their own behavior in the categories of "approving," "disapproving," and "instructional." Taking counts during 10-minute periods, they found that for one of the team members there were 44 instances of approving behavior, 42 of instructional, and one of disapproving. (An interesting sidelight to this experience for all the teachers was how little disapproving behavior they used when it was being observed and recorded.) Once the baserates were established, the team made systematic variation first in eliciting stimuli by introducing "fours" and later "fives," and found that the accuracy rate remained fairly constant. Then they lowered the amount of approving behavior to one third of what it had been but maintained a close approximation of the previous instructional and disapproving behaviors. They found that the accuracy rate held up. In other words, this little girl continued to learn at the same rate with less necessity for approval. The important thing here is that these teachers knew precisely what the youngster could do with specific materials and at what rate she learned these materials. They also gained some insight into their own behavior as it related to the learning process. They might have put a grade on her work but this would have been much less meaningful than the knowledge of what the girl specifically accomplished.

In another instance, to demonstrate a nonacademic behavior or group of behaviors, a team decided that their little 7-year-old boy was having great difficulty because he was emitting so many disruptive behaviors. He was doing things fairly continuously that interfered with learning since he could not attend to instructions while so engaged. Most of these were audible: grunts, groans, bang-ings, and all those things that active little boys can get involved in. The teachers took three 5-minute samples of the youngster's behavior during instructional time in which they counted all instances of audible disruptive behaviors. There were 46 of these altogether, or slightly over 15 per session. He was a fairly noisy little boy! To control this, the teachers put the boy on a *token system* and gave approval for quiet behavior (see Chapter 4), and these disruptive behaviors dropped to zero. They increased the sessions to 15 minutes and then 20 and 25 minutes. The behaviors remained at zero until they considerably reduced the approval, which resulted in a slight increase. The teachers demonstrated quite clearly that this child could change his behavior dramatically and that he was able to control those activities that would markedly interfere with his learning and be quite disturbing to the teacher and the rest of the class. The significant data are in Table 1. Note the dramatic change from the baserate. From an average of 15.3 disruptions for a 5 minute session or 46 for a 15-minute session he dropped to .8 and 4 respec-tively by the fifth day.

Table 1

	5 Minute Rate	Total Time (min.)	Total Frequency
Baserate	15.3	15	46
1st day	0	15	0
2nd day	0	15	0
3rd day	0	20	0
4th day	1.8	25	9
5th day	.8	25	4

These teachers were involved in other kinds of learning problems with this child, but they could not go on until they had helped him to control this behavior. We will discuss in considerable detail the techniques for controlling and changing behavior in later chapters. This simple example, however, graphically illustrates the value of the baserate and data collection in demonstrating the efficacy of teacher controlled variables.

Occasionally it is desirable to obtain a *multiple baseline*. For example a teacher may be interested in many disruptive behaviors and wish to check the effect of his behavior on all of them in some systematic way. He then obtains a baseline for each behavior under ordinary conditions and checks how, e.g., his decreased attention to these behaviors affect them. In order to know the specific effects he must change his behavior to each of the disruptive behaviors sequen-tially. Barton et al. (1970) were interested in the effect of a *time out* procedure on several eating behaviors of mentally retarded children. They systematically varied the time out for four undesirable eating behaviors and demonstrated that those behaviors did decrease in frequency. While this is a technique more frequently used in research than in a regular classroom situation it is one that can be helpful in determining the effects of teacher behavior on a multiplicity of student behaviors.

GATHERING DATA AND RECORD KEEPING

In this discussion of baserates, we have already given some ideas about data gathering and recording. Most teachers keep accurate records of their students' academic progress although these are not often kept as rates, i.e., the amount done in a given period of time. Most behavioral psychologists feel that the rate is a more desirable kind of record than just a percentage correct because it gives us a much more specific idea of how much a child can do as well as how accurately. Children who have the same accuracy score may have taken quite different amounts of time; we generally are concerned with increasing the rate at which a child learns as well as how accurate he is. For most academic responses, however, this means only a simple addition to the bookkeeping—that of recording the amount of time for the activity. During the usual school day it is not too difficult for most teachers to develop a routine of allotting certain times for certain activities. Then, for those students who seem particularly slow or fast, the teacher can gather accurate data and seek means to individualize the instruction.

But another aspect of data gathering is keeping records of behavior that is not usually recorded. This may take a little extra effort but, if the behavior is important, changing it can be of benefit to the child, the teacher, and the class in the long run. One device that is very useful for counting instances of behavior is the simple wrist counter such as golfers use. Lindsley (1968) describes one such device that gave satisfactory service over thousands of counts. It is unobtrusive and always available. It can be reset easily and you can readily transfer the data to a more permanent form. Suppose a teacher is interested in a particular youngster who is "never in his seat." This is a form of disruptive behavior that annoys the teacher and interferes with other children. However, with a wrist counter, the teacher can record all instances of this behavior from anywhere in the room, accumulate data for its occurrence at various times of the day and then accurately note changes as classroom conditions are changed. Many disruptive behaviors change dramatically when they are ignored by the teacher and the incompatible behavior (in this case sitting) is given some attention.

If more complex data are required, such as rates on individual children, these can be recorded at each child's desk by taping a data sheet on the corner of the desk which the teacher marks when necessary. A simple one would have the hours on the vertical axis and 5-minute intervals along the horizontal. This would provide a time record of a specific behavior or several behaviors. For each behavior the teacher could use a different symbol. Then there would be a continuous record of the time and quantity of the behavior. For example, a teacher might be interested in the number of teacher-initiated contacts as compared to the number of student-initiated contacts. These could be easily recorded at the student's desk and the data used for general or specific planning.

Perhaps the best way to record behavior is to have someone else do it. This is not as unreasonable as it may seem at first, for there is increasing interest in providing teacher aides for many classrooms. What better use is there for a teacher aide than gathering accurate data for the teacher so that he can maximize the effectiveness of his teaching? While it would be necessary to train teacher aides in these techniques (as it is also necessary to train experienced teachers), the task is not difficult and is much more relevant to the educational process than counting milk money or handing out papers. We envision the future classroom with the teacher as the director of the teaching process and with decisions based on accurate data gathered by paraprofessionals. Until that time, one may have the opportunity to utilize student-teachers, the principal (if he's going to be in the classroom anyway, put him to work), or some volunteer parents. The observer-recorder becomes more effective as a data gatherer as he becomes familiar with the classroom procedures and so accepted by the students and the teacher that he blends into the background. He is in an excellent position to make detailed observations over a long period of time. This frees the teacher to concentrate on teaching and behaving "naturally," something which contributes to the validity of the data.

In some instances students are required by the teacher to keep data on themselves. This presents some minor problems as far as reliability is concerned, although this can be controlled by occasional spot checks. A common side effect of this data recording technique is the diminution of some undesirable behavior if the student is responsible for recording its frequency. This is particularly true if there is some reward coupled with the diminution. One teacher reported that she had a youngster who was "always out of his seat." After all the usual admonitions failed, she had him record his own out-of-seat behavior by marking a data sheet on his desk each time it happened. He was easily convinced of just how much he had been moving around when he had to keep the records, and this behavior rapidly diminished under teacher praise for fewer marks. Before this she had been giving an unusual amount of attention to the inappropriate behavior and, as we shall see in Chapter 5, this only encouraged it.

SOME MEASURED BEHAVIORS

In this section we will examine some studies that illustrate further the process of measuring behavior and obtaining baselines. These are all actual cases of behavioral measurement, some involving psychologists who were doing research and were after rather complex data and others involving graduate students in a seminar on behavior modification. However, they share a common goal: to isolate behaviors and outcomes which could be measured and related to other student and teacher behaviors.

One graduate student was called on to improve the behavior of a 14-year-old girl in an eighth-grade junior-high-school science class. This girl was disruptive in the class, usually through talking to other students and "bothering" them. She also spent a lot of time "doing nothing" and very little time studying or doing the assigned work. After observing the girl and talking with the teacher, the graduate student decided that she would observe and record three categories of behavior: (1) talking (other than to the teacher or in line with the assigned work), (2) gazing (looking around the room, at the clock, or at other students without talking), and (3) working (any participation in the required laboratory work). She obtained her baseline data by observing and recording the behavior of the girl at 10-second intervals for 15 minutes of class on three days. She found, to no one's surprise, that the girl spent 40% of her time gazing, 45% talking, 2% working, and the balance in categories not classified. Percentages were used in this case since the graduate student wished to extrapolate her data to the entire period and she felt that this would be more meaningful to the teacher. These percentages, then, became the reference points from which she could measure any change. This was the "natural" behavior in the setting in which it was to be changed.

When modification procedures were instituted, in this case a token system, the behavior changed to 9% gazing, 13% talking, and 74% working. This was certainly a major shift and was very satisfying to the teacher. A change such as this would have been noticed without explicit data; however, they form a record of comparison at any future date. They provide observable, behavioral evidence of the efficacy of the procedure. The gathering of the baseline data in this applied study did not take much classroom time (45 minutes), nor did it involve very complex recording devices—one stopwatch, pencil and paper, and one graduate student. However, the results for the teacher and the girl were very significant. Not only was there dramatic positive change, but it could be measured, demonstrated, and replicated.

A much more complex series of measurements is illustrated in a study by Thomas et al. (1968). These research psychologists were interested in exploring the relationship between teacher behavior and the disruptive classroom behavior of primary age children. It is worth our while to take a detailed look at their method of getting baserates since they studied many behaviors, all of which interest teachers.

The teacher behaviors were frequency counts that fell into three major categories: (1) disapproving behavior, (2) approving behavior, and (3) instructional behavior. Each of these categories contained several subclasses. For example, disapproving behavior was further divided into (a) physical contact (grabbing, hitting, spanking, shaking, slapping, or pushing a child), (b) verbal (yelling, scolding, raising voice, belittling, or making fun of a child), and (c) facial (frowning, grimacing, side-to-side head shaking, and gesturing).

There were similar subclasses for approving behavior and for instructional behavior with just as detailed descriptions. The measures of these behaviors were also in frequency counts. Complex? Perhaps, but illustrative of the kinds of behavior that have significant impact on children.

The children's behavior was also divided into classes after careful observation and consultation. The research team recognized five classes of disruptive behavior: (1) gross motor (getting out of seat, standing up, walking around, hopping, skipping, jumping, rocking the chair, kneeling in the chair, arm flailing, etc.), (2) noise making (tapping feet, clapping hands, tearing papers, etc.), (3) verbalization (crying, screaming, singing, whistling, laughing, coughing, talking with other children, etc.), (4) orienting (turning head or body toward another person, showing objects to another child, looking at another child, etc.), and (5) aggressions (hitting, pushing, shoving, pinching, slapping, striking, poking with objects, grabbing objects from another child, destroying objects, etc.).

There was only one class within which appropriate behavior could be recorded (which may tell us something about children of this age!). At any rate, these behaviors were such things as looking at the teacher, raising hand and waiting for the teacher to respond, writing answers to workbook problems, reading assigned materials, etc. Then there was a category of "other tasks" which fit none of these aforementioned classes. All of these behaviors were measured under standard conditions, i.e., in the usual classroom setting, by trained observer-recorders. Once the baserates were established, it was possible for the research team to systematically modify the teacher's behavior and note the results on the various categories of student behavior.

This study illustrates very nicely that complex human relationships can be broken down for the purposes of research and classroom management into rather specific responses. We can then count these responses, introduce changes into the classroom, and measure the effect of these changes in a precise manner. Teachers who use behavioral techniques may not be involved in such complicated measurements as those in this experiment, but the process is the same. If the teacher wishes to know the effect that his behavior or some environmental modification is having on his students, he needs to record data. The data need to be relevant to the specific behaviors of the students so that they can be gathered again and again while the teacher introduces changes.

Let us look at one final example, a rather simple one in terms of data collection, in which a teacher was able to help a counselor make significant changes in the behavior of several first-grade boys by recording the necessary data.

The problem with these little boys was that they tended to fight on the playground during recess. The more the teacher attended to this, the more it seemed to increase, so that there was a kind of vicious circle going with the teacher getting increasingly upset and the little boys fighting more and more. At this point the counselor was called in and tried first to get the boys to change their behavior through a kind of play therapy. That is, they were taken out of the classroom at specific times for a period of special play with the counselor while he tried to help them develop better interpersonal relationships. This seemed to increase the playground fighting since the boys liked the counselor and the special attention and found that the best way to get it was to fight on the playground. The counselor then hit on a very simple idea. The teacher was to observe the youngsters during recess and if a child fought, his name was to be written on the board in the classroom. Thus the only information the teacher had to record was "fighting behavior" and this was pretty easy to observe. When the counselor came to get the youngsters for the special play period, he took only those whose names had not been written on the blackboard. Playground fighting soon ceased. There was no longer the constant friction between the teacher and the children, and learning proceeded in a much more orderly and friendly manner. What happened here was that the teacher and counselor stopped rewarding or *reinforcing* undesirable behavior and made the reward contingent on the desirable behavior. (These ideas are fully covered in Chapter 4.) Data keeping was not difficult but it was a very necessary part of the modification process.

To reiterate, then, the first step in good classroom management is to collect accurate information about what is going on. This can consist of academic response rates, error rates, accuracy rates, disruptive behavior rates, study behavior rates, or various aspects of the teacher's behavior. With good measurement the teacher can be much more efficient in controlling those variables which control the learning process. When data are kept regularly, there is a constant feedback of information as to the effectiveness of various teaching methods so that they can be maintained or altered to meet the conditions of the class or particular children. The net result is that the children benefit by having a more knowledgeable teacher, and the teacher benefits by having more control over what goes on in his classroom. With reference to our original question, he will know whether or not what he is doing makes a difference.

LEARNING TO GATHER DATA

No book can teach you to take data. You must get involved in the process in order to learn to do it reliably and accurately. However, here are suggestions of ways to learn to collect data that have proved successful with teachers in training. Probably the most difficult part is to decide on the specific and then attend only to that. It is very easy to get distracted until one has had a little practice, then data gathering becomes fairly routine.

A very good way to learn and to check the reliability of the data is to have a film or video tape of a classroom in operation. Decide first on some simple behavior such as a count of the number of times the teacher is verbally approving, and run the film or tape. At first there may be some disagreement as to the actual count but with repeats and careful delineation of the specific manifestations of the behavior, there will soon be surprising reliability among a large number of observers.

After this, it is desirable to increase the complexity a bit and record all instances of approving behavior whether verbal or nonverbal or, perhaps, both categories separately. Again, with the option of repeated use of the same sample of behavior, students of behavior modification can readily check their reliability against others. Then various pupil behaviors can be studied in the same way. The bvious advantage of the film or tape is repetition and the chance for checking.

We have found that once some facility is achieved in this technique, it is desirable to have students go in small groups (three or four) to a regular classroom and all take data on the same behaviors. They act as checks on each other, and if there are wide discrepancies in their observations, we attempt to determine why. Most often it is some problem with the definition of the category. The more specific the behavior, the more reliable seem to be the observations. For example, it is generally easier for one beginning to take data to be accurate with something like "out-of-seat" behavior than with a whole category of disruptive behaviors.

A final check for a teacher who wishes to gather his own data is to have someone check him on specific behaviors while he is trying to gather the same data. The teacher, for example, might be trying to record how many times he attended to a particular student, and it would be relatively simple to have someone check this.

In general, we feel that it is relatively simple to learn to take data and that the method outlined above is quite easy in addition to having built-in checks for accuracy. First there is simulation of some kind, then a move to a more realistic situation, and finally the teacher records his own data.

SUMMARY

When we conceive of the classroom as a teacher-controlled laboratory, the teacher's behavior is the independent variable and the student's behavior the dependent variable under the control of what the teacher does. For this to function efficiently, there must be accurate measurement of the relevant variables including teacher and student behaviors.

Teachers engage in three broad classifications of behavior: those which are designed to elicit student behaviors, those which are responses to student behaviors, and those which set goals for students. Students engage in two very broad kinds of behavior: those which are academic in nature and those which are nonacademic. While frequency of occurrence and rate are the most analyzed dimensions of behavior, duration, intensity, and appropriateness are also important if less available to precise measurement.

Teachers select student behaviors which they wish to diminish or enhance.

Then they systematically change classroom variables in order to accomplish their purposes. If the teacher is to know that what he is doing is effecting changes in the behavior of his students, he needs accurate data on specific behaviors. This is most often taken as some rate of occurrence with the reference point for change being the initial rate of the behavior in the natural situation.

The chapter illustrated that behavioral data are readily gathered for both academic and nonacademic behaviors as well as for many teacher behaviors. Learning to do this is relatively easy, but it must finally be practiced in the actual classroom situation. It is not enough to just read about it.

REFERENCES

Barton, E. S., Guess, D., Garcia, E., & Baer, D. M. Improvement of retardates mealtime behaviors by timeout procedures using multiple baseline techniques. *Journal of Applied Behavior Analysis*, 1970, 3, 77–84.

Lindsley, O. R. A reliable wrist counter for recording behavior rates. *Journal of Applied Behavior Analysis*, 1968, 1, 77–78.

Saslow, G., & Kanfer, F. Behavioral diagnosis. In *Behavior therapy: appraisal and status* (Cyril Franks, Ed.). New York: McGraw-Hill, 1969.

Thomas, D. R., Becker, W. C., & Armstrong, M. Production and elimination of disruptive classroom behavior by systematically varying teacher's behavior. *Journal of Applied Behavior Analysis*, 1968, 1, 35–45.

SUGGESTED READINGS

Baer, D. M., Wolf, M. M., & Risley, T. R. Some current dimensions of applied behavior analysis. *Journal of Applied Behavior Analysis*, 1968, 1, 91–97.

Birnbrauer, J. S. & Wolf, M. M. Classroom behavior of retarded pupils with token reinforcement. *Journal of Experimental Child Psychology*, 1965, 2, 219–235.

Lounin, J. S., Friesen, W. V., & Norton, A. E. Managing emotionally disturbed children in the regular classroom. *Journal of Educational Psychology*, 1966, 57, 1–13.

Martin, G. L., & Powers, R. B. Attention span: An operant conditioning analysis. *Exceptional Children*, 1967, 33, 565–570.

Zimmerman, E. H., & Zimmerman, J. The alteration of behavior in a special classroom situation. *Journal of the Experimental Analysis of Behavior*, 1962, 5, 59–60.

3
Setting Behavioral Goals

Implicit in our analysis of behavioral measures is the assumption that the measures are being taken for some good reason. That is, the teacher has some definite end in mind or some goal either for the class as a whole or for individual students. These goals may involve almost an infinite number of behaviors: increased accuracy in spelling or arithmetic; increased speed and accuracy with multiplication; increased (or decreased) verbal behaviors of various kinds; elimination of a multiplicity of disruptive behaviors; acquisition of a multiplicity of study behaviors; or anything that the teacher wants the children to learn.

As it is important to get precise measures of baserates to give us a starting point from which we can measure change, it is equally important to define the desired change precisely so it will be possible to determine (1) the steps to the goal and (2) the point at which the goal is achieved. It is surprising how many of our goals for students are so ill-defined that we really do not know when they have been achieved. We make up for our lack of precision with some sort of global statement in the form of a grade, like "C work." When one stops to think about it, does that statement tell the student very much about what he has done or, rather, is it a convenient way to avoid the issue?

Goals should include precisely defined steps for their achievement, with each step an important link in the learning process. This is particularly true of complex academic subjects but may be equally true in the modification of such activities as disruptive behavior where the teacher must select specific behaviors out of a context of many and focus on these one at a time. While it is an almost overwhelming temptation to want to change the "whole child" at one fell swoop, there is increasing evidence that this is neither reasonable nor efficient. It frequently leads to frustration for the teacher and an exacerbation of the problem behavior of the youngster.

In this chapter we will examine some of the common pitfalls in setting goals or *terminal behaviors*, some examples of terminal behaviors, and some examples of determining the next step in modifying a youngster's behavior. These steps toward the final goal can be construed as intermediate goals, each of which is a logical move toward the desired terminal behavior.

SOME PROBLEMS

Perhaps the greatest difficulty with teacher-set goals is their lack of precision. This is not to denigrate teachers, for much of what we learn to seek as desirable is some sort of abstraction. This book is being written during a presidential campaign, and anyone who has listened to the oratory of politics is all too familiar with vague objectives. We tend to do this because it is easier to handle a large number of specifics under some rubric than to deal with each of the specifics individually and concretely.

It is an interesting exercise to look at school-district curriculum guides with an eye to the objectivity of the proposed goals. Probably every one we have seen includes "good citizenship" as a very desirable outcome. Yet, consider this for a moment and think of all the possible behaviors that could be included or excluded, depending on who is defining the term. Is the good citizen obedient or challenging? Or does this depend on the circumstances? Is the good citizen other-directed or self-directed, or is there some optimum combination of these two? Does the good citizen speak only when spoken to? Does he always say that the teacher's ideas are best? It seems to us that the general statement "he's a good citizen" has little practical meaning. It is only when we break these goals down into their particulars that we achieve sufficient specificity to guarantee understanding.

Richard Harsh (1967), writing about the evaluation of educational objectives for disadvantaged children, states:

> This step (definition of objectives in behavioral terms) in the evaluation process is a rigorous and demanding activity, for it requires that objectives or anticipated outcomes be defined and described in terms of behaviors that may be observed, recorded, and analyzed. The test of behavioral definition is to find consensus that the behavior's presence or absence represents attainment or non-attainment of the objective.

It is relatively easy to determine the criteria for the goal if our objective is some simple behavior like remaining-in-seat or not fighting. It becomes much more complex if it is the development of reading skills or a level of mathematics achievement with which we are concerned. Traditionally, teachers have relied upon normative tests to give them this information. There are various achievement tests which have been standardized on a school-age population. The individual youngster's score can be compared with the averages in the standardization population, and the teacher will then know whether each child is average, or above or below average.

While these tests have value, especially if they are selected with the school curriculum and the normative population in mind, they can also be quite misleading. Recently we talked with some teachers about the reading skills of their youngsters and, during the course of the discussion, they mentioned their standardized reading test which they used as a basis for evaluating the students. The surprising thing was that none of the teachers knew anything about the content of the test or whether it really measured what they were teaching. The test was required by administrative fiat and administered by special personnel, and all they saw were the scores! Under these circumstances, they had no way of telling what the scores meant.

Harsh (1967) has this to say about these instruments:

> Too often general and "venerable" measures of achievement which have titles of tests of reading, language, math, or interest, etc., are assumed automatically to provide a measure of any and all behaviors that relate to that domain of development.

They quite obviously might not. For example, if there has been a significant change in how math is taught, then the specific objectives under the new method would not be the same as those under the old. Under these circumstances, a previous test of math achievement could be very misleading. Also, different cultural and socioeconomic groups respond differently to test items. Therefore the teacher should always be certain that his students are representative of the population of students on which the test was standardized and that the test measures what he has taught.

When tests are used as measures of objectives, it is best that they be devised locally with the specific behaviors required by the curriculum in mind and that they be standardized on the local population. Then there is complete control in defining the educational goal and the student behaviors which meet these goals.

However, normative data are not enough for helping individual children. Knowing that a child scores at the 3.8 grade level on a reading test when he is actually placed in the fifth grade does not tell us very much except that something probably needs to be done. Therefore, using standardized tests does not and should not preclude other forms of data gathering based on direct observations. In addition to accuracy rates and academic-response rates, it is often necessary to get very specific information of a programming sort—that is, just what can the child respond to accurately and just where lies the difficulty. We recently saw a little girl in the third grade who was having difficulty with arithmetic. The normative tests showed this as well as the classroom behavior. We had her work some problems and talked them through as she did. It became quite obvious that she knew many of the basic processes but somehow had missed out on some simple addition and subtraction facts. Without these she could not do the work, and arithmetic was becoming increasingly difficult as well as aversive for her. Once the specific problems were pinpointed, the teacher knew where to begin. This supports our contention that normative data by themselves are not enough. If the children are to achieve our academic goals, we must have specific information about where they are in the learning sequence in order to take them to the next step.

A second difficulty with some teacher-set goals is that the measured terminal behavior is not really a good measure of the behavior which is desired. This is probably most true when the teacher wants a behavioral outcome (i.e., wants the student to be able to "do" something) and measures this by means of verbal behavior tests requiring oral or written answers on an examination. The reader might well be able to pass an examination on the contents of this book, but this would be little evidence that its contents could or would be applied in modifying the behavior of children. In order to demonstrate this, the reader would have to apply the principles espoused here in some real situation.

A common goal in education is to teach children to have proper attitudes with the assumption that the attitude will then lead to the appropriate behavior. Suppose we wish to teach children to have positive attitudes toward minority groups. This is a very laudable goal and one with which few people would openly disagree. A typical way to go about this is to include a "unit" on race relations in some aspect of the social-studies curriculum. We might even use some attitude measure which contained a series of proposed behaviors toward members of minority groups. Would you invite them into your home? Would you take them to your church? Would you welcome them as neighbors? Etc. With this kind of measure, we are setting as our terminal behavior the student's ability to answer questions to previously learned verbal materials. These answers may or may not have any relation to a person's actual behavior with minority group members. While it may be inconvenient to get specific behavioral measures for many of our educational goals, the teacher should be aware that substituting a verbal terminal behavior for some other terminal behavior does not assure that the latter has been learned. The behavioral expression of attitudes and values is a much more significant indication of their relevance for the child than some verbal statement about them. The coach would hardly bring out a team who had only read and talked about the game!

A more subtle form of this problem with teacher-set goals is to have as an objective the "understanding" of some such process as multiplication or division. The key to this is for the youngster to be able to generalize and apply his knowledge in a new situation. He may well be able to give a rote verbal recitation without understanding, but when confronted with a not previously learned prob-

lem, he has no cues for his rote responses. However, he demonstrates understanding behaviorally, according to previously established terminal behaviors, when he is able to solve appropriate mathematical problems in several different contexts.

A third problem with teacher-set goals is that they are often limited by the teacher's global assessment of the child, and the goals are determined by an assumption based evaluation rather than a precise behavioral evaluation. Perhaps the most common example of this is the use of intelligence test scores (IQs) as a means of setting the limits of academic behavior for youngsters. In this case, terminal behaviors are prescribed by a test score, and the child is taught and placed in the curriculum on the basis of this global assessment rather than of a more detailed evaluation of his skills. In many states it is common to base assignment to some special education classroom on an IQ score rather than on more specific assessments. This practice has doubtful merit and may do positive injury to the "borderline" child who obtains a low score for environmental reasons (i.e., poor environmental background) and is placed in a curriculum which will not allow him to develop to his potential.

Even with rather severe retardates, we have seen many instances where children labeled as "trainable" or unable to be educated in the usual sense of obtaining academic skills have learned to read, write, and do simple arithmetic when their learning had been properly programmed both in terms of eliciting stimuli and reinforcement contingencies. Not that these children were without limitations, but the limitations were not nearly as great as had been supposed. The limitations or terminal behaviors had been set by global assessment and categorization. Once these children were labeled, there was no attempt to teach them more than the label suggested, until an enterprising teacher decided to ignore the label and see what could be done. The limitations were individual in nature and not a function of their being categorized. Thus, when behavioral goals are set on the basis of global assessments, we tend to achieve only those goals because we ignore other possibilities. Children are assumed not to be able to function on some particular level or other and are never given the kind of instruction which would determine if this were true.

A final problem of teacher-set goals is that they are frequently not stated in such a way as to be readily understood by the student. Assuming that it helps for a student to know what is expected of him, there is little assistance when the teacher substitutes some sort of rubric for specific guidance in learning. Such statements as "try harder next time" or "be a better citizen," while implying certain behaviors, do not specify them. If the student has been thoroughly schooled in what is expected of him in trying harder or being a good citizen, then the goals may be reasonably clear for him. However, many youngsters who are urged to try harder will diligently practice errors that will serve to increase learning difficulty. Unless a child is told specifically what to do and in what sequence, he cannot comply with the admonition. Both he and the teacher may end up being more frustrated because there was inadequate communication as to goals. Therefore, the terminal behaviors expected of students must be precise and stated in such a way as to enable them to follow a clear procedure to the final goal. This presents a problem in communication. The danger is that the teacher will assume a child knows what is intended and the child will be too confused to be able to ask the appropriate questions.

SPECIFIC TERMINAL BEHAVIORS

Specific terminal behaviors are those behaviors determined by the teacher to meet the objectives that he has set for the student. They may involve the learner in some physical activity, or in some verbal activity, or both; but whatever they are, they must be stated so that the teacher and others (including the student) can determine the point at which they have been achieved. From this point of view, "thinking" is not a terminal behavior. There is no way to observe it directly or get any consensus that it has occurred. Some oral or written statement or some physical action which the teacher may wish to take as evidence of thought may be defined as the terminal behavior. Many teachers, in order to instigate thought, ask questions in such a way as to minimize a kind of rote response from the student and maximize individual analysis. This product is then evaluated as either good or poor thinking. Most teachers we have talked to feel that teaching a child to "think" is one of the most difficult problems facing the teacher. We agree. Its difficulty lies to a large extent in defining those behaviors that are examples of "good" thinking, so that these can be used as models for the students.

Taking half seriously the idea that the goal of teaching is to make the student more like the instructor, one of the authors provided his students in educational psychology with complete answers to all the questions as soon as they finished an examination. Since the exams were about half objective and half essay, hopefully requiring thinking, he found it necessary to expose his thinking to their critical gaze for their commentary. The experience was useful in building toward some models of thought, even if a little devastating for the professor! Thus because the students had examples of written material on the same questions they were required to answer, the material was made relevant and established a basis on which to build toward the production of "thoughtful" material.

Thinking, or what is evidence of thought, is obviously a tough kind of problem to deal with behaviorally. But if one is to communicate with students with other than the rubric "THINK," he needs to define thinking explicitly. Let us look at another behavior which is not so complex but which also requires some analysis in order to define objectively the terminal behavior.

A pair of graduate students, experienced teachers, were working with a 10-year-old girl who had been referred for tutoring because of "poor attention span." Baserate data indicated that this was not the problem, at least not in this setting. If she did have poor attention span, this behavior did not generalize to the present situation. However, there did seem to be a problem with comprehension of the materials that she had read. Comprehension (or comprehension span) seemed to involve two variables: (1) the accuracy rate to questions covering the material and (2) the length of the readings. Difficulty was controlled by using materials of the same grade level throughout this little study. Having achieved perfect accuracy for 21 questions—84 lines of material—the teachers then proceeded to increase the length of the passages read while maintaining accuracy. After five sessions, the little girl was reading 134 lines with perfect accuracy. The number of questions had increased proportionally to 41. Data supported the observation that comprehension span had increased dramatically. The significant variable in this project seemed to be a special reinforcement. The little girl was very fond of grapes!

In relatively simpler behavior-modification tasks, the terminal behavior is often the elimination of an undesirable behavior and the substitution of some more desirable behavior. In a case previously cited, the elimination of fighting on the playground became the goal set for the first-grade boys. The teacher had to make a fairly simple discrimination between fighting and nonfighting and continue with the modification procedures until she was satisfied that her objective had been obtained. In this case it involved not putting their names on the board for the counselor.

The case of the junior-high girl, also previously cited, involved the modification of three behaviors to obtain the goal of "better study habits." These were defined as significant diminutions in gazing, talking, and a significant increase in working. While the term "significant," as used by the teacher, is not as precise as we would like it to be, it indicated that the teacher would accept even a reasonable change in the girl's behavior, not necessarily expecting her to be superior to the rest of the students. The data demonstrated a significant change, and the terminal behaviors were achieved to the teacher's satisfaction.

For many classroom tasks the terminal behavior selected by the teacher is a diminution in error rates or, more positively stated, an increase in the accuracy of responses. This is particularly true for such subjects as mathematics or spelling. An initial terminal behavior may merely be a diminution of the errors or increase in accuracy over a given period of time. Once the first goal is achieved, a new one is set so that the initial "terminal behavior" really becomes a step towards a more distant goal. It should be stressed here that terminal behaviors for most academic instruction are only terminal in the sense that they are the immediate objectives of instruction; what the teacher feels can reasonably be obtained within the allotted time. These are always subject to modification in the light of new data since one of the most significant aspects of individualizing instruction is that the teacher is ready to modify his behavior in the light of the new data. It has usually been the experience of teachers who practice these techniques to spend much of their time in setting new objectives as the students rapidly achieve the old ones. However, as challenging as this is, it is also very rewarding. The teacher sees children obtain specific goals, knows at all times both where the students are with reference to the behavioral objectives and that what he (the teacher) is doing is making a difference.

We would not want the reader to feel that we dismiss lightly the tremendous task of setting and planning for goals and defining the steps to reach them. Learning to be a teacher, at least one who is aware of what he is doing, involves this activity to a large degree. It is one of the most difficult of the teaching tasks, for it requires determining intermediate terminal behaviors and careful planning that helps the student move smoothly along to the more distant objectives. In order to do this the teacher must know both his subject matter and the baserate behavior of his students thoroughly. Then he develops the steps between the baseline and the terminal behavior and modifies these as learning progresses and as new data suggest changes. This process is called *programming* and is similar to the technique exemplified by programmed textbooks. (See Chapter 7.) There is one very important difference, however. We think of programming behaviors of all kinds, not just the verbal behaviors as given in a book. From our earlier discussion it should be clear that the more the student is involved in doing (not just talking about doing) the desired behavior, the better the learning. So if the task is to learn to do an experiment in physics, verbal instructions are useful, and necessary perhaps, but will only result in verbal learning unless the student is "programmed" through the experiment by actually doing it in a step-by-step manner. Under these conditions learning is to a large extent controlled by the teacher. If he is constantly gathering appropriate data on the progress of his students, he is in an excellent position to be flexible in his programming and to individualize the instruction for each student. It is our belief that "good" teachers have always done this when they were motivated to treat each child as unique. The old saying, "Start where the child is and take him as far as he can go," takes on new life in this context.

Nolen et al. (1967) describe this process in a study dealing with a junior high classroom for children with learning disabilities. The children were brought to a school where the researchers developed a program of study for them with particular emphasis on mathematics and reading. They discuss part of this process with reference to a student who was working with multiplication facts:

> In the junior high class, for example, a student was not merely working on multiplica-
> tion, he was working with multiplication of whole numbers defined in terms of
> repeated addition or reconstruction of multiplication equations with a missing prod-
> uct or missing factor in combinations 5×9 or studying in another area which had
> been analyzed with similar detail.

Once the basic analysis of the subject matter had been accomplished in this class, the teacher knew precisely where each student was in each skill at any time.

Then she could make certain that every child proceeded through the necessary steps to the previously determined goals.

We feel it appropriate, then, for a teacher or a curriculum committee to define the steps in the learning sequence. These steps form the basis of the record of the student's progress. This is not to argue that every student must do every step. Some very bright, perceptive, or creative students may very well "skip" steps and yet be able to demonstrate that they have acquired the requisite terminal behaviors. Fine! But the teacher still knows what the youngster can and is doing. He can provide for enrichment or an opportunity for accelerated learning.

When a learner has successfully completed one goal, he moves on to the next step at a pace that is individualized. No more "busy work" for the bright youngsters while the others catch up. No more leaving the "slow learner" confused and drifting further and further behind. In fact, it would be possible to build into this a kind of self-evaluation by the student: when he has achieved a step, he is ready to go on to the next. This does away with the necessity for grades as such since the criterion for each step will be stated so as to be open to the teacher and student. We believe that when behavioral goals are clearly stated and when intermediate goals are clearly defined, the teacher can individualize learning for each student and maximize the opportunity for him to succeed. It is clear that the vague definition of many of our educational goals are at the root of a significant amount of learning problems.

SUMMARY

We need to clearly define our objectives or terminal behaviors for students so that we can determine what the steps to these objectives are and when we have achieved them. There are four common pitfalls in teacher set objectives. These are (1) their lack of precision or objectivity (too often an abstraction is set as a teaching goal without clearly defining all the behaviors subsumed in it), (2) the substitution of some behavior (usually verbal) for the desired behavior (learning about an attitude is not the same as actually doing the things which reflect the attitude), (3) the utilization of global assessments and thus an assumption based evaluation (IQ for example, rather than a precise evaluation of the student in terms of the desired behaviors), and (4) their obscurity for the student who then does not know how to proceed to the goal or who may pursue a mistaken goal.

Some terminal behaviors are very difficult to define objectively (thinking, e.g.), but this does not make the task any less necessary. When the goals are described in precise terms, the teacher is in an excellent position to individualize instruction for the slow as well as the fast learner or even the average child. For the next step in learning is clearly defined, and any difficulties are readily pinpointed. The task, while challenging, is not impossible. The consequences are more efficient learning for the student and greater precision for the teacher.

REFERENCES

Harsh, R. J. Evaluating E.S.E.A. projects for the disadvantaged. *Educational Leadership,* 1967, **24** 453–461.

Nolen, P. A., Kunzlemann, H. P., & Haring, N. Behavioral modification in a junior high learning disabilities classroom. *Exceptional Children,* 1967 (November), 163–168.

SUGGESTED READINGS

Allen, K. E., et al. Effects of social reinforcement on isolate behavior of a nursery school child. *Child Development,* 1964, **35** 511–513.

Azrin, N. H., & Lindsley, O. R. The reinforcement of cooperation between children. *Journal of Abnormal and Social Psychology,* 1967, **72** 100–102.

Reece, M. M., & Whitman, R. N. Expressive movements, warmth and verbal reinforcement. *Journal of Abnormal and Social Psychology,* 1962, **64** 234–236.

Sherman, J. A. Modification of nonverbal behavior through reinforcement of related verbal behavior. *Child Development,* 1964, **35** 717–723.

4
Strengthening
Desirable Behavior

Perhaps it is a heritage of our Puritan Ethic that most of us will ignore children when they are doing what is "right" or expected of them. After all, we expect little Cedric to behave well, get his work in on time, and be nice to the teacher. He is only doing what he ought to do. Chances are if he continues in this vein he will be fondly thought of as a very nice child, and chances are he will not receive much attention because he doesn't need it. Why should he if he is behaving properly, is well mannered, and is unobtrusive?

But if little Johnny is being disruptive, slow with his assignments, and sassy to the teacher, he is likely to receive an inordinate amount of attention. Chances are if he continues still further in this manner of behaving, he will receive even more attention from the principal, the counselor, the school psychologist, and his parents. Again, why not? He is obviously a child with problems and needs this added attention to "straighten him out."

Another important factor in this selective attending is the number of children in the average classroom. With 35 students it is almost impossible to attend to everything that is going on, and in the interest of maintaining order, it is only natural to be concerned with deviation from the accepted pattern and not to be concerned with the "normal."

However, under these conditions (i.e., ignoring desirable behavior and attending to undesirable behavior) the behavioral psychologist would predict that the good behavior would gradually cease or diminish and that the bad behavior would be maintained or increase in frequency. The reason that it doesn't always work out quite this way in the average classroom is that few teachers are absolutely consistent in their reactions to children. They sometimes respond and they sometimes do not. Shortly we will consider evidence to show that teacher responses are of paramount importance in strengthening or weakening behaviors. Good classroom management, including the teaching of academic skills and appropriate social behavior, is based upon this principle.

In a previous section we stated that the teacher influences student behavior in the classroom whether the behavior is desirable or undesirable. We meant by this that the teacher's actions, particularly his responses to students, affect the behavior in fairly specific and determinable ways—that a detailed analysis of the variables of classroom management would show just what it was that the teacher did that was influencing student behavior.

In this and the following chapter we will explore the techniques the teacher may use to maximize the probability of desirable classroom behavior, whether in the academic or social sphere, and to minimize the probability of undesirable classroom activity. We should point out that we will not delineate specifically what is desirable and what is undesirable because, although we are interested in these problems personally, these decisions are primarily the responsibility of the teacher, the school administration, and the community. We have tried to select a broad spectrum of behaviors in order to illustrate that once the academic and social decisions are made, it is within the province of the teacher to utilize behavioral principles to implement these decisions. It is here, in the implementation of behavioral procedures, that the emphasis on data gathering and measurement pays off. For the most effective control of classroom variables depends on accurate and reliable measurements.

Now let us move on to a consideration of the basic principles of precise learning and examine in some detail the relationship between these principles and classroom management, how they are involved in maximizing appropriate behaviors and minimizing those that are inappropriate.

PRINCIPLES OF REINFORCEMENT

Most behavior is affected by its consequences, i.e., the probability of its occurring again is directly related to the effect it has on securing positive or negative outcomes from the environment. Even behaviors that were recently considered beyond environmental control are now being managed for the benefit of people with specific health difficulties. Patients are being taught to control various autonomic responses (Miller, 1969), and the whole impact of biofeedback is just beginning to be felt in medical and psychological therapies.

However, teachers are not usually interested in or trained to deal with these behaviors. But they are concerned with many things that children do, such as reading, writing, talking, running, spelling, fighting, whispering. The list is endless. These behaviors are affected by their consequences and belong to a general class that psychologists call *operant*, since they "operate" on the environment to secure various outcomes. They are also often thought of as voluntary behaviors as opposed to reflexive behaviors.

Teachers control many important consequences for students: They give praise, they punish, they give grades, they give and take away privileges; they sometimes ignore both good and bad behavior. With systematic application of these consequences, they can influence important student behaviors. They can increase the probability of some behavior occurring again by *reinforcing* it, or they can decrease this probability through some form of *punishment* or by instituting a procedure called *extinction*. Let us examine these processes closely for they are central to improved classroom operation. Careful control of these three kinds of consequences will help any teacher improve the quality of his instruction and the social climate of the classroom.

A *reinforcement* is an environmental event that increases the rate of a response which it follows. Praise a child for picking up some trash from the playground and it is highly likely that he will do it again, since praise is a very common form of *social reinforcement.* Likewise, smiles, hugs, money, candy, and awards of various kinds are frequently reinforcing for the behavior which they follow. There are an almost infinite variety of reinforcements, and we will look at the most important of these later in this chapter.

Reinforcements are sometimes categorized as *positive* and *negative.* Praising a child involves the use of positive reinforcement because you are presenting a stimulus (praise) that follows the desired behavior (picking up trash). Negative reinforcement consists of removing something that could be punishing, so the child avoids or escapes the punishing event by doing whatever is required. Negative reinforcement is one of the most common methods used to control the behavior of children and adults, and it most often takes the form of a threat. "If you don't finish your work, Cyril, you will have to stay in at recess." Presumably, Cyril will finish his work in order to avoid staying in the classroom at recess since being in the classroom at this time would be unpleasant or punishing. Then the teacher removes (verbally) the punishing event, Cyril goes happily outside to play with the other children, and we hope that his "finishing-work-on-time" behavior is reinforced by avoiding unpleasant consequences.

If one stops to think for a moment of the use of traffic citations, it is obvious that our own behavior is also controlled to a considerable degree by means of negative reinforcement. Traffic officers do not, as a rule, stop people to praise them for their driving well (this would be positive reinforcement), but they do constantly pose a threat of issuing a citation for improper driving. This threat is carried out just often enough to keep most of us honest. However, it has an interesting side-effect which we will discuss in more detail later. Most of us don't really like the people who give us citations.

However, parents and teachers as well as society in general use this type of control often because it is easy to administer. It requires the presentation of a threat, usually through some verbal means, and then the removal of the threat following compliance. One doesn't really have to do anything, just think of appropriate threats. However, if negative reinforcement is to continue to be effective it must occasionally be backed up. The youngster will have to stay in at recess, and we will have to receive a citation or two. At this point we are dealing with *punishment.*

Punishment is an environmental event which decreases the rate of the response which it follows. Adults use many kinds of punishment with children, from the physically painful to the psychologically painful. While there are generally some limits placed on how physically violent a teacher can become, there are plenty of opportunities for denial of privileges or shaming a student in front of his peers. However, punishment may and often does have some undesirable side effects that are detrimental to learning. The child may learn to avoid the teacher-punisher and develop a tendency to avoid school entirely. In view of this it seems strange that many schools use as the ultimate punishment expelling an "incorrigible" student. If indeed school has become so aversive that the youngster cannot conform to the regimen, then expelling him must be highly reinforcing for that very behavior the school personnel are trying to alter. True, his parents may become much more punishing so as to force him back into a school situation that is the "lesser of two evils." However, it somehow seems preposterous to confine a child in school primarily to avoid punishment of a higher order. We will be more deeply concerned about the effects of punishment in Chapter 5. Let us turn our attention now to another outcome which influences operant behavior.

In addition to reinforcement and punishment, there is another class of outcomes following behavior in which essentially nothing happens—at least nothing that can be classified as either reinforcing or punishing. We call this process *extinction,* and when it happens consistently, the behavior it follows decreases in rate until it is finally *extinguished.* This is a very common classroom practice, and teachers who set out to ignore certain behaviors with the idea that they will eventually "go away" are practicing extinction. That is, they are if they consistently and absolutely ignore the behavior, something that is not always easy to do.

However, one should be warned that when instituting extinction the first thing that will probably happen is that the behavior will get worse! For example, a youngster who has had temper tantrums and has been reinforced by adult attention will increase the duration and intensity of the tantrum at first because it has worked in the past. Morse (1966) explains this phenomenon as a function of the behavior having been reinforced in the past. It may also be considered under the concept of *expectancy* (see Chapter 6). Whatever the reason, the person who uses extinction should be prepared for the initial consequences or they will, like many parents, reinforce the heightened response.

These processes (reinforcement, punishment, and extinction) do not themselves distinguish between desirable and undesirable behavior. A teacher can extinguish desirable behavior by ignoring it just as easily as undesirable behavior, and perhaps more easily. This is because the latter is frequently reinforced by peers. If a child is consistently ignored when he raises his hand to volunteer, he will gradually cease to volunteer. On the other hand, a child who is consistently reinforced by teacher attention for deviant behavior will continue that behavior. If a teacher ridicules a child who is trying to answer a question, we would predict that he will reduce his participation as the teacher asks later questions. That behavior which is ignored will extinguish. That behavior which is reinforced will increase. That behavior which is punished will decrease. It all sounds very simple, but it requires careful consideration. For it is not always easy to ascertain just what is reinforcing and what is punishing for any individual child. It also requires alertness to administer consequences in a consistent manner since this is something we ordinarily do not do. However, for those teachers who master these processes and make judicious use of planned outcomes as consequences for student behavior, the reward is a more predictable classroom in terms of both learning and social behavior. Next, let us take a look at several principles that are basic to the utilization of reinforcement, punishment, and extinction with the purpose of refining our use of these variables.

Jack Michael (1967), in a splendid monograph on the arrangement of behavioral consequences in education, suggests several principles which are particularly appropriate for teachers intending to utilize behavioral techniques in their classrooms. These should be examined closely for they delineate clearly how the teacher may use consequences to the best possible advantage.

First, consequences (reinforcers and punishers) are defined only in terms of how they affect the learner, not how the teacher thinks they might affect the learner or how the same consequences have affected other learners. Nothing is truly a reinforcer for any child until it has been tried out and has been seen to increase that child's rate of response. Thus there is no a priori test of what is reinforcing or punishing; the only test is to try something and measure the effects.

However, the experienced teacher may make some educated guesses based on his experience or knowledge of the research literature. These will very often be accurate guesses because there are many kinds of things which have been shown to be reinforcing to many children. But, while most children respond to praise, some do not; while most people respond to money, some do not. It is this occasional person who does not respond to the usual or normal contingencies that makes this first principle so important. We can never be sure something will work until we try it.

Another complicating aspect is that the reinforcing characteristics of a stimulus will change from one situation to another. An adolescent may respond to praise only from his peers but not from the teacher. There are also hierarchies of reinforcement, i.e., for any person some reinforcers are more powerful than others. A child may respond reasonably well with verbal approval from the teacher but really blossom when given a pat on the head or a hug. These are two forms of social approval, and while one might expect children to respond equally well to both, this is not necessarily so. Our experience has suggested that many children who have difficulty with verbal expression are more responsive to nonverbal reinforcement. However, this is an impression and not the result of controlled research. For example, we saw a little girl recently who had been referred to a clinic for learning disabilities. Exhaustive diagnostic procedures did not reveal any major physical or psychological difficulties. However, we did learn that she seemed "immune" to the usual verbal social reinforcers. We asked the teacher to try hugs instead of words. The little girl responded very well. Since the teacher paired praise with the hugs the youngster soon came to respond to the praise as well. We could only surmise that somewhere in her history she had received many conflicting verbal messages from adults and for the time would only respond to "real love" in the form of physical contact.

Another problem concerns the use of outcomes which the teacher believes to be punishing but which are really reinforcing. Scolding a student or arguing with him until you "win" may seem to be aversive to the student from the teacher's point of view. However, teacher attention is a very powerful reinforcer for many children, and to these youngsters any attention is better than none. So the behavior continues or increases and the teacher attention (scolding, arguing, etc.) also increases. This can get to be a pretty trying experience! The only criterion that the teacher can use, then, to determine the nature of the stimulus event is the effect it has on the behavior of the individual student. This provides an objective and systematic way of determining what is maintaining behavior. *And if behavior is being maintained, it is being reinforced.* With systematic observation and consistent measurement there is no guesswork. We can proceed with modifications on the basis of knowledge, not on the basis of intuition.

A second principle for the utilization of consequences in the classroom is that the effects of reinforcement or punishment are automatic. The learner does not need to know or be able to verbalize about these consequences. Thus it is not absolutely necessary that the teacher and the student enter into some sort of verbal or written contract to effect positive change, although this is one ethical form of carefully spelling out the rules of the game and works very well with some children. This is especially important if the children are involved in keeping and recording some of the data so that they know where they stand at all times.

However, the work with very deviant children (autistic, schizophrenic, severely brain-injured) such as that reported by Lovaas and his associates (1966) clearly illustrates the automatic effects of consequences. The children that Lovaas worked with were mute, and his task was to teach them language. This was done by careful step-by-step training with reinforcement at every step. First the psychologists had to get the youngster to attend, then it was necessary to gradually develop imitative behavior, then to shape sounds and finally, words. It was quite obvious that these children could not verbalize about the relationship between their behavior and the consequences, nor was there any other indication that they "understood" (at least at first) about this relationship. Nevertheless, they learned rather complex verbal behavior through these techniques. We would recommend these studies, many of which are described in Chapter 12, for any teacher who is interested in the minute steps that are necessary to accomplish learning goals for certain children and in the careful control of consequences that contribute to this learning.

[A third principle in behavioral management is that the consequences, whether reinforcement or punishment, should be very closely related to the desired terminal behavior.]We use "terminal" here to mean the immediate goal of the teacher, not the long-range goal. This means that the teacher must be aware of exactly what it is he is trying to reinforce and then make certain that the reinforcement is contingent only on that behavior. For example, if accuracy in spelling is the goal and the teacher wishes to increase the number of correct responses a child can make in a given spelling assignment, then the teacher should reinforce the student for accuracy rather than for the amount of time spent on the assignment regardless of accuracy. While it may be appropriate to praise a child for "sticking to his assignment" regardless of accuracy, we must recognize that in such an instance we are basically reinforcing time spent and should not be too disappointed if the accuracy rate does not improve.

We recently had occasion to observe a third-grade boy who had been referred for a reading problem. As it turned out, his problem seemed to be primarily related to oral reading rather than silent reading, since he gave sufficient evidence for us to ascertain that he comprehended materials quite adequately when he read silently. We then discovered that as a consequence of his problem with oral reading, he was receiving the special attention of his own teacher, a remedial reading teacher, his mother, and to round it out, his grandmother. All of these people were to some extent involved in the remediation process, i.e., helping him with his reading problem, and there may have been still others of whom we were not aware such as siblings and his father. Assuming that attention from others, particularly adults, was very reinforcing for him (and we had evidence of this by observing his "attention getting" behaviors in other situations), he was being heavily reinforced for his problem behavior. Thus the more difficulty he had with oral reading, the more people he got involved with (including us!) and the more attention he received. We were all reinforcing the exact behavior we wanted to eliminate. So we gave instructions to reinforce him only for successful oral reading and to put the problem behavior on extinction by not attending to it. In this process we started him with reading materials we knew he could handle adequately so that he could emit the desired behavior and obtain reinforcement in the form of praise and attention. This little boy had been well on his way to establishing a persistent pattern of manipulating adults through his "infirmities" simply because he had learned that these deficiencies got the attention he craved so much. He had learned to expect rewards for failure. (See Chapter 6 for a more detailed discussion of *expectancy.*)

When we look at behavior, and particularly at what is being reinforced, we must pay very close attention to be certain that it is the educational goal that is being achieved and not something that is diametrically opposed or only tangential to our objectives.

⌐*A fourth principle involves consistency. The teacher must be consistent in how he responds to a child if he wishes to achieve specific educational objectives in a predictable manner.*⌐This is certainly not a new rule in dealing with children for psychologists have been urging it on parents and teachers for many years. The rationale, simply stated, has been that a child will feel more sure of himself and less anxious if the people around him behave in a reasonably consistent and predictable manner. From our point of view, the evidence is quite strong that consistency in the management of consequences is necessary if one is to know what is making the difference in the child's general behavior as well as in reaching specific goals. If a given behavior is sometimes reinforced and sometimes punished, depending on the whims of the teacher, it is not only confusing to the child but it is impossible to make predictable progress. We have seen instances such as the following: the teacher has been consistently and smilingly calling on a youngster when he has raised his hand because she wished to increase the rate of his "hand-raising" behavior and thus his class participation. This has been going on for several days and the child is becoming more and more involved in class activities because he is reinforced for participation (hand raising). Suddenly one day the teacher responds to his hand raising by remarking, "What's the matter, Byron, must you always be the star of the show? Put your hand down and let someone else have a chance for a change." He does, of course, and it becomes fairly difficult to reinstate his full class participation. Teachers are all too human and absolute consistency would be virtually impossible. Yet if we are involved in a very conscious effort to help a child change undesirable behavior to more desirable behavior, it is essential that we be consistent. One of the strengths of the behavioral approach is that it forces us into a position in which we have to examine our own behavior and relate it to student outcomes.

⌐*Fifth, consequences should closely follow the behavior on which they are contingent.*⌐There should be as little delay as possible between the child's behavior and the consequences. Human beings do have the ability to delay reinforcement or punishment because they have verbal means to mediate this delay. In fact, teaching a child to delay gratification is one of the major jobs of parents and society. We tend to think of adults who cannot do this as immature and childish. People do learn to work for distant goals such as a college degree. However, a careful examination of the situation surrounding such long range activities would undoubtedly reveal many reinforcements along the way that tend to maintain the behavior.

In trying to gain, maintain, or eliminate specific behavior in the classroom, we will have much more effect on the behavior of the student by using immediate consequences than by using delayed outcomes. Delay may have deleterious effects, and this is probably more true of younger than of older children because younger children do not possess the verbal skills required to handle the delay. We have all known parents who promise their, say, five-year-old child that if he is "good" all day (a nebulous goal), he will be rewarded in the evening. Of course, this is a very long delay for a small child. It is equally difficult for him to understand punishment that is delayed until his father gets home. The longer the delay, the less chance that the consequences are associated with the appropriate behavior. In fact, the reinforcement or punishment may become associated with stimuli that are not intended. For example, having a child stay after school and do his work as a form of punishment while his peers are playing and enjoying their freedom may result in getting the work done that time, but it may also make the work and school aversive. Scolding a student for something he has done earlier in the day when he has just come up to get help with his arithmetic may decrease the probability that he will seek help from the teacher the next time he needs it. In other words, outcomes must be planned, not just given at opportune moments. Surely one thing that is desirable in teaching is that the learner have positive feelings toward the teacher, the school, and the subject. Therefore, if we are to use consequences systematically, they must be carefully related to the behavior they are to change.

A sixth principle concerns the amount of reinforcement necessary for behavioral change. Most people underestimate this. Generally it is especially desirable to reinforce more frequently and with more potent reinforcers on tasks involving new learning. Later we will see that this point can be modified to maintain behavior.

In a previously cited study (Nolen et al.) the researchers determined that the amount of reinforcement was a very significant variable in improving the learning rates of junior high school students with learning disabilities. The more reinforcement, the better the learning.

Sometimes this principle presents some difficulty because the reinforcement itself is so time-consuming that any extension of it would seriously hamper the time for work. A common instance of this, employed by most teachers at one time or another, is to give a student time for "free reading" when he has satisfactorily completed some task. However, too long a period of free reading can markedly reduce the amount of time spent on more formal academic tasks for which a classroom environment is most appropriate.

One of the authors had a very cagey Latin teacher back in high school. There were three or four students who, because they were fairly proficient, were given the privilege of staying after school as a group and reading some of Cicero's letters. Somehow the group accepted this as a great reward, as recognition of their academic prowess, and they learned a lot more Latin (and history) as a consequence.

As one emphasizes a fairly heavy *schedule of reinforcement* only for new learning, he is actually making it more likely that there will be reinforcement for correct responses early in the learning sequence. It is important to do this to help prevent the student from emitting and practicing errors. For these early errors could become real barriers to learning later on in the sequence and increase the probability of failure to learn the more complicated material. Where succeeding steps depend on what has been previously learned and each step builds on the previous one as in a mathematical sequence, early reinforcement of correct responses is mandatory. This is handled fairly automatically in a programmed sequence in which the student is given immediate feedback as to the correctness of his responses. However, being correct is not always sufficient reinforcement and the teacher sometimes needs to supplement this with additional reinforcement. Then the student can move smoothly from one step to the next, both because he is correct and because he is recognized as successful.

A seventh principle is closely related to what has just been discussed. The student's work should be programmed (either formally or informally) so that there are many steps to be reinforced and the student can readily move from one step to the next. This approach is discussed in detail in Chapter 7 so we need not belabor the point here. A good program, and practically anything we require of the learner, can be presented sequentially and provides for an optimal amount of reinforcement and a minimal opportunity for error.

In this section we have discussed seven principles which are essential to the systematic modification of classroom behavior. They provide guidelines for adequate contingency management. In summary, they are: (1) Reinforcers are determined by their actual effect on the learner, not by their supposed affect. (2) Reinforcers affect behavior automatically. (3) Reinforcers should be clearly linked to the behavioral criteria of accomplishment. (4) Reinforcement should be administered consistently. (5) Reinforcement should follow immediately the behavior to be modified. (6) Reinforcement should be frequent and appear early in the learning sequence. (7) Reinforcement should be applied at each step of the learning sequence.

KINDS OF REINFORCEMENT

There are many ways that we could classify those outcomes which will increase the frequency of responses. In this section we will take a look at one such system, expand our analysis of positive reinforcers, and then make a more detailed examination of some that have particular usefulness in the classroom. Again we will rely on both personal experience and research, and trust that the suggestions here will stimulate the creative teacher to new and even better ideas.

Bijou and Sturges (1959) have classified reinforcers into five categories: (1)

consumables, (2) manipulatables, (3) visual and auditory stimuli, (4) social stimuli, and (5) tokens. We wish to add one more to this group which we will label "Premack" and will discuss a little later in the text. Thus, we will deal with six major categories of reinforcers.

While *consumables* have been used extensively in experimental studies, they do not lend themselves readily to the ordinary classroom. Usually parents have to be advised not to give their children breakfast, and this is not a very acceptable policy in most places. In addition, the distribution is sometimes a problem. However, if the reader is interested, he might well examine the study by Risley (1968), cited in Chapter 11, who used edibles and drinkables with great success to improve the social and verbal behavior of socially deprived 4-year-olds. In this case the reinforcers comprised an excellent dietary supplement for the children.

Manipulatables, such as toys and trinkets, might have some value in a classroom especially with younger children. Hobby items tend to be more useful with older children and adolescents. One of our student teams found that a 10-year-old girl who presumably was having difficulty with arithmetic was probably having more difficulty with communication. She was very shy and rarely volunteered anything. They discovered that her hobby was collecting bottle caps. It was not difficult to get a significant increase in spontaneous speech using bottle caps as reinforcers and pairing this reinforcement with praise.

Visual and auditory stimuli are frequently used as feedback to let the youngster know when he is right or wrong. This is difficult in the ordinary classroom although some sort of system could be built into an engineered classroom. However, we know one teacher who entered into a contract with a youngster in a sixth-grade class. This boy was very disruptive in what seemed to be an unthinking way. He talked too much and disturbed the other children with his noisy behavior. The teacher grew tired of reprimanding him, which was probably only reinforcing the behavior, so she set up a point system with which he could "buy" opportunities for game leadership, something he valued quite highly. This gave him the attention of the other students he so earnestly desired. She also installed a simple signal system to let him know when his behavior was appropriate and when inappropriate. This consisted of a paper disk hanging from a book end on her desk. It was green on one side and red on the other. If the green side was displayed "all systems were go" and the youngster knew that he was behaving within the limits, accumulating the necessary points to lead the team. However, if the red side was up he was losing points. This enabled him to become a self-controlled student and the system was no longer needed.

In the Risley study there was a need to get mothers involved in the teaching in order to have a more general effect on the children's behavior. The object was to obtain transfer of this behavior from school to the home, and it was hoped that the mothers would help bridge this gap. The researchers instructed the mothers to praise their children for successes, but these parents did not do so very readily. They were too accustomed to scolding the children and praise did not come easily. Part of the problem was a function of the mothers' working with their own children, but another factor was that there was no readily available outcome for the mothers themselves when they did give praise for a correct response. Their "praising behavior" was on extinction! In the second half of this research, the mothers were assigned to children other than their own and a red light flashed whenever they praised a child. Risley reports, "Under these revised conditions, all the mothers began to be much more liberal with praise. At the same time nagging and threats almost disappeared." The red light was an immediate indication that the mothers were doing the right thing. It was a potent reinforcer for their praising behavior.

MacDonald (1971) developed an ingeneous method to ensure the participation of adolescent boys with a history of delinquent behavior in academic pursuits. They divided the class into teams to compete with each other for a weekly prize such as a movie or a chance to go surfing on school time. Formerly, academic behavior had been disdained and there were powerful peer pressures to avoid it. Under the new conditions it became socially acceptable to excel. Thus peer reinforcement became contingent on good academic responses with the better students helping those with less skill. An interesting sidelight to this, though, was that the teams tended to rotate the prize. The students felt that it was not fair for any one group to win all the time.

Social stimuli comprise a very important category of reinforcers. Younger children are particularly influenced by the kind of responses they get from their teachers whether this be praise or punishment. However, a social outcome is almost always a significant factor in the behavior of students of any age. Social reinforcers comprise a significant part of what we might call "natural" reinforcers. That is, they are a common and usual part of social interaction and are not contrived, as are some that we discuss in this chapter. It should be the goal of every teacher to bring the behavior of children under the control of these natural reinforcers rather than rely solely on those that have been contrived for a particular situation. This is accomplished by always pairing the token or whatever you are using with social approbation so that gradually the approval alone will be enough to maintain the desired behavior. Approval, like reproof, is easy to use. It is a natural and simple part of teacher-student relations. It is not used nearly enough.

Peer approval or disapproval also exerts powerful control over the behavior of many children. This is particularly true with the adolescent. For some adolescents the history of reinforcement in school has been so sparse and the aversive outcomes so heavy that the students do not respond to usual management techniques. However, they frequently respond to reinforcement given by peers. In some cases it is possible to help a student change his behavior by arranging the course of peer approval. This is much easier to do with younger children than with adolescents. We have seen one teacher quickly stop the "silly" behavior of a 9-year-old boy by instructing his classmates to ignore it. The behavior was being maintained by their attention. The teacher then gave her approval for the appropriate behavior, and the boy was soon as well behaved as the rest of the class.

In another instance, this time involving a small class of emotionally disturbed children of about sixth-grade level, the teacher hit on a method of providing a particularly obstreperous youngster with massive reinforcement from his peers. The entire class was on a point system with the points exchangeable for desirable activities. Points were earned for various academic and social behaviors. The teacher told the boy that if his behavior were adequate, and this was carefully spelled out, she would double the points for the whole class. When this happened and the other children were informed that they had double points that day because the one youngster had been able to be a "good citizen," they were lavish in their attention and praise of him. The beauty of this method was that the boy could not take anything away that the other students earned, his action could only make a very positive difference.

Recently Meacham and Gall (1970) prepared an annotated bibliography of research studies based on the use of behavior modification techniques with children in school settings. The studies were selected so as to exclude most of the work with very deviant children and concentrate on "normal kids in normal classrooms" as much as possible. We originally became interested in these studies when considering social reinforcement since many of them seemed to use this kind of reinforcement variable. Consequently, we decided to take a closer look at them and record for each age level the kind of reinforcement that the researcher had used. The results are in Table 1. Note that we list six categories of reinforcement, having added "Premack" to the usual five categories of reinforcers. This Premack technique is explained fully later in the chapter.

First a caution about this table. We do not suggest that this is a random sample of all the research done with children using behavioral techniques. These studies were selected because they tended to deal with normal children and young

Table 1. THE BEHAVIOR OF THE BEHAVIORIST
CATEGORIES OF REINFORCEMENT FOR VARIOUS AGE LEVELS
IN 63 RESEARCH STUDIES

	Consumables	Manipulatables	Visual and Auditory	Social	Tokens	Premack
Preschool	4	6	0	14	1	1
Primary	0	2	2	6	0	0
Elementary	4	1	1	8	4	0
Jr. High	0	0	0	1	2	1
Sr. High	0	0	1	0	1	0
College	0	0	1	1	0	1
Totals	8	9	5	30	8	3

adults such as those we find in normal classrooms. We do feel, however, that we have a fairly representative sample.

Two things stand out when we take a close look at this table. (1) The predominant reinforcement used with relatively normal children in this sample of research studies has been the natural social reinforcer. If we think of token reinforcers as also involving social contact, then the figures are even more impressive. At any rate, almost half of these studies, all of which resulted in significant behavioral changes, used social rather than contrived reinforcers. (2) There is much more research reported with younger than older subjects. We evidently need to do a more thorough job of analyzing the behavior of adolescents. Much is written of this group but evidently very little of an objective behavioral nature, i.e., with the intent of systematically isolating the variables that are significant for enhancing learning.

Runyon and Williams (1972) studied the reinforcement selections of 200 seventh graders. They used a paired comparison scale for the purpose of predicting reinforcer effectiveness of 15 stimuli. These stimuli were selected from three categories of reinforcement: (1) verbal and social, (2) tangible and manipulatable, and (3) knowledge of progress. While the scale was determined to be moderately reliable, the validity seemed to be somewhat in doubt. On the validation tasks the students performed equally well for the most and least preferred reinforcers. The results suggest that these students, when selecting from several reinforcers, cannot choose those which are most effective for their own behavior. It is interesting to compare how the self-imposed contingencies work compared to teacher imposed contingencies, as will be noted in later chapters. At any rate, the article suggests that behavioral observation should be an important adjunct for determining the effectiveness of reinforcers.

We consulted in a central-city school project for two years and as a part of this were involved in selecting tangible reinforcers for adolescent youth. Asking them did not seem to produce very good results by itself, but a combination of asking and testing plus some sheer luck did seem to work. We developed some very powerful reinforcers such as basketball tickets, lunch tickets, and record albums but also found that many other things simply did not "sell."

Deci (1972) reports an interesting study in which he had college students work puzzles which he had previously determined were intrinsically interesting to them. He wanted to determine the differential effects, if any, of kinds of contingencies on subsequent interest in the tasks. Some students were given money, some were praised, and some were threatened with a punishment that was rarely administered. The students who were given money contingent on success later showed less interest in the tasks. Those given money simply for doing the task showed no change. Those threatened with punishment showed a decrease in interest. The students who showed a definite increase in interest were those who had been praised. While the author suggests that too much praise might make a person dependent on that kind of extrinsic reinforcer, it did seem to help develop intrinsic motivation. Intrinsic motivation is a primary goal of a humanistic behaviorism. While contrived reinforcers are useful and often necessary to help develop motivation, the normal social reinforcers seem much more desirable in maintaining behavior and developing self-motivation.

Another kind of reinforcer, already alluded to several times, involves the use of *tokens* or some symbol that the learner can later trade in for something that he wants. These tokens may be gold stars, plastic disks, or any convenient object which the teacher dispenses for desired behavior. The token has real meaning only in terms of what it will "buy," so just how many are given for selected behavior depends on the teacher and his estimate of the sort of things that his students will work for. We have seen token systems in which students were paid off for accuracy and speed of academic responses. They could then buy toys with the accumulated points. There were several toys available but the point price of each was established so that a student could earn a fairly important toy in one day but had to spend several days of accumulated earnings for the more desirable expensive toys. This system has two things in its favor. First, it increases accuracy and speed, maintaining a high rate of student participation. Second, it teaches some students to delay satisfaction, something that becomes very important as we expect young people to work for long range goals.

We had an opportunity to observe another classroom (for retarded children) in which a mark system was in operation. Each child received a mark for any correct response. They accumulated these marks and could trade them in at any time for some desired activity. One adolescent girl liked to listen to the record player. She was allowed 10 minutes at the record player for every 20 tokens. As she finished the requisite responses and received her tokens, she went to the record player, put on the earphones and her favorite music, set the timer for 10 minutes, and listened until the alarm sounded. Then she went back to work to earn more tokens. This girl had been labeled "trainable retardate" in a category oriented school setting. However, under this reinforcement system she was learning to read, write, and do arithmetic, skills that were thought impossible for her. Needless to say, she now had a teacher who didn't believe in limiting children by categories but who started with what the student could do and tried to take her further. This teacher's only complaint was that he had to spend so much time developing new materials as his "trainables" learned the old.

Tokens are often used in conjunction with the *Premack principle* (Premack, 1965). Simply stated, this means that a behavior that naturally occurs with a high frequency can be used as a reinforcer for a behavior with a low natural frequency. Teachers have used this principle for a long time but have never bothered to give it a name or scientific validity. Such teachers find out what the child likes to do and then allow him time to engage in activity if his required work is accurate and has been accomplished within a set period of time. Probably the most common application of this principle is to let the child read his favorite book when he has finished his assigned work.

When the Premack principle is used in conjunction with tokens or points, it provides the teacher with a splendid opportunity to bring many different kinds of behavior under the reinforcement contingency. Points are allocated for academic responses as well as for desired social behaviors, and all of these add up to time in the desired activity. Once the child has accumulated the requisite number of points, he can cash them in at any time. It is very important to allow the student to decide upon the cash-in period. Then it occurs at a time when he really wants to do something, thus maximizing the effect of the reinforcement.

Occasionally this results in a rather amusing side effect. In a nearby school a teen-age girl who was doing poorly academically and socially agreed to a point system which allowed her time out of class for relatively free play, reading, or whatever else she wanted to do. She started to accumulate points very rapidly but would not trade them in. At the end of several months, during which her academic and social behavior improved markedly, she accumulated enough points for several days out of class. However, she did not want to trade them in. She preferred accumulating and recording them to spending them. At the time this is being written she is still accumulating points with no intention of using them. She likes school much more than she previously did and probably the social reinforcement of teacher praise has taken over the task of maintaining her behavior. Yet she is not quite willing to give up on the accumulation of points.

But there are many instances in which children simply asked to be taken off the extrinsic reward system. We have frequently seen instances in which youngsters say, in effect, "I don't need that anymore" and are now able to function quite well under intrinsic motivation and the normal social reinforcers of praise and success. We feel that this should be the goal of any behavior-modification system, that the youngster learn to function on his own and become self-directed as much as possible.

Tokens may also have interesting effects on the teacher's behavior. In fact, many psychologists believe that the most significant effect of a token system is to teach the teacher when to respond to a youngster. For every time one gives a token there is a social contact based on some desirable behavior. The teacher is scheduled to respond at the right time. Mandelker et al. (1970) studied the effects of a token system on a teacher's rate of social contacts with the children in her class. They varied the conditions from contingent to noncontingent tokens and found that the children who were given contingent tokens received the highest social contact. Thus with social contact as a desirable goal, the token system facilitates this behavior in teachers.

Generally, observers have found that under free-choice conditions, academic behavior has a lower probability of occurrence for most children than nonacademic behavior. This provides an interesting insight into our educational system and is probably linked to the aversive nature of the usual classroom controls. In other words, when given the opportunity for free choice, most children would rather not do school work. They would rather do any one of a number of other things. It is by observing these freely chosen activities that the teacher learns what the youngster values most. We recommend observing the child's choice as well as asking him what he likes because children will often try to have their choice reflect what they think their teacher expects them to like. This may please the teacher but may not result in very effective behavioral management.

The teacher who is going to use the Premack principle in his classroom should develop for each child a hierarchy of behavior frequencies based on his observation of the free choices of the pupil. Once he obtains the hierarchy he can use those behaviors that occur most frequently to reinforce those that occur less frequently. Of course, safety and other factors should enter into the teacher's decision as to what preferred activities to permit. A typical hierarchy for a fourth-grade boy might have some physical activity or sport at the top and reading at the bottom. Then the time permitted for the sport is arranged so that it is contingent on a specified amount of reading. One must always assume, however, that the teacher is programming the reading materials in such a way as to enable the youngster to accomplish the academic goals sufficiently to allow him to participate in at least a minimum amount of athletic activity.

Let us refer back to the junior-high-school girl who was having behavioral problems in her science class. She earned tokens for adequate behavior and these were given to her at the end of each class. She used the tokens to buy time in group counseling sessions. Evidently she enjoyed these sessions because they provided an opportunity to talk about her problems. Prior to the token system, the counseling sessions had not changed her general behavior in almost a year. (It is possible the unearned sessions had actually reinforced the deviant behavior since this was the reason she was sent to counseling.) Once the token system was introduced, however, and she could go to counseling only if her behavior in science was adequate, she improved markedly. In another class she was similarly rewarded and used these tokens to buy time as an office worker. There was high status attached to such positions by the eighth-grade girls, probably because of the high degree of visibility. She worked conscientiously in class in order to earn the privilege of working in the office. Given free choice, group counseling and office work were high frequency behaviors for this student. They became reinforcing for low-frequency behavior (studying) through the mediation of a token system.

Another way of applying the Premack principle is through "high strength" areas in the classroom. Research at the Experimental Education Unit of the University of Washington employs this principle (see Haring and Hayden, 1966). Part of the classroom is designated as a "probable high-strength area" and contains various games and toys which appeal to children of the class' general age group. The academic part of the classroom is designated as a "probable low-strength area." This approach, as it is utilized at the E.E.U., is discussed in detail in Chapter 10.

High-probability behaviors are powerful reinforcers and probably have not been investigated or utilized enough. They offer a particularly interesting way to motivate older teenage students. This is a highly active group usually interested in getting involved in activities that have some relevance to their goals and ideals. They are particularly prone to scorn "busy work." While many rebel against the system, it may very well be that the system does not seem particularly relevant to their goals. We have wondered, e.g., why the very bright or gifted adolescent could not earn time out of school for other productive activity if he is capable of finishing the required academic work in 3 or 4 days a week instead of 5. There are probably many alternatives to a full academic day that could enhance rather than hinder academic and social goals.

Earlier in this chapter we alluded to one of the most important of all reinforcers—teacher attention. Let us take a closer look at this very significant variable and examine further how it operates in the classroom.

Teacher attention, like any reinforcer, will maintain the behavior it follows. The little boy with the reading problem discussed earlier was being heavily reinforced by teacher and other adult attention for his reading problem. So it continued until we reserved attention for acceptable oral reading. The junior-high-school girl, after beginning her token reward system, remarked to the teacher, "The only time you paid any attention to me was when I was bad." She was able to state her need clearly and once this was satisfied by attention following desirable behavior, she changed dramatically. This suggests, incidentally, that the main power of a token or point system may be that it focuses teacher attention on the desired behavior. Perhaps the "real" reinforcer here is social and not the token or what it can buy.

Recent research also confirms the power of teacher attention in influencing classroom behaviors. Hall and others (1968) studied the effect of teacher attention on the study behavior of one first-grade and five third-grade children who had "high rates of disruptive and dawdling behavior." The investigators obtained baserates on three variables: (1) study behavior, (2) nonstudy behavior, and (3) teacher proximity. These data were gathered over a 2-week period with two to four 30-minute observations each week on each child. The data were recorded at 10-second intervals. That is, the observer noted what the child was doing every ten seconds during the half-hour rather than keeping a constant record of the child's behavior. This is easily accomplished by having an interval timer attached to a clipboard that gives a visual or auditory signal at the specified intervals.

The investigators then set out to change the teacher's behavior so that she would be giving attention (reinforcement) for appropriate behaviors. During the reinforcement period the observer would hold up a small square of colored paper and the teacher would use this as a signal to attend to the designated child both physically (moving closer, giving a friendly pat on the shoulder) and verbally. In this way it was possible for the observer to systematically control teacher attention. The changes in student behavior were quite convincing. From a baseline of about 25%, their study behavior increased dramatically to about 90% after only 10 sessions of controlled reinforcement. To further demonstrate the effectiveness of teacher attention, the contingencies were reversed, i.e., the teacher returned to attending to nonstudy behavior. Contingency reversal is often used in research of this kind so that there can be no doubt that the independent variable is effective. As a result of the reversal in this research, the study rate of these children dropped back to 40%. Then reinforcement was reinstated for study behavior, the contingencies were reversed, and the study behavior increased again. The increased rate continued to hold up even after the cueing of the teachers was discontinued, suggesting that they had learned to attend more to study than to nonstudy behavior among their students.

This research was carried on in crowded classrooms in schools within an urban poverty area. However, the investigators report that the research procedures did not seem to interfere with the ordinary classroom routines. On the contrary, even after the investigators and teachers achieved their goals, the atmosphere in the rooms was greatly improved and the teachers had more time to devote to teaching.

One of us was recently a consultant in a program which was aimed at changing teaching behavior. When a teacher made a referral of a problem to the staff of the project he was obliged to bring his class to a special room for a week of observation and teacher training. The staff made many video tapes of the class, modeled appropriate behaviors for the teacher, and "wired him for sound," i.e., equipped him with a small FM radio and an ear plug so that he could receive directions from a staff member behind one-way glass. This proved to be a very effective way of changing behavior just as it was occurring.

Becker and his associates (1967) also studied the relationship between teacher attention and disruptive classroom behavior. Ten children from five different elementary school classes served as subjects for this experiment. This particular school was also in an urban ghetto. The observers selected two children in each class who exhibited high rates of disruptive behavior and these became the "target" children for behavior modification procedures. Baseline measures showed that these children had an average deviant behavior rate of 62.13% which seemed to bear out the original impression they made on the observers. Teachers were instructed, in general, to ignore the deviant behavior and give positive attention to the desired behaviors. As in the previous study, the teachers were to give praise and approval to the youngster when he was doing the "right" thing and ignore him when he was not. But this was to be done for all the children, not just the target children.

The experimental period lasted approximately 2 months and, while there was some variation among the 10 children selected for specific study, the average rate of deviant behavior dropped to 29.19%. This is a substantial change from 62%. In addition, there were some beneficial side effects which, while not measured, were still rather obvious. The general tone of the classes improved markedly and there was much more time available for academic pursuits since so much less was spent in discipline.

The investigators also found that the children were helped when the modes or models of desirable behavior were explicitly pointed out by the teachers as they reinforced this behavior in other youngsters. By observing the reinforced youngsters, the more obstreperous ones learned how to receive positive teacher attention. This emphasis on positive teacher attention paid off in still another way. The teachers were so busy reinforcing desirable behavior that they had little time or opportunity to attend to the undesirable. This rather automatically put the deviant behavior on extinction and thus helped to maintain this aspect of the modification procedures.

The investigators conclude:

> The results of these investigations demonstrate that quite different kinds of teachers can learn to apply behavioral principles effectively to modify the behavior of problem children. These results extend to the elementary classroom, with normal teacher-pupil ratios, the importance of *differential* social reinforcement in developing effective social behaviors in children. Work now in progress suggests that rules alone do nothing and that simply ignoring deviant behavior actually increases such behavior. *The combination of ignoring deviant behavior and reinforcing incompatible behavior seems critical.*

It seems to us that these conclusions are particularly important for the teacher who is trying to use these techniques in the average classroom with the average number of children. It is *not* enough to just ignore the deviant child. In fact, this may be impossible, and it is likely that he will always get a little attention (reinforcement) for his deviant behavior. To most efficiently modify the child's behavior, the teacher must reinforce an incompatible behavior. Study behavior is incompatible with nonstudy behavior. Quiet behavior is incompatible with talking. The child learns the incompatible behavior because it is the one that receives the reinforcement.

In another study, Thomas and others (1968) systematically varied teacher behavior in such a way as to produce or eliminate disruptive classroom behavior. (See Chapter 2 for the baseline data.) The class used in this research was once again an elementary school class with 28 children ranging in age from about seven to eight. The teacher was in her second year of teaching and volunteered for the project.

After the baserates were obtained on the various measures of student and teacher behavior, modification procedures began. These consisted of varying teacher approval and disapproval of student behaviors. In the initial baserate conditions, i.e., the natural classroom conditions, the student disruptive behavior occurred 8.7% of the time. During this time the teacher was responding to the students with 7.1% approval and 4.3% disapproval. The first experimental condition was "no approval." The teacher was instructed to try very hard not to approve of any student behavior and to increase her disapproval. She dropped her approval to .6% and increased her disapproval to 10.7%. Under these conditions of frequent disapproval and infrequent approval, the disruptive classroom behaviors climbed to 25.5%. One can see a "vicious circle" operating here. The more the teacher disapproved, the more the students misbehaved. After all, this was the behavior that got teacher attention.

Then the experimenters asked the teacher to return to baserate conditions. Disruptive behavior dropped to 12.9% somewhat higher than the original baserate but significantly lower than under the first experimental condition. Next, the condition of no approval was reinstated and the disruptive behaviors rose to 19.4%, and then climbed still higher to 31.2% when she was instructed to be very disapproving.

Now this teacher was behaving as many of us might as a matter of course when confronted with a class full of problem behavior. Fortunately, we are now in a far better position to understand the processes which influence behavior, thanks to systematic examination of important variables. These investigators demonstrated that they could markedly alter the behavior of the children by changing the behavior of the teacher. The teacher could now take a more influential role in managing the classroom. They also noted, "The frequency of Relevant Behaviors was high whenever Approving Behaviors followed Relevant Behavior, and decreased whenever Approving Behaviors were discontinued." They go on to make two very interesting observations:

> First, the teacher who uses her Approving Behaviors as immediate consequences for good behavior should find that the frequency and duration of appropriate behaviors increase in her classroom (at least for most children). On the other hand, the teacher who cuddles the miscreant, tries pleasantly to get a child to stop behaving disruptively, talks with a child so that he "understands" what he is doing wrong, or who pleasantly suggests an alternative activity, is likely to find an increase in the very behaviors she had hoped to reduce.

We have included a fairly detailed look at the research reported in this chapter because it repeatedly demonstrates the validity of the basic thesis of this book: teacher behavior is closely related to that of the students and the teacher does, for good or ill, influence the classroom. He has the potential for greater precision if he arranges important contingencies in a systematic manner. Probably the most important of these is his attention as manifested through approving and disapproving student actions.

Note that much of the research reported here has involved ordinary classrooms with the usual number of children. Teachers, albeit with observer-recorders, have modified the behavior of children consistently and significantly. The behavioral techniques do work in the usual classroom. It may take a little ingenuity to get the appropriate data and find adequate reinforcers, but this is only a challenge to the creativity and flexibility of the teacher. The system works.

By this point, the reader may surmise that a very close relationship exists between strengthening desirable behavior—the focus of this chapter—and eliminating undesirable behavior—the topic of the next. This tends to result in some unavoidable redundancy later on, though the emphasis will be rather different.

These same principles which we have been discussing hold when we are concerned with academic behavior. Reinforce that which is desirable, and extinguish that which is undesirable. Try marking only the correct responses on a spelling paper. Make them stand out, not the incorrect. Positive reinforcement is a teaching tool through which education can be converted from a trying experience to an enjoyable one. It would be quite an educational triumph if, in the usual hierarchy of probable behaviors, study behavior became so strong that it could be used as a reinforcement for nonstudy behavior, and a student would only be permitted to do his arithmetic after he had successfully completed recess.

SCHEDULES OF REINFORCEMENT

No discussion of objective teaching would be complete without some reference to *schedules of reinforcement.* How much, how often, and when should we reinforce? We stated earlier that it is generally better to reinforce a child frequently but, while this general rule is true, it is often impractical. A teacher has only so much time to give to the 30 or so students in his class (about 12 minutes per student in a 6-hour day), and he cannot reinforce every response that the students make. However, we have seen that there are ways of building up the quantity of reinforcement. A point system for correct academic responses makes it certain that these will be reinforced even if the teacher is not present each time one is made. Not only can one arrange formally written programmed materials so as to enable the learner to respond correctly most of the time, but also he can add appropriate encouraging phrases as additional reinforcement. For example, on some teaching machines the student may be congratulated by the machine after a given number of correct responses. This is especially true with computerized instruction. It is almost as if another person is overseeing the student's work when the machine types back encouragement or even a reprimand.

Recently we were involved in a demonstration of computer techniques and were asked to engage in a dialogue with the computer wherein it would "ask" questions and we would provide (hopefully) the appropriate answers. This series happened to be on the physics of light and the computer asked, "What major invention preceded the laser?" Trying to throw the machine off a bit, we typed back, "The candle," whereupon the machine retorted, "Don't be ridiculous!" After that we gave reasonable answers.

It will probably be a long time before machines take over much of the teaching function and until they do, the teacher still has this problem of how much time to devote to reinforcing student behavior. In general, the teacher should reinforce most heavily when the student is learning a new task and less when he is maintaining a behavior that has been well learned. Therefore, for most academic work that involves new learning, reinforcement should be frequent and consistent on what is called a *continuous schedule of reinforcement.* Such a schedule requires that each correct response obtain reinforcement. If the learning task is reasonably well programmed so that the steps in the learning provide many opportunities for success, there is a built-in quantity of reinforcement since success provides automatic reinforcement for most students. If not, then a token system coupled with a generous amount of teacher approval may eventually make success more reinforcing.

When the desired behavior is social rather than academic and is to be maintained over a long period of time, the teacher may turn to an *intermittent schedule of reinforcement.* In such a schedule, several correct responses may be required for reinforcement (ratio schedule), or a given time may have to elapse before it is given (interval schedule). As an example, let us assume that the behavior in question is class participation as indicated by a child's raising his hand in order to comment or answer questions. He has been rather heavily reinforced for hand raising by teacher approval (on a continuous schedule) until he has acquired a very high rate of this behavior. At this point the teacher wishes to "thin out" the reinforcement but still maintain the behavior. One way to do this would be to gradually decrease the number of times that the teacher called on this student (moving to a ratio or interval schedule), but to do this in a random and nonsystematic fashion. In other words, the child would not know when he was going to be called but would know just that he would be called if he continued to raise his hand.

Schedules of reinforcement, then, imply the rate at which reinforcement is dispensed for desired behavior. Since continuous reinforcement requires a reinforcement for each correct response, the ratio of reinforcement in a continuous schedule is often written 1 : 1.

Ratio schedules may be either *fixed* (FR) or *variable* (VR). In a fixed ratio, the subject obtains a reinforcer only after a given and fixed number of responses. Thus, if a child were required to solve 5 multiplication problems before being given his reinforcer (say, a token), he would be on a fixed ratio 5 : 1. However, if he were required to do 7 problems before reinforcement, he would be on an FR 7 : 1.

A variable ratio schedule calls for reinforcement to be dispensed according to number of correct responses, but the number required is systematically varied. In some cases, the subject may have to make 4 responses (4 : 1) to receive reinforcement, but the next time he may be required to make more, say 6 (6 : 1) and then 8 (8 : 1). The number of responses required for reinforcement is averaged to determine the exact variable-ratio schedule. In this case, 4 : 1 and 6 : 1 and 8 : 1 are averaged and the variable ratio is 6 : 1.

For example, we were consultants for two years in an inner-city middle school. We had discovered several extrinsic reinforcers that seemed to do an excellent job of motivating the students. These were at first contingent on the student completing carefully prescribed academic tasks at a level of 80% accuracy. They were rewarded on a continuous schedule. We soon found that the students would hurry through the tasks, get their reinforcer, and then become fairly disruptive for the remainder of the class time. We increased the number of tasks before reinforcement but this still resulted in some of the faster students finishing and disturbing the slower students. We could have increased the tasks even further but we didn't want to discourage the slower students. In addition, we wanted to maintain the sense of fairness the students felt about the procedure. We also could have put some sort of contingency on appropriate behavior, but we wanted to keep the emphasis on academic behaviors in this class reasoning that if we could keep the students busy on a productive task we would not have disruptive behaviors. So we informed the students that they would no longer be rewarded after, in this case, three tasks, but that their reward would be indeterminate. They would never know ahead of time which task would be reinforced.

The students grumbled a little at this but soon accepted it. We marked the teacher's assignment book in a manner which enabled her to know which tasks were to be rewarded. Thus, we gradually thinned the schedule over several weeks so that students were eventually doing about twice as much work as previously for the same rewards. They also worked the entire class time! A significant aspect of this "thinning" of extrinsic reinforcers was to increase teacher praise regarding objective improvement so that normal social reinforcers would become more palatable to youngsters who had considerable distrust for adults. Thus as we cut back on the contrived reinforcers we attempted to bring about a better relationship between the teacher and her students. While our data showed that this occurred in the available time we were never able to drop the tangible rewards.

Interval schedules, generally less frequently used in education, provide for reinforcement to be obtained for the first response following a given interval of time, say 10 seconds. Just as in ratio schedules, the time interval may be fixed or varied from time to time.

Very high rates of responding can be maintained by a variable-ratio schedule. This schedule, as other intermittent schedules, is also far more resistant to extinction than continuous schedules. In other words, if a child is reinforced on a continuous schedule (1 : 1) but then reinforcement is discontinued, he will rapidly stop responding. However, he will continue to respond long after the discontinuance of reinforcement if he has been reinforced on a variable-ratio schedule.

Let us look, now, at what happens when a teacher uses a *fixed-ratio schedule* in maintaining hand raising behavior. We recently had a graduate student observing in a classroom in which the teacher complained of the lack of participation of one little boy in particular. He spent a significant amount of his time in nonstudy behavior and seemed to be paying little attention to the usual classroom procedures. While other children recited or answered questions, he gazed out the window or did other things that were very distracting to the teacher.

This teacher's method of gaining class participation was to call on the class in a fixed order. She started with one row, went completely through this, then on to the next. This was actually a fixed-ratio schedule because the frequency with which a child's hand raising response was reinforced was fixed by the number of students in the class. Thus, if there were 30 students, the youngster in this example was on a fixed ratio of 30 : 1. Under this schedule there was a general current of unrest in the room although this little boy did stand out. When his turn came, he participated briefly and then went back to doing other things. It was highly likely that his nonstudy behavior was being reinforced by teacher attention. In this situation there was a long interval in which the only way the student could receive reinforcement was by doing those very things of which the teacher disapproved. When, with the encouragement of the observer, she changed her behavior and began to call on her class according to a much more variable schedule (variable ratio), the little boy's nonstudy behavior dropped off significantly. What we are saying here is that reinforcement is much more effective if it is certain but unpredictable. The economy of the state of Nevada rests to a significant extent on this very principle.

Fixed schedules of reinforcement do have a place in the classroom, however, when they are properly associated with the desired behavior. For example, it might be very appropriate to teach a child better study habits by reinforcing him for fixed intervals of studying. He could be reinforced on a fixed-interval basis, say every 10 minutes, if during the period of observation he had met the criteria for appropriate study behavior. Once this interval was fairly thoroughly established, the teacher could increase the study time required for reinforcement and gradually build up study behavior so that it was a reasonable part of the child's repertoire. At this point, some variable schedule would become more appropriate for maintaining the behavior.

A common classroom practice is to offer the students some reinforcement after a fixed amount of work is done (a fixed ratio schedule) or after a specific period of time if the work is done. A major problem with the fixed ratio schedule is the tendency to reinforce speed rather than accuracy. So the teacher must be certain that the ratio is stated in terms of accurate responses, not just total number. In the case of the fixed-interval schedule, there is a danger of reinforcing nonstudy behaviors because the brighter children will tend to dawdle during the first part of the interval and then work rapidly as the time runs out. Then one of the things being reinforced here would be "dawdling behavior" on the part of the bright student. Probably a fixed ratio schedule is best for most classroom activities where the teacher can stipulate that the reinforcement—for example, free reading—is available as soon as the student has done the required work accurately.

One final word about reinforcers. Many of them tend to "run out." There is probably a satiation principle applicable here much as there is with food. We think this is particularly true of the contrived reinforcers, although a token system avoids this to some extent by allowing the youngster several choices for his tokens. It is also probable that the natural reinforcers do not loose their properties so readily. We all seem to like lots of attention and approval and rarely seem to become satiated.

As teachers devote more attention to contingency management and utilize the principles espoused here, school will become a more positive experience for most children and learning will increase proportionately. Once positive reinforcement is given its rightful place in the teaching process, significant advances will occur in rates of learning and other aspects of academic achievement.

SUMMARY

Most behavior is affected by its consequences. These consequences are reinforcing if, as a result, the behavior increases; punishing if the behavior decreases. If there is no consequence, the behavior will tend to extinguish and we call this process extinction.

There are two basic kinds of reinforcement, positive and negative. Positive reinforcement involves the presentation of a rewarding stimulus following the desired behavior, while negative reinforcement calls for the removal of a punishing stimulus following a given response. Both increase the frequency of the desired response.

The seven principles of contingency control that are related to good classroom management are as follows: (1) Reinforcers are determined by their effect on the learner. (2) Reinforcers affect behavior automatically. (3) Reinforcers should be clearly linked to the behavioral criteria of learning. (4) Reinforcement should be administered consistently. (5) Reinforcement should follow immediately the behavior to be modified. (6) Reinforcement should be frequent and should appear early in the learning sequence. (7) Reinforcement should be applied at each step of the learning sequence.

There are 6 major categories of reinforcers: (1) consumables, (2) manipulatables, (3) visual and auditory stimuli, (4) social stimuli, (5) tokens or points, and (6) high-strength behaviors (Premack principle). Among these six, the most "natural" for the teacher are the social reinforcers, and these have also proven to be among the most potent. Teacher attention, teacher approval, and teacher disapproval are powerful factors in student behavior, and they can by systematically varied to produce both desirable and undesirable behavior. In utilizing this inherent power, however, the teacher must be sure to reinforce desirable behaviors as well as to ignore the undesirable if he is to achieve his goal of maximizing learning.

While it would be desirable if the teacher could reinforce all appropriate student behaviors, this is practically an impossibility. It is important to reinforce new learning as much as possible on a continuous schedule of reinforcement. To maintain behavior, a variable schedule in which reinforcement is certain but unpredictable is frequently used. Predictable or fixed schedules do have value when applied to certain categories of behavior. A common problem is that the wrong behavior may be inadvertently reinforced.

REFERENCES

Becker, W. C., Madsen, C. H., Arnold, C. R., & Thomas, D. R. The contingent use of teacher attention and praise in reducing classroom behavior problems. *The Journal of Special Education*, 1967,1, 287–307.

Bijou, S. W., & Sturges, P. S. Positive reinforcers for experimental studies with children —consumables and manipulatables. *Child development*, 1959, 30 151–170.

Deci, E. L. Work—who does not like it and why. *Psychology Today*, 1972 (August), 57–ff.

Hall, R. V., Lund, D., & Jackson, D. Effects of teacher attention on study behavior. *Journal of Applied Behavior Analysis*, 1968, 1, 1–12.

Haring, N., & Hayden, A. The program and facilities of the experimental education unit of the university of washington mental retardation and child development center. In *Special education programs within the United States* (M.V. Jones, ed.). Springfield, Illinois: C.H. Thomas, 1966.

Lovaas, I., Beberich, J. P., Perloff, B. F., & Schaeffer, B. Acquisition of imitative speech in schizophrenic children. *Science*, 1966 (February), 151, 707.

MacDonald, W. S. *Battle in the classroom: innovations in classroom techniques*. New York and London: Intext Educational Publishers, 1971.

Mandelker, A. V., Brigham, T.A., & Bushell, D. The effects of token procedures on a teacher's social contacts with her students. *Journal of Applied Behavior Analysis*, 1970, 3, 168–174.

Meacham, M. L. & Gall, R. S. *Behavior modification in the schools: a selected annotated bibliography*. University of Washington, School Psychology and Counseling Laboratory, January, 1970. (Mimeographed).

Michael, J. Management of behavioral consequences in education. Southwest Regional Laboratory for Educational Research and Development, Inglewood, California, 1967.

Miller, N. Learning of visceral and glandular responses. *Science*, 1969, 163, 434–445.

Morse, W. H. Intermittent reinforcement. In *Operant behavior: areas of research and application* (W.K. Honig, ed.). New York: Appleton-Century-Crofts, 1966.

Premack, D. Reinforcement theory. In *Nebraska symposium on motivation* (D. Levine, ed.). University of Nebraska Press, 1965, 123–180.

Risley, T. Learning and lollipops. *Psychology Today*, 1968, 1 (8), 28–31 & 62–65.

Runyon, H. L., & Williams, R. L. Differentiating reinforcement priorities of junior high school students. *Journal of Experimental Education*, 1972, 40 (3) 76–80.

Thomas, D. R., Becker, W. C., & Armstrong, M. Production and elimination of disruptive classroom behavior by systematically varying teacher's behavior. *Journal of Applied Behavior Analysis*, 1968, 1, 35–45.

SUGGESTED READINGS

Bijou, S. W. Patterns of reinforcement and resistance to extinction in young children. *Child Development,* 1957, 28, 47–53.

Glynn, E. L. Classroom applications of self-determined reinforcement. *Journal of Applied Behavior Analysis,* 1970, 3, 123–132.

Griffiths, W. J. & Griffiths, M. T. Reinforcement schedules and response variability. *Journal of General Psychology,* 1965, 107, 23–28.

Homme, L. E., deBaca, P. C., Devine, J. V., Steinhorst, R., & Rickert, E. J. Use of the premack principle in controlling behavior of nursery school children. *Journal of Experimental Analysis of Behavior,* 1963, 6, 544.

Lovitt, T. C., & Curtiss, K. A. Academic response rate as a function of teacher and self-imposed contingencies. *Journal of Applied Behavior Analysis,* 1969, 2, 49–54.

O'Leary, K. D., & Becker, W. C. Behavior modification of an adjustment class: a token reinforcement program. *Exceptional Children,* 1967, 33, 637–642.

Powers, W. T. Feeedback: beyond behaviorism. *Science,* 1973, 179 (4071), 351–355.

Wiesen, A. E., G. Hartley, C. Richardson, & Roske, A. The retarded child as a reinforcing agent. *Journal of Experimental Child Psychology,* 1967, 5, 109–113.

5
Eliminating Undesirable Behavior

When a young child enters school, he is entering what amounts to an educational lottery. If he is lucky, he will be assigned a teacher who understands the principles of objective teaching, one who relies heavily on the development of positive expectancies and on positive reinforcement to promote learning. If he is unlucky, he will be placed in a class operated on the erroneous idea that punishment and threat facilitate education, and he will develop an aversion toward school and toward learning.

It is the school's responsibility to develop in each child a favorable attitude toward learning. In the early grades, the development of this attitude is particularly crucial. It is essential to realize that an individual's ability to function in an advanced society requires a high level of education. If later pursuit of education may reasonably be associated with positive expectancies resulting from positive learning experiences in school, it becomes apparent that an individual's personal growth and his potential contribution to society can be enhanced by early positive school experiences. Conversely, it would also follow that aversive experiences in school can seriously limit both an individual's personal development and his contribution to society.

SIDE EFFECTS OF PUNISHMENT

There are strong indications that anxiety arising from an aversive school environment produces a physical-and/or emotional-avoidance response. The aversive elements in our educational system establish active or passive resistance to

63

learning. Specific manifestations of punishment pose problems directly affecting the society. Absenteeism, often culminating in the act of dropping out, can be seen as the most direct avoidance response attributable to the aversive techniques employed by schools to "motivate" students. Vandalism in the schools often reveals just what is thought of these techniques and of the experiences they offer. Anxiety, fear, and conformity, though more subtle, are also the result of punishing experiences and result in emotional escape from the classroom. Often the "good" student is really so frightened and intimidated by his teachers and the system that he readily relinquishes creativity for passing grades, originality for conformity. Daydreaming or apathetic inattention may become the escape routes chosen by students who are subjected to negative emotional experiences in the classroom.

The historic and continued use of punishment and other forms of aversive influence reveals at least covertly a predominant view of the nature of man. We tend to act as though man is inherently evil and unless he is controlled and suppressed, he will behave accordingly. In the classroom, aversive techniques range from the raised eyebrow of the teacher to outright humiliation by peers, extra assignments, a dressing down by the principal, or even corporal punishment. While these may temporarily suppress undesirable behavior, the emotional responses they produce usually generalize to other aspects of the school program,[1] and the result of frequent use of aversive procedures may be an overall reduction in degree of participation by students who seek the safety of anonymity. Students may begin to arrive late, complain of physical symptoms which release them from school, or may actually become more disruptive.

School phobia, the intense fear that is generated by the prospect of another school day, has received considerable interest in recent years (Patterson, 1965a). Traditionally, this problem has been considered to result from an internal conflict usually exacerbated by poor familial relations. Assumptions of this nature fail to take into account the actual aversive properties of many schools. Remaining at home, even in a state of family disruption, is often selected as the lesser of two evils.

The degree to which aversive practices such as constant disapproval will actually increase disruptive classroom behavior is illustrated in the study by Thomas et al. (1968) mentioned earlier. Very well-behaved 7- and 8-year-old children were observed through various periods as teacher behavior was varied. At one stage in the study, the teacher stopped giving approval and actually began a policy of severe disapproval in which no positive reinforcement was given. During this period, disruptive behavior was found to rise from the low-initial-baserate average of 8.7% to 31.2%, an increase of over 200%. In other words,

---

[1]John B. Watson's famous experiment in which Albert learned to avoid objects similar to a white rat which had been paired with a loud, sudden noise illustrates the degree to which fear may become generalized.

by employing a critical, derogatory approach toward discipline, the teacher not only failed to improve discipline but actually created "monsters" out of the usually pleasant youngsters in the classroom. Noise and general activity level increased markedly and what had been an orderly classroom, became a sort of educational nightmare. Fortunately, the situation was systematically returned to normal as the last phase of the study.

In addition to a specific increase in overt disruptive behavior, another side effect of an excessively punitive classroom environment is that of a general increase in aggressive preoccupation among the students. The teacher who employs a series of punishing and threatening actions for classroom management may be setting a precedent for his students to the effect that such tactics are not only acceptable but also immediately successful. Students may then imitate or model (see Chapter 6) this approach in their own dealings with others, primarily those they consider to be in a subordinate position. The degree to which a punitive teacher may actually encourage a similar behavioral predisposition among students is well demonstrated in the research of Kounin and Gump (1968).

The students who served as subjects were 74 boys and 100 girls, all in the first grade though in three different schools. Six teachers were selected, three rated as punitive and three as nonpunitive. These were first selected by the principal and assistant principal. Additional ratings were made by the investigators and a student-teacher supervisor. No pair of teachers was employed in the study unless all five raters agreed that the pair represented a true dichotomy of punitiveness-nonpunitiveness. The three punitive teachers were recorded as using severe threats of harmful consequences to the children and as generally indicating a readiness to use punishment for infractions of classroom regulations. The three nonpunitive teachers received high ratings in the category "does not punish and does not threaten."

Each child was interviewed separately during the third month of school attendance. Each was asked his opinion regarding the worst thing a student could possibly do in school, followed by a further question as to why the act selected was so bad. The same questions were asked in regard to a child's actions at home. The replies were carefully coded within various content categories by the researchers, and the reliability among the researchers was about 90%.

The results strongly indicated that even the relatively short-term contact in the classroom between teacher and students had rather dramatic effects on the children. Children who had experienced a punitive classroom environment had much more aggressive and violent action in their replies than children from a nonpunitive class. The latter group of students tended to give replies in which the "victim" of the misdeed suffered psychological consequences rather than physical assault. The significance of this difference can be more clearly understood when we look at how the 84 children in the punitive group and the 90 children in the nonpunitive group responded. In the punitive group, 31 replied that physical assaults were of major concern while the rest cited school violations and other infractions. However, in the nonpunitive group, only 15 were preoccupied with accounts of physical assaults, the rest being school violations and miscellaneous misdeeds. In general, students who had nonpunitive teachers were more concerned with values directly related to the school situation. They tended to talk more about academic achievement and learning than children from a punitive environment, the latter emphasizing physical aggression not unique to the classroom.

When we consider the evolutionary nature of society and recognize the tremendous impact of a child's classroom experiences on his overall attitudes and behavior, it becomes apparent that a punitive classroom environment may sow the seeds for aggression even beyond the limits of the school and well into the future. In controlling children through punishment, threat, and coercion, the excessively punitive teacher is, in effect, teaching the children to be aggressive by serving as a model of aggressiveness. The emergence of imitation as a powerful force in learning (see Chapter 6) was perhaps insufficiently recognized by such writers as Freud and Lorenz who, in viewing the history of aggression among men, attribute it to an instinctual factor over which we have little real control.

The nonpunitive, positive atmosphere we advocate need not be one which is overly permissive. We believe that children must be increasingly exposed to the logical consequences of their actions as they develop into maturity. They must assume a greater degree of responsibility for their actions. But while young children need some guidance so that they can adequately learn basic academic skills, they need not learn to be authoritarian in the process.

To a greater degree than we might expect, our own student experiences influence the kind of experiences we provide our students. This kind of behavior modeling largely accounts for the continuation of aversive practices from generation to generation and impedes progress in the development of more rationally based methods of education. The time is now ripe for a critical look at the philosophy and traditional practices upon which classroom teaching has been based. There is now little doubt that habitual use of punishment creates far more problems than it solves and that at best it suppresses undesirable behavior, but does not extinguish it. The use of an aversive approach is rarely justified, but failure to link it up with a contingency program in which a student's objective learning is warmly received places it on exceedingly thin ice.

IDENTIFYING INTERFERING BEHAVIORS

In recent years a great many educators and psychologists have begun to recognize that certain kinds of behavior compete with or totally preclude the learning of other, more adaptive behavior (Bijou, 1968). While many behaviors may actually interfere with new responses, the concept of *interfering behavior* is reserved here for those specific behaviors which are not only themselves undesirable, but occur so continually, and at such a high rate, as to reduce markedly the probability of any other responses being made. It is quite possible that much of the behavior currently resulting in a diagnosis of "mental retardation" or "childhood autism" will eventually be viewed as merely severe interfering behavior.[2]

While the more severe examples of this behavior are frequently found in institutions for the retarded or so-called mentally ill, it is not uncommon in the average classroom, particularly among younger children.

High rates of general activity described as restlessness or hyperactivity are frequently seen in younger children and are often automatically reinforcing because they enable the children to expend energy and escape the aversive properties of sitting still. In some cases, high activity rates are reinforced by the attention of either the teacher or classmates and interfere with a child's ability to attend to presented material.

A broad range of behavior, including constant talking, looking around, throwing objects, poking other students, etc., is often reinforced by teacher or student attention, preventing learning by the child emitting such behavior and impeding the work of his classmates.

Aggressive and destructive behaviors are particularly disruptive and are often rewarded by peers who are in turn reinforced by the temporary diversion provided. While peer reinforcement exerts powerful influence beyond the boundaries of the classroom, the teacher can influence the direction of behavior within the classroom by systematic control of reinforcers.

In general, the assumption that children are naturally restless and must, therefore, be expected to display high rates of undirected behavior leads to exactly that. Excessive movements may serve as a signal for the teacher to unknowingly provide more interesting material, change the activity, or permit recess. This approach, designed to attract or divert student interest, often tends to reinforce the restless or disruptive behavior which interferes with successful learning.

SETTING LIMITS

While the need to set limits on behavior is generally accepted, all too often either the limits themselves, their enforcement, or both, are relatively capricious.

[2]Interfering behavior may be inadvertently reinforced by even the experienced researcher. One of the authors found that while he was attempting to reinforce specific responses by a youngster, he was also reinforcing certain perseverative responses such as saying yellow in reaction to any color. The experimenter was correcting too much and the attention served as a reinforcer. This was corrected by the experimenter removing the tangible reinforcers he was using whenever a perseverative response occurred.

The combination of arbitrary limits and punishment produces an environment in which students have little way of knowing what is permissible in the classroom, but are nevertheless apt to be punished for infractions. A typical student response to this kind of environment is to determine the teacher's mood on a given day and use it as a cue. They usually learn that when a teacher is in a good mood, they can behave inappropriately with a low probability of punishment. However, on those days when the teacher is more irascible, disruptive or noisy behavior may be suppressed. Of course, this also produces an environment in which students are negatively reinforced (escaping punishment) for learning a difficult "mood" discrimination. Other students, less capable of making subtle distinctions of this nature, find themselves in an unpredictable environment and may experience a considerable degree of anxiety. Furthermore, this kind of classroom situation promotes behavior that is commonly referred to as manipulation—a behavior which is of dubious ethical value in a free society.

These problems can be overcome by establishing a classroom environment in which desirable and undesirable behaviors are clearly stated and whenever possible, mutually agreed upon by student and teacher; one in which classroom standards are planned, made clear to the students, and maintained consistently, largely through an atmosphere of creative learning enhanced by positive outcomes.

A first step, then, is to select those behaviors which interfere with previously established academic goals and social learning goals. We cannot stress enough the need to encourage student participation in this selection (as well as in the selection of desirable behaviors) so that they have a greater role in classroom policy making. There is growing evidence that student involvement in the establishment of contingencies may be as critical a factor as the nature of the contingencies themselves (Lovitt and Curtiss, 1969). Once established it is particularly useful to make a list of undesirable behaviors, which might look as follows:

Undesirable Classroom Behaviors

1   fighting
2   yelling
3   destroying property
4   poking or pulling other students
5   disturbing other students
6   making loud noises, etc. (depending on the makeup of the class)

Once these interfering behaviors have been defined, the goal is *not* to set up a system of punishment for occurrences, but to plan the classroom environment so as to markedly reduce the probability of these responses being emitted.[3] There is now increasing belief (see Chapter 6) that the environment, and more

[3]A consideration touched upon by B.F. Skinner (1968), but not elaborated upon.

specifically the "setting events" within it which serve as cues for behavior, has great influence. Student seating must be arranged so that there is sufficient space between students to reduce the chance of pushing or accidental bumping which is distracting and which may result in other undesirable behaviors. This is particularly the case with younger students. A generally bright and attractive classroom atmosphere is certainly advisable. If a particular student is highly distracting, seat him near students who have the highest rate of attending-to-teacher behavior so that he will not obtain reinforcement from them. By careful design of the classroom environment, you can immediately enhance the probability of desirable learning activity being pursued and can reduce the frequency of counterproductive behaviors.

EXTINCTION OF UNDESIRABLE BEHAVIOR

While careful design of the classroom can certainly reduce the frequency of undesirable behavior, certain students, nevertheless, will present problems which disrupt ongoing activities. The teacher must then make specific decisions as to the means he will employ in changing the behavior of these students, but certain factors must first be taken into account.

The teacher must observe the behavior to determine whether or not it belongs to the category of undesirable classroom behaviors or is sufficiently undesirable to warrant addition to the list. If the behavior does not interfere with a student's performance and does not interfere with the rest of the class, there is probably little reason to modify it. Thus a behavior may annoy one personally without justifying remedial action. Students may scratch their heads, pull their ears, wear their hair long, have unusual opinions or odd facial expressions, but unless these are genuinely interfering, the teacher need not be concerned and should make every effort to be tolerant of irrelevant individual differences.

Assuming the behavior is interfering with either individual or class learning, the teacher is faced with a decision as to how to reduce or eliminate it most efficiently. He must take into account the various possibilities open to him: punishing the undesirable behavior, extinguishing the undesirable behavior, reinforcing a competing desirable behavior, or simply removing the student. Being consistent with contemporary knowledge, we will focus mainly on the extinction of undesirable behavior while strongly acknowledging the necessity to simultaneously encourage competing desirable behavior through positive reinforcement.

Extinction, you will recall, is the gradual weakening of a response as a result of nonreinforcement. Careful observation of undesirable behavior usually enables the classroom teacher to define the reinforcing outcome which sustains it (attention, peer approval, etc.) and provides valuable information about how to effect its systematic removal, bringing about extinction.

As an example, teachers working with kindergarten or first-grade children occasionally come upon the excessive crier, the child who cries at the slightest provocation, particularly in the presence of adults. Observation reveals that this behavior is typically preceded by the child's looking around to make certain that there are adults available to provide the attention and sympathy which serve as reinforcers for this behavior. Further light was shed on this problem by Betty M. Hart (1964) and her associates. Teachers carefully avoided giving attention to the crying responses of two boys when they were not based on actual injury. In the course of a week, excessive crying was virtually eliminated and more appropriate responses to mild stress, which had been simultaneously reinforced by the teachers, took over as ways of dealing with stressful situations.

There is now considerable evidence that many kinds of troublesome behavior are easily eliminated by systematic withdrawal of attention. Temper tantrums, particularly common in younger children, are generally easily handled by complete withdrawal of attention and refusal by parents or teachers to yield to the child's demands during a tantrum. The classroom teacher must be careful to avoid reinforcing interfering behavior, then, by attention or concession. This requires considerable patience and maturity because many of the undesirable behaviors emitted by younger children in school are designed to attract attention by their dramatic or demanding nature.

A pertinent example appears in the study by Hall et al. (1968). A young male student was observed to spend about 75% of his classroom time in a variety of activities which interfered with studying. Included among these were talking to fellow students, playing with milk cartons, and removing toys and other small objects from his pockets and playing with them. Only 25% of his time was actually devoted to studying. It was observed during the recording of baseline data that the teacher tended to ask him repeatedly to begin work and put his things away. More than half of the teacher attention he received followed behaviors which interfered with studying. Clearly, teacher attention was a powerful reinforcer for this young student. By carefully redistributing the attention, that is, by rearranging the situation so that attention only followed one minute of solid study, the studying rate was brought up from 25% to almost 80%.

Another pattern of undesirable behavior which clearly contains interfering elements has been investigated by Quay et al. (1966). This pattern of behavior, fairly familiar to most teachers, consists of defiance, overactivity, aggression, and a general tendency to be irresponsible as far as academic work and punctuality are concerned. The child who displays this kind of behavior has been termed the "conduct problem child." Such a child has not only failed to develop the prerequisite social skills necessary for adequate classroom functioning but actually has opposed the situation rather openly. The researchers were charged with an especially difficult responsibility—to implement a reinforcement program in a classroom consisting entirely of conduct problem children. Fortunately, they had sufficient authority to regulate class enrollment and started off with just a small number of children. This enabled them, working directly with the teachers, to establish classroom procedures and routines with a few students before having to implement them with an entire class. Consistency was thus facilitated as additional students entered a structured classroom environment in which the teachers had already developed behavioral goals and had already set the limits of acceptable behavior. The program itself combined extinction and positive reinforcement in the form of candies. There was, however, a new twist. A box, which the teacher could light up from a central classroom position, was placed on each child's desk. Since a major problem was inattention, increased attending behavior by these active children was a primary goal. Each time a student looked up at the teacher for a given time while the teacher was talking or presenting material, the box on his desk was lit. This indicated to the student that he had earned a piece of candy. This simple and relatively inexpensive use of easily available equipment provided for instant reinforcement with minimal teacher time and no disruption of ongoing activity. Its effectiveness was demonstrated by a marked increase in rate of attending by the students. Concurrently, much of the disruptive behavior which had been so prevalent earlier was extinguished through simple lack of reinforcement. This approach enabled the teachers to extend reinforcement procedures to an entire special class without much additional help. Furthermore, since the teachers themselves could directly implement the program without requiring continuous psychological consultation, this gave additional support to their growing independence. Knowledgeable employment of selective reinforcement and extinction by the teacher frequently makes it unnecessary to obtain other professional consultation. As a matter of fact, in some cases positive reinforcement plus extinction of undesirable behavior may overcome conduct problems which have evaded the complex efforts of other professionals.

Once extinction is initiated, the teacher must make every effort to *totally avoid reinforcement for the undesirable behavior at any time in the future.* Merely waiting until one can no longer stand the inappropriate behavior is not only insufficient, but actually makes the undesirable behavior much more difficult to get rid of. This is because the child soon learns that if he is persistent enough in his behavior, the teacher will eventually yield. In other words, this practice puts the child on an intermittent schedule of reinforcement (as discussed in Chapter 4) which is constantly being stretched as the teacher tries harder not to give in, but finally does. This schedule of reinforcement results in behavior which is extremely difficult to extinguish, so the teacher is wise to avoid any attention or concession for undesirable activity, thus enabling rapid extinction and less of a headache for all concerned.

A rather intriguing problem confronting teachers is how to extinguish behavior reinforced by other students' attention. This was the kind of problem which faced G.R. Patterson (1965b) in his effort to reduce the extremely active classroom behavior of a 9-year-old boy. Earl's behavior consisted of talking, moving about the room, hitting, and generally disturbing other students by excessive movements. Occasional reinforcement was given by the other students who found some of his antics rather entertaining. Since Earl's classmates were the major source of reinforcement, Patterson set up an ingenious situation whereby both Earl and his fellow students obtained reinforcement in the form of candy or pennies from a "magic teaching machine" whenever Earl displayed ten seconds of attending behavior. In addition to Earl's being rewarded for sitting still, his classmates were reinforced for withholding their attention during his antics. In other words, Patterson got the students to put Earl on extinction by rewarding them for doing so. The result was a significant drop in hyperactive behavior. In four weeks Earl was a much quieter boy, and near the end of this period his behavior did not differ significantly from that of his classmates. By reinforcing students for not attending to a particularly disturbing child, the teacher may obtain rapid extinction and in turn be reinforced by a more favorable classroom atmosphere.

It is important to remember that there may be marked individual differences among students as to what is reinforcing. Until the particular reinforcer is clearly identified, systematic extinction cannot be achieved. Furthermore, an attempt to establish a uniform punishment for all students often results in certain students actually being positively reinforced. For example, having a child leave the classroom until he can "behave himself" may sound like a reasonable practice, but to some students this provides an opportunity to explore the building, meet with friends, and obtain other kinds of reinforcement.

Extinction is also effective in reducing the undesirable behavior of older students. Attention and peer recognition usually function as important reinforcers for teenagers. Often, by attending to the disturbing behavior of junior high or high school students via scoldings or lectures, the teacher sets up a situation whereby the disturbing student is then reinforced by his peers who attribute his behavior to courage. When this is observed to be the case, it is wise to ignore as much of this behavior as possible and attempt to set up situations in which the disturbing students can succeed easily on learning tasks and obtain positive outcomes.

Certain kinds of undesirable behavior, such as truancy or failure to do homework, can best be handled through a joint effort of home and school. Many powerful reinforcers which are immediately available to the parent are not within the control of the teacher. A good illustration of what may be accomplished through the close cooperation of parent and teacher is a study reported by Thorne et al. (1967). Claire, a bright 16-year-old high school student, was about to be expelled for truancy and related poor grades. Though she was quite capable of performing well once in school, she had illegally missed 30 of the last 46 school days. As a punishment, her mother had deprived her of all phone and dating privileges without clearly informing her of how she might regain them. Claire was threatening to leave home and tension was at critical point when intervention occurred. The counselor requested a temporary postponement of expulsion while a contingency program was set up. Since phone and dating privileges were important to Claire, they were used as positive reinforcers for school attendance. Each day that Claire attended all of her classes she was given a note to that effect. Her mother then permitted her to use the phone on that evening. One date night per weekend could be earned if notes were presented 4 out of 5 days, and five out of five notes permitted Claire to have two weekend dates. The frequency with which formal notes were given was gradually decreased. The results were both swift and impressive. During 3 months of the project she was out illegally only twice, and after the project terminated she was never illegally absent again. What is of major significance here is that the thoughtful use of reinforcement kept Claire in school.

The problem of truancy, a pattern which may well be considered the most critical of all school avoidance responses, requires a thoughtful approach. MacDonald et al. (1970), using a procedure similar to that employed by Thorne and his colleagues in the study previously noted, were able to substantially reduce the absence rate of ninth-grade students. Mediators from the immediate community, including a pool hall operator, worked in harmony with school personnel to establish contracts (deals) with students in which they received privileges or other positive outcomes at home and in their neighborhoods contingent upon specific improvements in their attendance. Contact counselors, however, who provided no positive outcomes per se, achieved *no* significant increase in their students' attendance.

A problem which occasionally arises is that in which the teacher serves as a highly reinforcing figure for the student. This may be due to the teacher's physical attractiveness or other features admired by the student. In these situations, the teacher may unwittingly reinforce the student for either disruptive behavior or merely mild, but annoying attention seeking. Here, reinforcement may be given by the teacher in the form of extraneous discussions after class about why a student should behave better, or in the case of the excessive attention seeking student, repeated compliance with the student's requests for clarification of points discussed, etc. Students may also attempt to have daily after-class chats with teachers between classes, believing this may improve their grades. Unless the teacher wants to maintain these kinds of counterproductive interactions, and there is little reason that he should (though he may choose to participate in meaningful after-school activities with his students), he is well advised to avoid this pattern, particularly when undesirable behavior is being reinforced. This does not mean, however, that the teacher should not encourage legitimate questions or enter into thought provoking discussions with his students.

A combined procedure involving both extinction and expectancies of positive outcomes for desirable behavior can certainly be carried out simultaneously, and it is usually highly appropriate to do so. What is really involved is a systematic redistribution of reinforcers, be they tangible or social, so that undesirable behavior is deprived of reinforcement but competing desirable behavior is heavily reinforced. When attention proves to be an effective reinforcer, which it so frequently does, the teacher can promote a surprising amount of academically and socially acceptable behavior simply by directing his attention to a student only after he has made a desirable response.

To review briefly, after it is definitely decided that a specific disruptive behavior interferes with successful classroom performance, the following steps will lead to effective extinction. For extinction you should:

1 Obtain a stable baserate of the undesirable behavior if possible (Chapter 2).
2 Observe closely and determine the reinforcer.
3 Set up your program so that the reinforcer does not follow the disruptive behavior.
4 Take periodic samples of the behavior to ensure that extinction is occurring,[4] and record the rate.

Simultaneously you should. . .

5 Select a desirable competing behavior (such as appropriate class participation).
6 Use the original positive outcome or another reinforcer to strengthen it.

REMOVAL OF POSITIVE REINFORCEMENT

Since the hazardous side effects of punishment and threat preclude their routine use, another method may be used to reduce undesirable behavior too disruptive to the student or the class to permit its simple extinction. In a classroom operating largely on positive reinforcement, rapid reduction of such behavior can often be accomplished by removing the possibility of reinforcement immediately following an undesirable response. Thus, for example, a student may temporarily be refused participation in an activity which offers potential reinforcement. Whether or not this "time out from positive reinforcement" may in itself may be considered punishment is academic, but the overall advantages it offers over traditional punishment may prove to be significant.

Having a student stay after school is a traditional example of time out. But because the student anticipates later positive reinforcement through, for example, rejoining his friends, he may be regarded as having an expectancy of a positive outcome. Because the outcome is an expectancy rather than an actuality, it may be more accurate to regard such an approach as a mildly aversive outcome.

[4]In certain cases it is appropriate to do a reversal. The teacher responds as she did before extinction (reinforcing inappropriate behavior) to determine further whether or not attention was in fact the reinforcer. Of course, extinction is then repeated.

Ramp et al. (1971), however, argue that delayed time out, in this case confinement to a time-out booth for short periods, has the saving grace of permitting the recently disruptive student to remain in the classroom and avoid missing further work. In this effective study, the researchers were confronted with a 9-year-old elementary school boy who had a very high rate of out-of-seat and talk-out behavior. They mounted a red light on the boy's desk. Each time he disruptively left his seat or talked out in a disturbing fashion, the teacher activated the light on the student's desk. Each time the light went on, the boy lost five minutes of free time scheduled for later in the day. While his classmates were enjoying this recess, he was required to spend one or more 5-minute periods in the time-out room. The boy's very high rate of out-of-seat behavior was reduced from 23.7 per 15-minute session to zero. His talking out rate shrunk from 17.1 per 15-minute session to less than one.

Several precautions are necessary in this technique. If employed at all, time out should be used only for short, controlled periods with elementary school children. It should not be considered unless systematic positive methods have failed and the behavior in question is so highly disruptive as to seriously impair the educational rights of the other children. The teacher who decides to employ a time-out room for such highly disruptive behavior should ensure that the room chosen is completely safe, lighted, ventilated, out of the immediate classroom area, and subject to inspection by the teacher or other classroom personnel. Confinement should generally be limited to 5-minute units and any child who is placed in time out on a regular basis for several days without objectively measured improvement should certainly be treated some other way. While it is difficult to specify the maximum permissible time-out period, the study cited above provided solid evidence that time out need not be long to be highly effective. We can foresee very few instances in which time-out periods of more than 10 or 15 minutes in a single day will ever be required. The objective teacher should rarely, if indeed ever, choose to employ a time-out procedure, but if he does, he must take full responsibility to ensure that precise guidelines, such as those above, are carefully followed. Finally, the teacher should be prepared to furnish exact records to parents and administrators regarding those students with whom time out was used, frequency, duration of each incident, purpose (specifically stated), and the objective results.

In classrooms operating on a token or mark system, removal of earned points may also serve to decrease undesirable behavior. In this approach, warnings should be followed up consistently, or their effectiveness as discriminative cues will be diminished.

Using this general procedure in an unusually effective yet easy manner, Sulzbacher & Houser (1968) employed what they termed a "group contingent consequence." While retarded students served as subjects in their study, the level of functioning appeared to be somewhat irrelevant and their technique may well be applicable to the normal classroom.

Fourteen students, seven boys and seven girls, ages six to ten years, were the subjects. As is typical in many classrooms from time to time, these children had picked up a harmless though annoying gesture which became a major source of amusement to the other students. The gesture was a so-called "naughty finger" which involved a raised first with the middle finger extended. Not only was the gesture itself disruptive, but each time a student displayed the naughty finger, many of the other students began to make verbal references to it, laugh, or inform the teacher of this villainous act being perpetrated by a classmate. Since most teachers are confronted with similar problems occasionally, particular attention to the method may well prove helpful.

The teacher placed 10 cards, numbered 1 through 10, on a bracket in front of the classroom and announced that a special 10-minute recess period would be permitted with the following contingencies:

> From now on there will be a special ten minute recess at the end of the day. However, if I see the naughty finger or hear about it, I will flip down one of these cards, and you will have one minute less of recess whenever this happens. Remember, every time I flip down one of these cards, all of you lose a minute from your recess.

The results of this simple procedure are noteworthy. This undesirable classroom behavior was reduced from an average of 16 occurrences per day to about two. With no extra equipment, elaborate procedures, or outside help, the teacher was able to eliminate the kind of interfering behavior often so costly of critical school time. Furthermore, punishment was avoided and the students could obtain a desirable outcome dependent upon their behavior. An additional benefit may be seen in that the outcome, contingent upon group behavior, provided a group goal. The children were part of a vivid demonstration of group cooperation serving the mutual interests of the individual members. This technique, providing an extra and positive outcome, is not open to the criticism so justly earned by a group punishment technique in which all students may be unfairly punished for the misconduct of a few. As such, it is a useful addition to the objective teacher's repertoire and will be discussed later.

GROUP OUTCOMES

While fairness alone precludes the use of group punishment, we have seen that extra positive outcomes for group cooperation can be effective in reducing disruptive activity. Barrish et al. (1969) played a "good behavior game" in which the teacher divided the class into two teams and gave a mark to a team if one of its members left his seat in violation of class rules or talked out inappropriately. The team with the lesser number of marks were given "victory badges" to wear and other special privileges for the remainder of the day. But if both teams had fewer than ten points against it, irrespective of which had less, both teams were declared winners and the whole class enjoyed extra privileges. This easy-to-apply approach resulted in a marked reduction in class disruption without punishment.

In an attempt to reduce classroom inattention, Packard(1970) used a group outcome with classes at various grade levels. The class as a whole received special privileges contingent upon an increase in the percentage of time the students spent attending to the teacher and to their work. The improvement in the students' attention rate was encouraging.

A combination of praise to an entire class of secondary school students for overall appropriate behavior and rebuke immediately following the inappropriate behavior of a few students resulted in a reduction in disruptive talking out and, to a lesser extent, in inappropriate turning around (McAllister et al., 1969).

STUDENT ASSISTANTS

In recent years there has been a growing trend toward using the services of students to facilitate the learning and social development of their peers. Students can be quite effective as teachers and may themselves benefit from the experience of teaching a younger or less able student a particular skill.

Bailey et al. (1971) found that boys could successfully act as "speech therapists" for their peers. Acting in both individual and group situations, these boys reduced articulation errors in two of their classmates. The study was conducted in Achievement Place, a special living and training situation for predelinquent youngsters in which earned points were used as currency. The student assistants earned points by detecting articulation errors in the speech of their two peers. The two boys with speech problems lost points for every articulation error they made. In a short time the student assistants succeeded in reducing the frequency of their peers' articulation errors about 90% on certain words and there was evidence that their articulation also improved on words other than those specifically selected for improvement. This improvement proved to be quite durable; there was no evidence to suggest a return of the original high error rate after the procedure was terminated.

With the help of a fifth-grade student, Surratt and his colleagues (1969) were able to reduce the disruptive behavior of four first graders. The fifth grader activated lights on their desks which served as cues to the first graders that they could expect positive outcomes for working during that period.

The employment of students as assistants to the teacher offers great promise in the difficult job of providing more individualized attention to students. But it is necessary to remember that the students serving in such a capacity must not be hampered in their own educational pursuits in the process of helping their classmates improve their performance.

SELF-RECORDING

One technique that has proven encouraging in applying objective teaching to the elimination of undesirable classroom behavior is the use of self-recording procedures. In this method the student is asked to maintain records of his/her own behavior, academic or nonacademic, and report results back to the teacher for agreed upon outcomes. While studies indicate that there are frequently divergences of opinion between students and teachers as to the accuracy of the student's self-score, with the student tending to amplify his/her performance a bit, still the overall approach holds substantial promise for the busy teacher.

In an applied study by Broden and others (1971), a teacher asked a fifth grade student to keep a record of the number of times he talked out inappropriately in class. Even without any external reinforcement, the mere act of self recording by the student led to a reduction in his rate of talking out from 1.1 times per minute to .3 per minute. While fear of punishment for lack of progress might have been the motivating factor in this case, evidence from other studies suggests instead that the student's intensified observation of his own behavior, and possibly a reinforcing effect of watching his behavior improve on paper right before his eyes, was the critical variable. Nevertheless, when self recording is used it is a good idea for the teacher to check for student reliability from time to time.

Elaborate systems of punishment or even extinction of undesirable behavior cannot alone prove effective in promoting desirable behavior, but must play a minor role in a classroom in which positive expectancies and outcomes are frequently and systematically provided for appropriate responding. By taking a fresh look at the potential for positive reinforcement in the form of tangible items, opportunities for preferred activities, and attention, the classroom teacher will find powerful ways of promoting desirable classroom behavior and eliminating the avoidance response which has plagued our schools too long.

SUMMARY

In this time of rapid change, it is becoming increasingly important for the educational system to provide not only the technical skills but the positive attitudes toward education which prevent the school avoidance response and general disinterest. If enthusiasm is stunted by a poor school environment, the student may discontinue his education as soon as possible, missing out on many opportunities which require academic achievement.

The use of punishment and threat as a means to control classroom behavior was strongly discouraged, not only for ethical reasons but because of the side effects of punishment which tend to impede the learning process. While we recognized the need to set limits in regard to classroom behavior, we urged a fair and objective approach to limit setting and suggested that only genuinely *interfering behaviors*, student responses which impede the learning process, are fair game for modification. Several kinds of interfering behavior were examined and representative research was presented to provide further insight into the elimination of this behavior.

We cited several examples of the elimination of undesirable behavior through both extinction and the positive reinforcement of specific desirable responses which compete with the undesirable behavior. Various ways in which extinction and the removal of positive reinforcement can be employed by the teacher were discussed, and the importance of accurate record keeping was reiterated.

We discussed what we considered to be a fair way to promote positive classroom behavior through a group outcome method, though we pointed out that careful study of each aspect of the procedure be made before it is implemented.

The use of student assistants offers great promise for the busy teacher who wishes to use objective teaching methods to reduce disruptive behavior, and student self recording of undesirable responses provides still another practical application of objective methods in the classroom.

REFERENCES

Bailey, J. S., Timbers, G. D., Phillips, E. L., & Wolf, M. M. Modification of articulation errors of pre-delinquents by their peers. *Journal of Applied Behavior Analysis*, 1971, 4, (4) 265–281.

Barrish, H. H., Saunders, M. & Wolf, M. M. Good behavior game: effects of individual contingencies for group consequences on disruptive behavior in a classroom. *Journal of Applied Behavior Analysis*, 1969, 2 (2), 119–124.

Bijou, S. W. The mentally retarded child. *Psychology Today*, 1968, 2, 47–50.

Broden, M., Hall, R. V., & Mitts, B. The effect of self recording on the classroom behavior of two eighth grade students. *Journal of Applied Behavior Analysis*, 1971, 4 (3), 191–199.

Hall, R. V., Lund, D., & Jackson, D. Effects of teacher attention on study behavior. *Journal of Applied Behavior Analysis*, 1968, 1, 1–12.

Hart, B. M., et al. Effects of social reinforcement on operant crying. *Journal of Experimental Child Psychology*, 1964, 1, 145–153.

Kounin, J. S., & Gump, P. V. The influence of punitive and nonpunitive teachers upon children's concepts of school misconduct. In *Studies in educational psychology* (R. G. Kuhler, ed.). Waltham, Mass: Blaisdell Publishing Co., 1968.

Lovitt, T. C., & Curtiss, K. A. Academic response rate as a function of teacher and self-imposed contingencies. *Journal of Applied Behavior Analysis*, 1969, 2, 49–54.

MacDonald, W. S., Gallimore, R., & MacDonald, G. Contingency counseling by school personnel: an economical model of intervention. *Journal of Applied Behavior Analysis*, 1970, 3, (3), 175–182.

McAllister, L. W., Stachowiak, J. G., Baer, D. M., & Conderman, L. The application of operant conditioning techniques in a secondary school classroom. *Journal of Applied Behavior Analysis*, 1969, 2 (4) 277–285.

Packard, R. G. The control of "classroom attention": a group contingency for complex behavior. *Journal of Applied Behavior Analysis*, 1970, 3 (1), 13–28.

Patterson, G. R. A learning theory approach to the treatment of the school phobic child. In *Case studies in behavior modification* (L. P. Ullmann and L. Krasner, eds.). New York: Holt, Rinehart & Winston, 1965a.

Patterson, G. R. An application of conditioning techniques to the control of a hyperactive child. In *Case studies in behavior modification* (L. P. Ullmann and L. Krasner, eds.). New York: Holt, Rinehart & Winston, 1965b.

Quay, H. C., Werry, J., McQueen, M., & Sprague, R. Remediation of the conduct problem child in the special class setting. *Exceptional Children*, 1966, 32, 509–515.

Ramp, E., Ulrich, R., & Dulaney, S. Delayed timeout as a procedure for reducing disruptive classroom behavior: a case study. *Journal of Applied Behavior Analysis*, 1971, 4 (3), 235–239.

Skinner, B. F. *The technology of teaching.* New York: Appleton-Century-Crofts, 1968.

Sulzbacher, S. I., & Houser, J. E. A tactic to eliminate disruptive behaviors in the classroom: group contingent consequences. *American Journal of Mental Deficiency*, 1968, 73, 88–90.

Surratt, R. E., Ulrich, R. E., & Hawkins, R. P. An elementary student as a behavioral engineer. *Journal of Applied Behavior Analysis*, 1969, 2 (2), 85–92.

Thomas, D. R., Becker, W. C., & Armstrong, M. Production and elimination of disruptive classroom behavior by systematically varying teacher's behavior. *Journal of Applied Behavior Analysis*, 1968, 1, 35–45.

Thorne, G. L., Tharp, R. G., & Wetzel, R. J. Behavioral modification techniques: new tools for probation officers. *Federal Probation*, 1967, 31, 21–27.

SUGGESTED READINGS

Allen, K. E., Turner, K. D., & Everett, P. M. A behavior modification classroom for head start children with behavior problems. *Exceptional Children*, 1970, 37, 119–129.

Anderson, E., Jr., White, W. F., & Wash, J. Generalized effects of praise and reproof. *Journal of Educational Psychology*, 1966, 57, 169–173.

Doubros, S. G., & Daniels, G. J. An experimental approach to the reduction of overactive behavior. *Behavior Research and Therapy*, 1966, 4 251.

Fine, M. J. Some qualifying notes on the development and implementation of behavior modification programs. *Journal of School Psychology*, 1970, 8, 301–305.

Nolen, P. A., Kunzelmann, H. P., & Haring, N. G. Behavioral modification in a junior high learning disabilities classroom. *Exceptional Children*, 1967, 34, 163–168.

Rhodes, W. C. The disturbing child: a problem in ecological management. *Journal of Exceptional Children*, 1967, 33, 449–455.

Wetzel, R. J. Behavior modification techniques and the training of teacher's aides. *Psychology in The Schools*, 1970, 7, 325–330.

Wiesen, A. E., & Watson, E. Elimination of attention seeking behavior in a retarded child. *American Journal of Mental Deficiency*, 1967, 72 50–52.

6
The Learning Environment and Imitative Learning

The unfortunate tendency to equate technological advancement with educational improvement has thrown education violently off course in the last two decades. In the absence of an effective educational model and meaningful criteria of learning, unnecessarily elaborate equipment and expensive gymnasiums have prevailed as the symbols of academic progress. This is an example of what one of the authors has termed dialectic evolution, the process by which an inherently irrational idea manifests itself via its evolution to an irrational course of large scale action in economic, social, political, and educational spheres.

The erroneous idea that better education equals technological advancement has generated design and equipment programs in schools which are both expensive and ineffective. The learning environment must be designed from the inside out, not from the outside in. Objectively defined educational goals, attainable through objectively observable and flexible means, should determine the physical and organizational design of the learning environment. As any architect or social scientist knows, the shape of the physical environment has a considerable influence upon the shape of the behavior which people display within it. If the shape of that behavior is to conform to the contours of our goals for high academic achievement in our schools, those very same goals must direct the design of the learning environment which helps shape that behavior.

The development of an adequate learning environment requires a sufficient number of teachers, teacher's aides, and other personnel trained specifically in objective teaching. Inadequate student-teacher ratios, as exist in most schools, severely handicap the learning environment. Essential materials and relevant equipment are too often sacrificed for "showcase" items which impress everyone but the overpressured teacher and neglected student. When objective teaching methods are consistently employed, the school budget, while not necessarily lowered, will be expended in an effective manner for the promotion of improved education.

An objective approach to the teaching of content material requires a precise description of terminal behavior and of the process by which academic goals will be met. Terms cannot be ambiguous and course description must convey accurately just what is to be taught. Consequently, broadly defined course curricula such as "social skills" and "personal development" should be avoided in favor of precise course curricula which are easily understood by teachers, administrators, parents, and, of course, students. This means that teaching techniques must be explicit; they must be sufficiently definable to permit uniform application, and they must be amenable to evaluation.

Objective teaching emphasizes well-defined educational goals in regard to content material and provides students with information as to how these can be achieved. This prevents students from being confused as to what is expected of them and permits them to spend more time on work and less on trying to determine what a particular assignment requires. Pop quizzes are also avoided as they are based on motivation through avoidance of failure and related anxiety and do not really strengthen the overall learning process.

Large amounts of content oriented material can best be learned if presented in a logical and systematic sequence with a number of opportunities for the student to compose responses according to explicit questions. Fill-in items or other questions are meant to help a student learn rather then to confuse him, and teachers have always recognized that such items are most beneficial when they are an integrated part of the educational experience, not just tests.

Our emphasis on objectivity and specificity should not be taken to mean that new educational techniques cannot be explored; on the contrary, progress cannot occur without innovation. Clarity and precise instruction to students does not mean lack of creativity on the part of the teacher, but indicates that he has a depth of understanding about the goals he has established with his students. Students appreciate this approach. Even creative writing and art classes need not be based on vague instructions, but present a unique challenge to the teacher to convey to his students the various possibilities attainable through the different techniques. Creativity is desirable behavior and warrants positive recognition.

It is also very important for teachers to be explicit in defining the kind of academic responses to content material which are most desirable, and to provide an environment in which cues are presented in a manner which enhances the probability of correct responding. Teachers too, working with programmed materials discussed in Chapter 7, know precisely what kind of response they wish to obtain from each student at a given time. This does not mean that teachers must give answers away, but merely that cues must be reduced gradually enough to ensure a high rate of success on each response, at the same time encouraging movement to the next.

CUES AND BEHAVIOR

Behavior which is appropriate in one environment may hardly be applicable to another. A *cue* is really that aspect of the learning environment that provides an individual with information about what he needs to do if he is to receive a positive outcome; that is, which responses are and which are not likely to be reinforced at that time, place, and condition. The student is required to make particular kinds of discriminations according to his general environment such as the specific class he is in, and very precise cues, such as a fill-in question in which only the correct response gets reinforced. A *prompt* is a highly specific cue which is geared to promote a rapid emission of an already learned response. The prompt helps the student by greatly increasing the chance that he will make a correct response, one that is relevant and subject to positive reinforcement. Prompts may be verbal, as in the case of a foreign language in which the instructor says the word and the student echoes it, or they may be nonverbal, as when the teacher presents a picture and the student must respond with the correct word or phrase.

The objective teacher is concerned with providing a classroom environment in which new and difficult material is presented with a considerable number of clear cues and prompts. As material is presented and correct responses made, cues and prompts are gradually *faded* out until even minimal cues are sufficient to permit correct responses. For example, in teaching children to print the alphabet, a teacher may have a child trace each letter on very thin tracing paper, then on denser paper, still denser paper, and so on until he can print the letters without the necessity of tracing. This general idea can be applied to junior high and high school students learning advanced subject material. Students frequently use this method themselves when they are studying for examinations by gradually covering up the material they are learning until they can duplicate it without requiring the cueing or prompting provided by the material itself. The essay examination is an example of a minimal cue calling for a long chain of complex written responses. Sometimes cues are too vague or too ambiguous and prevent a student from giving desired responses, although had he been given a cue more closely associated with the learned material, he would have demonstrated a complete grasp of the area. For example, asking a student to discuss the Pythagorean theorem is far better than asking him to explain "the geometry problem we studied yesterday." Whether they be words, figures, pictures, or questions, the teacher must be careful to avoid giving those cues for which there is a low probability of correct responding or he will encourage failure, an outcome that really does little to enhance learning in the long run.

A positive outcome may itself serve as a cue for another response in a behavioral chain. Bijou (1968) has noted that research indicates a strengthening effect of a positive outcome for a response on the cue which precipitated that response. But frequently the outcome itself appears to act as a cue for behavior. In this commonly seen chain, a child receiving a particular positive outcome behaves as if the outcome itself has triggered a repetition of the specific response. There is some difficulty here, however, as the positive outcome may produce a perseverative pattern as each positive outcome serves to promote a response almost identical to the previous one. The cue value of the positive outcome may prevail over a newly introduced cue, particularly when the positive outcome has remained qualitatively similar over repeated responses. This may lead to high error rates and difficulty in shifting from one response mode to another. Thus, when using positive reinforcement in the classroom it is often best to establish a waiting period of 5 to 15 seconds between the delivery of the positive outcome and the presentation of the next cue.

INCREASING STUDENT ATTENTION THROUGH CUES

Attention may be considered a first step in learning, and unless a student attends to the relevant features of a problem, he will not be able to learn it. Merely using bright colors or shapes indiscriminantly may not only fail to improve learning but may actually draw a student's attention away from the really critical aspects of the task at hand. For example, if a child prefers a particular color which is not a relevant part of the problem, he may tend to pick items or select answers which appear in the preferred color, thus he will operate at a chance level of problem solving. Trabasso (1968) urges that teachers "pay attention" to the problem of attention. He notes that extraneous stimuli may distract students and that students have a difficult time learning to make important discriminations in such an environment. Much problem solving begins with essentially chance or random responding. As the student progresses, he no longer attends to those aspects of the problem which do not contribute to finding a correct solution. For example, in learning to identify the shapes of different objects, he must abandon size or color cues. The sooner he abandons irrelevant cues, the faster he improves his rate of problem solving. Trabasso, then, suggests that teachers systematically select those cues which are critical to the solution of a problem and accentuate them while simultaneously avoiding cues which are irrelevant and distracting. The first step is to "impoverish" the learning environment, that is, impoverish it in regard to distracting stimuli. The next step is to use arrows, marks, underlining, etc., to embellish the critical features (e.g., shape). It is also possible to focus attention on a particularly crucial feature by embedding it among irrelevant features so that it stands out more clearly. Actually, this is often done in the classroom when the teacher gives hints by modulating his voice in various ways.

The teacher can also decrease the initial chance responding period by providing several relevant cues. An *apple* is not only *red* but it is also roughly *"round"* and is a *fruit* which has a *skin*. By planning for the systematic presentation of relevant cues which are both numerous and accentuated, and by eliminating distracting material, the teacher can certainly expect to increase the rate of learning.

The term *setting event* has been used increasingly to describe the essential stimulus or pattern of stimuli which serves to promote specific behavior. Frequently the setting event is the teacher's behavior which provides significant cues as to expected behavior. Often, too, the teacher may himself promote or discourage certain behavior by his very presence or absence, a fact which is hardly surprising to most teachers. But the presence of the teacher plays another important part: it serves as both a source of adult behaviors to model and a potentially reinforcing audience for successful imitative behavior.

THE TEACHER AS A MODEL

The continuity of a culture appears to be maintained by man's high rate of imitative behavior and by the reinforcement he obtains by imitating those about him. Bandura (1962) and his associates have shown that social learning is heavily influenced by an imitative process in which the adult serves as a model for a child's behavior. Once the adult's behavior is imitated by the child, it is strengthened by reinforcement. This work also indicates that an adult can increase the tendency for his behavior to be modeled if he himself is associated with the pleasant outcomes he has provided the child in the past. The average parent, of course, generally conforms to this pattern; thus his behavior has a very high likelihood of being imitated by his child.

Peterson (1968) emphasizes the importance of distinguishing between imitation or modeling and what he terms observational learning. While both modeling and observational learning share the basic feature of behavioral similarity, they are really different phenomena. A response may be termed imitative "when one individual behaves to match the response of a model, and in that instance only." Observational learning, while also involving behavioral similarity, is not imitative in that the key cues do not necessarily come from a particular model. For example, a number of students singing a national anthem are not generally modeling from one another (unless perhaps some of them have forgotten the words), as the major cues tend to be the previous lyrics and the music.

The tendency to model is especially vital to the development of language. While shaping appears to play an important role in the refinement of verbal responses once they are emitted by the child, linguistic skills can hardly be expected to develop through shaping alone. Without verbal modeling, the entire process of language development would take far longer, if, in fact, full language ability would be achieved at all. This is easily understood when one considers that shaping is dependent upon some approximation of the particular response being made in the first place. Shaping would require that each individual sound be learned through a tedious and time-consuming process beginning with a rough approximation of the sound and ending with an accurate verbal production. This would require many in-between steps with reinforcement occurring at each successive approximation to the desired sound. This process would probably severely limit the size of our vocabularies. Perhaps the significance of modeling in language development may best be grasped by those of us who have attempted to learn another language such as German or French. We can probably recall the degree to which we relied on imitation to learn the strange new sounds and phrases, and can very likely imagine how much more difficulty we would have experienced if it were not for the degree of modeling encouraged by the teacher. Furthermore, in language development there is evidence that the mother's voice, through its association with tangible reinforcement such as food or escape from discomfort, takes on secondary reinforcing qualities. The young child has the opportunity to reinforce himself by acting like his mother; that is, by imitating the sound of her voice and repeating it in her absence.

The teacher, acting as a model[1] for the young student, is actually providing very precise cues to the child as to what he is expected to do—cues which are so precise, in fact, that the probability of incorrect responding is markedly reduced. By imitating the behavior of his teacher on request, the child has a good chance of obtaining reinforcement from his teacher, or obtaining it directly from being "right." Modeling, then, is a valuable tool in objective teaching. By demonstrating exactly what he wants his students to do and by reinforcing their successful efforts at imitation, the teacher can frequently overcome problems that would otherwise consume much more time and effort. This is not to imply that objective teaching thrives on turning out carbon-copy students. What is being referred to here is the learning of content-oriented material, such as mathematics and spelling, in the most efficient and satisfying way possible. As this task is handled in a systematic fashion through modeling, reinforcement, and programmed learning (Chapter 7), the teacher will have the time to see his students as individuals with unique interests, abilities, and ways of thinking. He will be in a far better position to encourage individuality and creativity, but individuality and creativity supported by academic proficiency.

A most impressive application of modeling procedures is demonstrated in a study reported by Baer et al. (1967). While this work was done with retarded

[1]In the United States the teacher has traditionally been expected to be, in a sense, a model for the community. A strong spokesman for middle-class values, the teacher has been viewed by his students as typifying acceptable ideas and actions and, thus, being reinforced by the community. Today, however, as the value system is subjected to youthful scrutiny, the teacher too may become a focus of reexamination by students. Here we present the teacher's role as a model within a narrower teaching context.

children and was essentially geared toward the development of speech, it provides a good example of the potential use of modeling in rapidly building the behavior of younger children. The objective was to explore the extent to which imitation could be developed by reinforcing responses which closely approximated those of the experimenters who served as models. At first, a great deal of help was given to enable the children to imitate the early simple responses (e.g., raise left arm) which obtained food reinforcement. Gradually, more complex responses (e.g., move hat from table to desk) were introduced and successful imitations continued to be reinforced. As the children began to imitate consistently, several responses were linked together and modeled by the experimenters, reinforcement being contingent upon imitating the entire chain of as many as five separate or discrete responses. Vocal responses such as "ah," which had not generally been imitated when presented alone, were then introduced at the end of chains of motor responses. This modification made the difference and some of the children began to imitate spoken sounds for the first time. As they began to develop imitative vocal sounds, the early nonvocal (motor) parts of the chain were gradually shortened trial by trial until only the vocal sounds were presented for imitation. Not only were vocal responses imitated, but this procedure permitted the children to learn specific words through shaping, a procedure to be discussed in Chapter 7. After only 20 hours of training, these children, who had never spoken before, learned as many as 10 usable words including their names.

The teacher, then, can view himself as a model for the learner, providing clear-cut examples through his actions whenever possible. As students imitate his responses they receive either tangible reinforcement (for younger children) or social reinforcement (for more advanced students).[2] While some imitative responses may occur without reinforcement, the process is strengthened through actual reinforcement of a correctly imitated response. This technique is particularly useful when the subject being taught requires highly specific kinds of vocal or motor behavior. Included in this category, of course, are speech, foreign languages, vocational skills, specialized technical skills, athletics, dancing, and many professional skills. While modeling can serve as a shortcut to learning, the teacher serving as a model must be careful that his performance is free of errors so that his students do not pick up incorrect behavior. Video tape recordings are extremely useful in this regard, in that a teacher can view his performance and correct errors before presentation to his students. Bandura's work suggests that visual techniques, such as movies and now video tape, can themselves be used with the teacher filming or taping a performance in such a way as to enable students to imitate the model's recorded behavior. While reinforcement is sometimes automatic in these situations and the "rightness" of a response is often

[2]One might certainly put forth a strong argument that the teacher can better serve as a model of the enthusiastic learner if he is seen by his students as heavily reinforced by the society, e.g., by receiving a better salary.

sufficient to keep a student motivated, this is not always the case. In an important piece of research, Steinman (1970) found that generalized imitation may in fact be heavily dependent on several setting events. The subjects in this study were 6 public school girls, ages seven to nine. The girls were requested to either imitate or not to imitate the adult model under conditions such as the presence or absence of reinforcement. The results indicated a strong natural tendency for these students to imitate even when no reinforcement was forthcoming. Steinman concluded that social-setting events, such as the degree to which the model is associated with reinforcement, the continued surveilance of the students by the model while the students were imitating him, and the students' previous experiences with adult models, all interact to affect the likelihood of imitation.

The importance of the adult model as a setting event for imitative behavior is firmly supported in an imaginative study by Peterson & Whitehurst (1971). Working with normal 5-year-old children, these researchers learned that imitation is a very durable kind of behavior once it is initially reinforced. They, just as Steinman, studied generalized imitation, a pattern in which the child tends to imitate not merely those responses for which he has been reinforced, but other actions demonstrated by the model even though they have not been specifically reinforced. This tendency to imitate is so strong once it is initiated that it appears necessary to actually reinforce the child for nonimitation or incorrect imitation to diminish the pattern of generalized imitative behavior. Yet even this approach cannot always successfully eliminate it completely.

The essential variable, according to these researchers, is the presence or absence of the model immediately after the model has performed his to-be-modeled behavior. Observed through a one-way screen, the child typically continues to imitate the model, even without reinforcement, when the model stays on to observe the child's imitation. But if the model leaves immediately after he completes his to-be-modeled performance without waiting to see the child's imitation, the child frequently fails to imitate the behavior completely.

This finding has immediate application in the classroom. Many teachers, unfortunately, tend to demonstrate academic behaviors to students but walk away without any assurance that their performance is imitated correctly or indeed at all by their students. Whether it is penmanship for early graders or microscope techniques for advanced science students, it is important that the teacher both model the desired behavior and observe the student as he attempts to duplicate it. This, followed by feedback delivered in a helpful, positive manner by the teacher offers promise for the enhancement of learning through imitation.

Probably the most comprehensive work on the use of modeling and imitation among a school-age population was conducted by Sarason & Ganzer (1971). The project was carried out at the Cascadia Center in Washington State among a population of adolescents referred there for a variety of juvenile offenses. In the main study, which was conducted over a 16-week period, the boys attended weekly 1-hour group sessions. The purpose of the study was to explore the effectiveness of modeling procedures as compared to structured discussions of the same material on the adaptive behavior of the boys. A control group, which did not participate in the programs, served as a further basis of comparison. Half of each treatment group was permitted to view their role imitations or group discussions on video tape.

The measures used to determine the effectiveness of the modeling procedures versus the discussion and control groups included various self concept, attitude, and behavioral data. The modeling groups were conducted in a carefully structured manner. Adult models acted out various social situations from precise scripts using fairly authentic figures of speech and real-life problems (e.g., dealing with a policeman, on the job problems, avoiding an argument with the boss, dealing with angry parents, etc.). The boys in the modeling groups both acted out the various roles and observed the other boys acting out the roles as originally performed by the adult models.

The results of this approach were striking. The boys who participated in nontelevised modeling groups "demonstrated the strongest and most positive changes in their attitudes and rated behaviors of any of the experimental or control subgroups. Subjects in the nontelevised modeling groups also were given more favorable case dispositions (e.g., parole) than were subjects in other groups."

An additional finding was that more passive boys, those requiring more externally imposed guidelines, showed the greatest receptivity to the approach. Surprisingly. the groups given televised feedback showed regression rather than improvement, possibly a result of wrapping up the problem area rather than leaving it open for the students to deal with as an unsolved problem requiring further attention. Even 4 months later, most of the boys in the nontelevised modeling groups maintained or improved their newly acquired behavior patterns.

Perhaps what is of greatest relevance in this study for the classroom teacher is the diversity of the scripts employed by the models. A straightforward modeling technique expands the choices of behavior available to students and permits them to find new modes of interacting with one another and with adults. Not only does this method offer promise for dealing with disruptive behavior, but it opens up a whole new realm of creative problem solving possibilities in academic areas. A wide range of academic behavior is amenable to imitative learning. The use of models depicting various interpersonal situations appears useful in social-science areas, enabling students to see portrayed, to portray themselves, to choose, and to create the roles they seek to play in their lifetimes.

In vocational areas, modeling might well deal with the physical and social aspects of a job and techniques for obtaining employment. Here too there are many possibilities available to the objective teacher who is aware of the potential of modeling techniques for promoting learning.

THE STUDENT AS A MODEL

Certain students may themselves appear to be modeled by other students. Behavior and modes of dress, for example, are often initiated by an inner circle of students or one student and quickly imitated by others. This is not really modeling in the sense that we use it above because the individual whose behavior is imitated is not really helping others learn new behavior. He is merely allowing his behavior, and the reinforcement it obtains, to be an example of how others should behave to receive similar reinforcement. Thus, if a student learns behavior which is particularly successful in obtaining reinforcement in the classroom, others may observe the behavior and emit similar responses to obtain the reinforcement given the first. If the behavior is desirable, this is to the teacher's advantage, but if not, students will pick up undesirable behavior which will impede the overall learning process. Very young students are particularly likely to imitate the behavior of their classmates when they observe their classmates receiving positive reinforcement for their responses. Barnwell & Sechrest (1965) found that first-grade children selected a task on which they viewed their classmates receiving praise and avoided a task on which they witnessed other children receiving reprobation. Third-grade children also imitated the rewarded selection, but were far less reluctant to choose the punished task than the first graders.

The learning environment may provide conflicting models for students. Bijou (1968) has noted that "patterns of behavior strengthened in one situation may be aversive to the members of another peer group or to an adult dominated group." Thus, the behavior desired by the teacher in the classroom may directly oppose the kinds of behavior held in esteem by the students. This dilemma challenges the teacher to assess the kinds of roles which are acceptable and unacceptable to his students. But this does not mean a simple acquiescence to all student demands. Frequently models have a broader basis of acceptability than to merely one type of group. In the Sarason and Ganzer research, the models depicted behavior which was both socially adaptive and immediately relevant to the boys' lives. The thoughtful introduction of this large reservoir of acceptable roles may offer new modes of behaving to students who have previously depended on disruptive peers as their primary role models. Frequently, too, students may reject a role considered socially desirable in the adult community (e.g., a stable contributor to the community) simply because they themselves lack the necessary skills to play that role. This "sour grapes" response appears quite prevalent, but the introduction of socially adaptive behavior through modeling offers students a wider range of social skills than generally offered by peers. By providing students alternate modes of behavior which obtain positive outcomes, disruptive patterns often slip quietly out of existence.

But student leaders, those students adept in influencing the behavior of their peers, have acquired control over many social outcomes which might also be of use to the teacher. By careful observation of the student leader, it is possible to learn more about the distribution of social reinforcement. However, leadership may be acquired and maintained largely out of class and merely carried over to the classroom. In such a case it becomes difficult to ascertain the kind of reinforcers employed by the leader.

Since the leader's behavior is often imitated, it is sometimes possible to promote useful learning by focusing on changing the leader's behavior first. This approach becomes more feasible as one deals with older students because, while younger students' behavior is influenced more easily by tangible reinforcers and other reinforcers within the teacher's control, the behavior of older students is somewhat more subject to change through the subtle social contingencies in the hands of the peer leader. The teacher, then, must occasionally "share" leadership with certain students who control reinforcers either not typically available to the teacher, or of little practical use to him. Because the teacher may be able to redirect any dysfunctional behavior of the peer leader toward functional activity, he is in a better position to change the behavior of the entire class. The existence of this situation has long been acknowledged by teachers who may refer to this tactic as "winning over" certain influential students.

The procedure first requires an observation of student behavior long enough to determine which students tend to exert influence over their peers. When this is done, the teacher then determines those modifications of the learning environment that will successfully redirect the leader's behavior; either social reinforcement or preferred activities are typically useful. The leader's desirable behavior is then encouraged and reinforced in such a manner that his encouraged and reinforced behavior and its outcome is observable by the class. The final goal is to help students imitate desirable classroom behavior displayed by the leader. When this is accomplished, those students that imitate the leader's adaptive behavior should also be reinforced. As an example, the leader might be asked to respond in the area of his greatest competence so that he will be very likely to respond appropriately and receive reinforcement (e.g., a history question which he has answered successfully in the past). Correct responding by the leader is then subject to imitation by others. This is far better than attempting to "show up" the leader by pointing out his inadequacies because such a tactic may merely increase the leader's oppositional tendency to exert his influence in an effort to impede class functioning. When objective teaching becomes predominant in the school system and when a child learns primarily through imitation of appropriate adult models and positive outcomes from his first day of school to his last, the teacher will not have to depend on influencing the behavior of leaders to modify the behavior of others. In today's large and frequently overcrowded classrooms, however, such an approach often proves to be the lesser of several evils, though open to question on some ethical grounds. For example, by supporting the leader-follower concept among students, one may be contributing to the breakdown of individuality and strengthening an authoritarian process. Present indica-

tions are that imitation and positive reinforcement must function as solid part-
ners to enhance and maintain desirable behavior in the classroom.

GENERALIZATION

Still not completely answered is the question of whether or not behavior
learned in one setting will necessarily carry over into another. Research suggests,
of course, that the similarity in quality and quantity of the stimulus components
of two learning settings is an important factor. In practice, however, it is frequently difficult to predict whether or not improved behavior at school will
generalize to the home or vice versa.

Wahler (1969), working with two boys, one five and the other eight, attempted to deal with precisely this question. Careful records were kept at regular
intervals of Steve's cooperative and oppositional behavior and Louis's disruptive
and study behavior. The findings were disappointing but useful. The boys had
been referred to an outpatient clinic for behavior problems. For each, the undesirable behavior occurred both at home and at school. A reinforcement procedure
was conducted at home for these boys, with no attempt to carry out similar
procedures at school. The results: the boys' behavior improved while at home,
but there was no significant corresponding improvement in classroom behavior.
It was not until positive reinforcement was initiated in the classroom that their
school behavior showed improvement.

This finding raises several questions. Why did the boys' undesirable behavior
seem to generalize from one setting to another but not their newly learned
desirable behavior? Is it possible to promote generalization by reinforcing certain
key behaviors or changing essential aspects of the learning environment? Is it
necessary to use a separate procedure in each learning setting? Are there fundamental personality variables which must be changed before overall behavior
patterns can be altered?

While research is continually exploring these areas, practical experience
points to the close cooperation between home and school as an important factor.
As we will show in later chapters, involvement of the family and the community
as well as the school may provide the consistency necessary to ensure overall
improvement in behavior and personality.

EXPECTANCY OF OUTCOME

Those studying the process of learning have often suggested that it is not
merely the outcome that determines whether or not a child will learn a particular
behavior but the child's expectation of the outcome his behavior will produce.
Unfortunately, definitive studies of the role of expectancy are lacking, partly

because of the reluctance of strict behaviorists to give much credence to so "mentalistic" a variable. Objective teachers, however, must remain open to approaches which take into account the student's ability to conceptualize the contingencies in his environment rather than treating him as if his behavior was directed only by its consequences. The ability to anticipate important environmental events may well be a key factor in classroom learning and self direction.

SUMMARY

The superior learning environment is designed to meet the genuine needs of teachers and students. Extraneous and superficial school facilities must give way to facilities whose design arises from the objective requirements of the learning situation. Improved staffing is of higher priority than an overly elaborate gymnasium.

Asking questions or giving hints really involves providing a student with *cues* as to what is the correct or desired response that you are seeking from him. A *prompt* is a more specific kind of cue and is generally used to get a student to quickly make a response he has already learned.

It is important to be consistent in the use of cues so as to avoid confusing the student. Cues and prompts should not be used to trick the student but should be employed in a systematic manner in an effort to increase the chance that he will actually learn the desired behavior.

Cues and prompts may be gradually *faded* out in such a manner as to require the student to complete more and more of the desired response without them. A typical method of studying for an examination is to refer back to the required material less and less as studying proceeds so that the student eventually need not rely on the written material to reproduce it. Fading is particularly effective in programming and may be used in a variety of creative ways.

It is possible to increase the rate of correct responding by students by eliminating extraneous stimuli which may serve as false cues and by increasing both the number and salience of relevant cues. The study of modeling and imitation has taken on new importance in recent years. The teacher may serve as a model for his students by making a desired response so that his students can learn to do it through imitation. Studies were presented which pointed out the applicability of modeling to the classroom, particularly in regard to the language development of young children and retarded children. Modeling serves a shortcut function in speech development.

The model and his behavior act as *setting events* which define the behavior expected of the student. Because the presence of the model during the student's imitation is critical, the teacher must not merely demonstrate the desired behavior but must observe the child's imitative response as well, reinforcing it appropriately.

The teacher may also serve as a general model for the learner by expressing positive attitudes toward the process of learning.

Students, too, may serve as models for other students. Unfortunately, students may imitate the undesirable behavior of their classmates, particularly if they observe them receiving reinforcement. Various ways to prevent the modeling of such undesirable behavior were suggested.

The degree to which behavior learned in the home generalizes to classroom behavior was discussed. The similarities of the environments are important, but so too is the involvement of the entire community in educational matters.

The teacher must regard the student as capable of acting in accordance with his expectation of the outcome his behavior may produce. The ability to conceptualize the contingencies in the environment may prove to be a critical factor in learning.

REFERENCES

Baer, D. M., Peterson, R. F., & Sherman, J. A. The development of imitation by reinforcing behavioral similarity to a model. *Journal of the Experimental Analysis of Behavior,* 1967, 10 405–416.

Bandura, A. Social learning through imitation. In *Nebraska symposium on motivation* (M.R. Jones, ed.). Lincoln: University of Nebraska Press, 1962.

Barnwell, A., & Sechrest, L. Vicarious reinforcement in children at two age levels. *Journal of Educational Psychology,* 1965, 56, 100–106.

Bijou, S. W. *Reinforcement history and socialization.* Paper presented at Miami Symposium on Social Behavior, Miami University, Oxford, Ohio, October 31–November 1, 1968.

Peterson, R. F. Imitation: a basic behavioral mechanism. In *Operant procedures in remedial speech and language training* (H. H. Sloane, Jr. and B.D. MacAulay, eds.). Boston: Houghton Mifflin Co., 1968.

Peterson, R. F., & Whitehurst, G. J. A variable influencing the performance of generalized imitative behaviors. *Journal of Applied Behavior Analysis,* 1971, 4 (1) 1–9.

Sarason, I. G., & Ganzer, V. J. *Modeling: an approach to the rehabilitation of juvenile offenders.* Final report to Dept. of H.E.W. for partially supporting grant No. 15-P-55303, June, 1971.

Steinman, W. M. The social control of generalized imitation. *Journal of Applied Behavior Analysis,* 1970, 3 (3), 159–167.

Trabasso, T. Pay attention. *Psychology Today,* (1968), 2,

Wahler, G. Setting generality: some specific and general effects of child behavior therapy. *Journal of Applied Behavior Analysis,* 1969, 2, (4), 239–246.

SUGGESTED READINGS

Bandura, A. Behavioral modification through modeling procedures. In *Research in behavior modification* (L. Krasner and L. Ullmann, eds.). New York: Holt, Rinehart & Winston, 1966.

Boles, R. C. Reinforcement, expectancy, and learning. *Psychological Review*, 1972, **79** (5) 394–409.

Burgess, R. L., Burgess, J. M., & Esveldt, K. C. An analysis of generalized imitation. *Journal of Applied Behavior Analysis*, 1970, **3** (1), 39–46.

Haring, N. G., & Lovitt, T. C. Operant methodology and educational technology in special education. In *Methods in special education* (N. G. Haring and R. Schiefelbusch, eds.). New York: McGraw-Hill, 1967.

Patterson, G. R. A learning theory approach to the treatment of the school phobic child. In *Case studies in behavior modification* (L. Ullmann and L. Krasner, eds.). New York: Holt, Rinehart & Winston, 1966.

Stephens, T. M. Psychological consultation to teachers of learning and behaviorally handicapped children using a behavioral model. *Journal of School Psychology*, 1970, **8**, 13–18.

Walls, R. T., & Smith, T. S. Voluntary delay of reinforcement as a function of model status. *Journal of Educational Psychology*, 1970, **61**, 123–126.

7
Programming for Successful Learning

⌐The recent emphasis on individualized instruction grows out of an increasing awareness that we can no longer afford to overlook the substantial differences in skill levels among students grouped by grade. Frequently a child feels he is over his head in a sea of academic requirements for which he has not yet acquired necessary skills. While some students sink beneath their classmates' level of performance, and indeed well beneath their own potential, others feel thwarted by an academic program which requires them to repeat academic work which they have mastered long ago. Good programming does not mean planning for the average level of the group, but planning for the individual requirements of each student to the greatest degree feasible. While completely individualized attention is not always possible, it can be far more closely approached through the methods we will presently describe.⌐

Our system of graded schools is based on tacit recognition that an individual must acquire certain skills before he can progress to more advanced tasks. Yet far more frequently than we wish to admit, a student is advanced without even approaching the standards he is supposed to fulfill, and rumors of "social" promotion are often well founded. In a nation which emphasizes individual achievement, it is surprising to see so many students virtually herded from grade to grade as part of the pack with their individual levels of skill subordinated to their grade standings. This is mass education. It does not fit in a world in which we would like to see individuals count for something beyond being part of a group. It can be changed through objective teaching.

THE AGE-GRADE FALLACY

Just because most infants develop basic motor skills such as standing and walking at approximately the same age, there is no reason to assume that they will acquire similar academic skills at similar ages. Our entire educational system, for example, adheres to the idea that a child is not really ready to be educated until he is about 5- or 6-years-old. At this point he enters kindergarten or first grade to be promoted from year to year as long as he can even barely keep up with the class. At 7, a child is studying what other 7-year-olds are studying, and at 14, what other 14-year-olds are studying, and so forth. Thus, while we give lip service to individual differences, we really fail to view the student as a unique individual with a unique background of experiences and a unique rate of learning new material. Objective teaching, on the other hand, considers such individual differences carefully. A student moves from one academic step to another when he successfully completes the former, not when he reaches a prescribed age. And that makes a good deal more sense.

Donald Baer has pointed out (1966) that our entire concept of child development, resting heavily on the traditional but poorly supported notion that rigid maturational stages dictate level of performance, must be reexamined in light of current findings. According to Baer, the reason that older children can do more complex tasks than younger children is not so much that their bodies or brains have matured in some unknown way, making more advanced learning possible, but rather that they have had certain sequences of experience which are denied to younger children simply because the older children have been around longer. In other words, beyond that period of real neurological and general physical development, the age factor is irrelevant to learning. What is relevant is the sequence of learned responses which an individual has in his repertoire at a given point and which indicates the next logical step he should take to advance further. This line of reasoning is well supported by Baer who cites research in which children were systematically taught in just a few sessions to do tasks which they had been unable to do before (e.g., raising their left and right hands on request), tasks which are characteristically performed only by much older children.

While it is risky to rule out the possible existence of certain age-related stages of development, particularly in light of contradictory findings, we support the general concept that optimal rearrangement of learning sequences promotes optimal learning. At the same time, however, we must recognize that there are clear-cut organismic changes with age. The response repertoire available to a 3-year-old is far more limited than one available to a 7-year-old. We are, in a sense, dealing with a different kind of organism. These differences are partly physical and partly the result of learning. An interactional explanation, rather than a strictly environmental or strictly biological one, seems to offer the greatest promise.

Looked at in another way, it may be assumed that there is enough consistency in the social system so that most children of the same age have had access to similar kinds of learning experiences. This basic similarity in sequence of experience could certainly account for most of the resemblances in behavior and levels of skill seen in most children of the same age group. But since these experiences are provided by our natural environment, they tend to be randomly distributed rather than arranged in the logical step-by-step fashion that seems to enhance learning. Thus, particularly at the preschool ages, learning is a haphazard affair, with luck rather than reason playing the major role. Obviously, the child living in an enriched, stimulating environment has the advantage over the deprived child because he has a wider range of experiences and a greater probability of responses being reinforced, responses which are frequently important prerequisites for more advanced behavior.

But random experiences in the natural environment could not alone explain the uniformity of behavior among age groups. Another factor plays an important part in limiting and defining the kind of experiences the child will have, the kind of responses he will make, and the specific responses which will tend to be reinforced. This factor is expectation. If a child of a certain age is expected to learn certain behaviors, his parents will tend to structure his environment in such a manner as to increase the chance that he will learn just those behaviors. He will be coaxed, cajoled, and sometimes forced to make the necessary responses, and will then obtain positive reinforcement (usually social) or negative reinforcement through escaping the punishment he might receive if he failed to make the correct response. Widely read "baby books" which provide parents with charts of behavior to be expected at various age levels help define the expectations, thus setting the stage for the child to conform to the behavior expected by his parents. With such culturally defined expectations, it is hardly surprising to see the degree of uniformity in behavior within age levels. Even when the possible effects of biologically influenced changes are accounted for, the culture still plays a powerful role in defining a child's behavior at a given age.

When a child enters school, age and grade based curricula restrictions contribute to the uniformity already molded by cultural expectations. The result is even greater regimentation of the learning process and a further decrease in individual differences in rate and degree of learning. Even in the midst of these two powerful forces toward uniformity in learning, an occasional student deviates so markedly from others that he creates a serious educational challenge. Whether his academic skills are inferior or superior in relation to the rest of the class, he presents a problem to the educational system which must choose a course of action. The usual approach is to develop special courses with special curricula, but these too are often inadequately designed to meet the present educational needs of the student and may themselves create new uniformity, only at different levels. The solution offered by objective teaching involves dissolution of grade levels based on rigid, preconceived and self-perpetuating expectations of maturation and readiness. They would be replaced by an educational structure which takes into account a student's present level of educational skill. Objective teaching provides a logical sequence of steps to move the student as far as possible. This does not necessarily mean that exhaustive and totally unique academic plans must be drawn up for each separate student; it requires the design of sequential programs so that each student starts off at a point below which he has learned practically everything, and beyond which he has yet a great deal to learn. Only occasionally is it necessary to significantly alter the sequence of an existing program for an individual student, especially if the program is skillfully designed.

What we are saying is that what is learned is what is taught by the learning environment through reinforcement, imitation, and other interactions which involve contingencies. The teacher can be a powerful presence in the student's learning environment by enhancing the student's interest in learning, or he can become a figure to be tolerated as a necessary evil. In the latter case, the teacher may simply be avoided through truancy or other escape routes.

While every teacher is not inherently rewarding to all of his students, his careful programming of learning materials can overcome a wealth of shortcomings in his delivery. A sequential programming of academic content material frequently engages a student's interest whereas the identical content, presented in lecture form by the teacher, may merely promote painful boredom. The effectiveness of programmed material is frequently increased by diversity, humor, and positive outcomes which occur as the student reaches progressive steps in his learning sequence.

ABILITY GROUPING

The idea of grouping students within the classroom according to ability in various academic subjects has become a controversial topic in recent years. While some argue that it facilitates teaching, and consequently learning, the parents of a child in the lowest reading group in his class may argue that their child's confidence has been shattered, that his self-esteem rises and falls on his academic position among his peers. We feel that it is the teacher's responsibility to meet the educational needs of *all* the students in the classroom, and any classroom design that seriously sacrifices one student's progress for another's needs alteration. If a teacher decides to employ ability grouping, she must take an objective measurement of all the students in her classroom to ensure that all of her students are making gains, not just those in the less advanced groups or those in the more advanced groups. When a teacher expends most of his effort upon just a few students at the expense of the others he is not distributing his teaching skills fairly or effectively.

The teacher deciding to employ ability grouping will find it useful to advise parents of the purpose of such an approach so as to avoid misunderstanding and resentment. He might explain to the parents that no student is locked into his or her group permanently, but that each will be encouraged to improve his skills with the precise purpose of facilitating rapid movement to a more advanced group. It is further advisable to assure parents that ability grouping is merely a method of giving a student more individualized attention, never a method of stigmatizing less advanced students. Finally, it might be wise to explain that a student can achieve more positive outcomes when he is placed in a group of students whose skill levels approximate his own. Less of the work is over his head; failure experiences are infrequent.

Even when a teaching pyramid is used (i.e., the teacher teaches skills to advanced students who in turn teach others until the entire class achieves the skill), the teacher must keep directly in touch with each of his students individually.

One relatively untested idea which incorporates principles of good sequential programming with positive reinforcement is that of progress grouping. A student might be placed in a group (not in terms of location in the classroom but in terms of special privileges and special recognition) not merely for absolute progress but for relative progress; that is, how much he himself has advanced his particular skills in given areas. We would welcome reports of such programs in action.

BEHAVIOR SHAPING AND PROGRAMMING

Continuing allusion to "programming" without specific definition and description of the concept would itself be indicative of poor programming on the part of the authors. At this point, then, let us turn to this important aspect of objective teaching.

An elementary example of programming lies in what is termed behavior shaping or just *shaping*. Like all programming, *shaping consists of a plan or program by which a complex terminal behavior* (see Chapter 2) *is achieved by designing a sequence of successive steps which approximate the terminal behavior.* A correct response on each step leads to reinforcement for that response. In shaping, the reinforcement tends to be tangible or social, while in formal programmed instruction it tends often to be automatic—for example, being "right" on a response.

Shaping is used to build a complex behavior which an individual does not yet have in his immediate repertoire, although he has the physical capability required for the behavior. All he need be able to do is make a response which even barely approximates the desired terminal behavior for shaping to begin. Let us suppose that a kindergarten teacher wants disinterested children to learn to draw with paper and crayon without having to enforce it or set it up as a formal exercise, thus avoiding an aversive quality to the task. A table might be set up with paper, crayons, and a few chairs. The terminal behavior, drawing, may be approached as follows:

1   Reinforce a child for looking at or asking about the table, using either primary rewards, social reinforcement, or marks depending on the child.
2   Once he begins to do this with increasing frequency (which you could ascertain by recording the frequency of these responses over, say, an hour), require that he be within a certain distance of the table and oriented toward it before giving reinforcement. For example, you might require that he be within 10 feet.
3   When your records indicate that he is now within 10 feet of the table quite frequently (say, he comes within that distance 8 or 10 times in an hour, whereas before it was only once or twice), the next step could be to require that he be within 8 feet before reinforcement is given.
4   Repeat this procedure until he must come within 6 feet, 4 feet, 2 feet, and so forth, on successive steps until reinforcement is contingent upon his actually sitting at the table.
5   Once this is accomplished, make reinforcement contingent upon touching the crayon, holding the crayon, and, finally, only upon scribbling on the paper. Gradually you might successively reinforce for straight lines, circles, colors, or various combinations.

However, these should be only short exercises. Once the teacher observes that the child has reasonable control over his artistic medium, she should encourage and reinforce the child primarily for effort. While carefully defined terminal goals and learning steps may be programmed for much academic material, essentially esthetic areas need not be so carefully structured. Demands for excessively precise artistic techniques in such subjects as drawing or creative writing can be so aversive as to destroy a student's interest in the subject even before it develops. The objective teacher assumes an attitude which encourages creative expression within classroom limits. She is as quick to reinforce the relatively unskilled student for his genuine efforts as she is to reward the more advanced student for his esthetic achievement.

The shaping process, quite obviously, involves breaking the complex terminal drawing behavior into meaningful successive steps toward the goal. Each step is itself quite easy, making only a minimal demand on the student. But gradually, as he moves through each step of the sequence, he completes the final complex drawing behavior.

Since reinforcement of a response strengthens that response, caution must be used in reinforcing the successive steps employed in shaping. The final goal, the terminal behavior, cannot be reached if the student is so heavily reinforced at particular steps that he keeps making these early, simpler responses rather than moving ahead to more advanced steps. In the previous example, it is necessary to reinforce each successive step to the terminal behavior, drawing, just enough to establish it as a kind of foothold for the next step, but not enough so that the child looks at the table frequently but does not approach it. Suppose a child is reinforced for coming within 6 feet of the table for several days and receives 75 reinforcements. The next shaping step would be to get him to come within 4 feet. But reinforcement has occurred so heavily at 6 feet that a "come-to-within-6-feet" response has been firmly established, and movement to 4 feet is difficult. One session in which seven or eight reinforcements were given at 6 feet would probably have been sufficient to establish the response just firmly enough to ensure rapid movement toward the table in later steps.

Just as excessive reinforcement at a given step can slow down learning, insufficient reinforcement at a response step can put the brakes on progress. Shaping involves a dual process in which responses are reinforced only to be extinguished to make way for the next response in the sequence. But this next step, as each response step before it, must be developed strongly enough so that it actually does serve as a foothold for the subsequent response. In other words, equal care must be taken to avoid excessive reinforcement and under reinforcement. Through practice and experience, the objective teacher will be able to shape behavior efficiently without getting held up at a particular response step.

While modeling, as discussed in the previous chapter, is frequently the approach of choice when the subject being taught requires highly specific motor or vocal behavior, shaping has a very wide range of application and can often be used in situations in which modeling would prove to be impractical. In many cases the teacher desires to establish a general category of behavior which will later be refined further. An example of this might be "studying" behavior or, more precisely, "looking-at-printed-material" behavior. In the study by Hall and his associates discussed earlier, one of the students, a young girl, had an extremely low rate of studying in the classroom. Since studying behavior occurred so infrequently that it would not have been feasible to wait for it to be emitted before reinforcing it, a shaping approach appeared to be in order. As soon as the student displayed behavior which was a preliminary to studying, she was reinforced. At first she obtained reinforcement for the roughest approximations to studying behavior, such as taking out pencils, paper, books, or other written material. The next step involved the reinforcement of those behaviors which involved orienting toward work. For example, she obtained reinforcement when she merely had her book out, then it became contingent upon her turning pages although without necessarily reading. Finally, she was given reinforcement when actual studying behavior was observed. In this case, the shaping of an early approximation to studying behavior set the stage for more advanced approximations to this behavior. By reinforcing these early responses, the probability of studying was gradually increased in successive steps until studying itself emerged, to be reinforced and consequently strengthened. Of course, had the early approximations to studying been excessively reinforced, you might have seen a student who spent a good deal of time getting ready to study, but one who did little actual studying.

Shaping is particularly effective in changing the general behavior patterns of young school and preschool children, and is often used to transform undesirable behavior into socially acceptable modes of responding. This use of shaping is exemplified in a study by Hart, et al. (1968). In this study, a 5-year-old female preschool child was systematically reinforced for successive responses approximating the terminal behavior, cooperative play with other children. Before shaping, the child was observed to have spent most of her time away from the other children. The few interactions she displayed were short-lived, often aggressive and marked with outbursts of undesirable language. Using social reinforcement in the form of praise and attention, the teachers began to systematically shape the desired cooperative behavior. The first step in shaping involved the reinforcement of any verbalization which was responsive to another child while in his proximity. As this behavior began to increase, verbal communication was reinforced only in those situations in which there was a potential element of cooperativeness. Soon pleasant interactions began to develop and by the seventh shaping session, clear cut cooperative behavior, consisting of such activities as pulling a wagon with another child in it, being pulled by the other child, handing an object to another child, working on a task together, and sharing, finally emerged.

Shaping, of course, is used to develop skills among older students. Actually, it is perhaps the basic approach in training athletes in the schools and elsewhere. At first the athlete, let us say a track man, will receive reinforcement from the coach if he completes a run in a given time. Gradually, however, the coach will withhold reinforcement until he completes his event in faster time, still faster time, and so on in successive steps until, hopefully, he breaks the existing record. In academic areas, the terminal goal, a level of proficiency in a given subject, should be reached through easy successive steps. Even among older students, however, it may be necessary to shape the prerequisites to actual study behavior as described above. Since the technique has a broad range of practical application, through practice you will no doubt find many new and creative uses for this systematic teaching procedure.

BACKWARD CHAINING

A very effective variation on shaping is known as backward chaining. This procedure may be successfully used when the task is a complex one, requiring several operations before it is completed. For example, in teaching a young child to undress and dress, a useful method is to assist fully in every step until the very last (i.e., climbing out of his clothes), for which you reinforce the child. Then, once the child has mastered this step, reinforce him when he completes not only the last step, but also the next-to-last step (i.e., tugging on his clothes properly to loosen them just before stepping out of them). Gradually the child moves "backward", doing more and more of the undressing task until he can complete the entire task all the way back from the beginning. Teaching a child to dress follows the same pattern. First a child might be rewarded with tangible reinforcers and/or abundant praise for merely pushing his foot into his sock. Then, once he has mastered this final act, reinforcement might be contingent upon his tugging his socks on as well as pushing his foot in, etc., until the child can go through all the steps from the last to the first with each garment.

In the classroom, backward chaining can be used in teaching spelling and writing. A student might be given a model word (e.g., HOUSE) and beneath it the unfinished word HOUS__.He is asked to finish the word. When he learns to fill in the letter "E" to complete the word, the incompleted word HOU__ __ is presented, etc., until he can duplicate the model. Then the model word itself might be gradually faded out until only the verbal cue "HOUSE" is enough to promote an accurate spelling response. When the terminal behavior requires several steps in a fairly complex pattern, the objective teacher may find that this technique can be used effectively in teaching a wide range of skills.

PROGRAMMED INSTRUCTION

Despite the aversive experiences that many of us have had at one time or another while attending school, we are apt to remember at least one special teacher that had a knack for conveying even the most difficult material with clarity and meaning. To our great surprise, we may have become interested in a subject in which we had no business being interested, such as mathematics or history. Such a situation arises relatively infrequently in our present system, but this need not be the case. The answer does not lie in intuition or hidden talent unique to one teacher but forever denied to another. Nor is it alone a special personality trait which enables a magical rapport to develop between teacher and student. Every teacher has the potential to be the extraordinary teacher and every subject offers the possibility of attracting profound interest. It is largely in the manner of presentation—the way the material is organized and the opportunity it provides for reinforcement.

Programming, as you will recall, is the arrangement of material in a particular sequence: a series of successive steps moving toward a final goal. It is a logical approach to the presentation of content material and one which contributes to the increasing resources of objective teaching. Programmed instruction is neither a passing fad nor a gimmick. It has been used with great success for many years in specialized educational areas and will play a major role in teaching from now on. You can be certain that your familiarity with this approach will prove to be of great value to both yourself and your students.

The above definition applies mainly to *linear* programming. Another programming method called *branching* is generally used to denote two other programming operations. The first way in which the term branching is used refers to a multiple choice format in which the student, upon making a wrong choice, learns why it is wrong and then has a chance to try again. The second use of the term refers to an adjustment which is made in the level of difficulty of the material according to the number of incorrect responses made. The authors tend to agree with B.F. Skinner (1954) who suggests that these two operations, generally considered to be within the realm of branching, are actually employed in linear programs as well. Furthermore, since linear programs are more amenable to presentation in book form or with the help of relatively simple teaching machines, whereas branching programs often require more mechanization and even computerization, we will restrict our discussion to linear programming.

CONSTRUCTING AN ACADEMIC PROGRAM

The recent recognition of the usefullness of programmed material has resulted in the increasing availability of commercially produced programs in a wide range of academic subjects. But frequently the particular area of study is unique and there are no such commercially prepared academic programs available for that topic. For this reason, we feel it is important that the teacher knows how to use and construct academic programs.

Since a program moves through successive steps to the terminal behavior, it is clear that decisions have to be made regarding the kind of terminal behavior desired, the size of the steps, and the sequence in which the material is to be presented.

The terminal behavior in academic programming is a certain level of proficiency in a subject or subtopic. The educational ideal, of course, is for the student (and, hopefully, the teacher) to have a complete grasp of the subject; that is, to know all that is known in an area. Secondary education, however, has more limited goals and a high school graduate is generally expected to have sufficient knowledge to perform his duties as an informed citizen and to have some acquaintance with a wide range of topics in the sciences, arts, and social sciences. The exact point at which secondary education terminates and higher education begins is difficult to define, and it is very likely that the progress of objective teaching, and particularly programmed instruction, will raise educational achievement and goals at all levels. For the time being, however, the goals with which we need be concerned are quite explicit; they are specific, predetermined levels of skill in given academic areas. Thus, an entire program in high school mathematics might end with an introduction to calculus. A program in American history might cover all major events, but without the degree of detail to be expected in a college program. Eventually, graded schools will very likely be replaced by ungraded schools in which graduation is determined more by the completion of certain programmed steps than by how many years one has attended school. To facilitate the construction of programs, overall subject material is broken down into segments such as "the industrial revolution," "mathematical set theory," and so on. Related field trips, museum visits, etc., might then be contingent upon completion of a program covering a specific segment of material.

With the selection of the desired terminal behavior, a decision must be made on the size of the steps which will move the student toward the goal with greatest efficiency. The material presented at each step is written in a unit technically called a *frame.* A complete academic program may consist of hundreds or even thousands of frames. If the steps are too large, it will be more difficult for the student to move easily from one frame to another and, consequently, the number of correct responses and reinforcements will be reduced. Although smaller steps require more effort on the part of the teacher-programmer, they increase the probability of success on each frame and keep the student better motivated. For these reasons, it is desirable to construct a program in which frames are close enough to ensure almost totally correct responding (95% correct responding is a usual goal). In this way, a student progresses from frame to frame experiencing success on almost every response he makes. Success itself is often a powerful reinforcer, assuring continued responding throughout the program until the terminal behavior is achieved. However, there is no reason why external rewards cannot be granted for the successful completion of a program or a segment of one, and such an approach would be especially desirable with younger students. Such a system may be considered to involve two kinds of reinforcement operating simultaneously: automatic reinforcement (being correct) is given on a continuous schedule while external reinforcement (tangible items or preferred activities) is provided intermittently. At any rate, careful planning of frames encourages movement without coercion and at the same time offers success. By sparing the academic rod, you spare the student.

The sequence in which items are presented is a key factor in programming. Unlike simple behavior shaping in which the next step is obviously determined from the step before, programmed instruction is directed toward a far more complex terminal behavior and, therefore, it is not always as easy to know just what direction the next frame should take. A good academic program may employ various techniques in the construction of frames. Certain frames may consist basically of words which serve as prompts through familiarity and experience. Other frames may merely introduce new material and ask easy questions about it. Logical order is another criterion used to determine the next frame to be presented, and degree of difficulty is still another consideration. At various

Table 1. SAMPLE PROGRAM

Sentences to be Completed	Word to be Supplied
1. In a written program, each unit of material is called a frame. An entire program may consist of_____ frames.	many
2. Frames are put in a sequence which moves toward a desired terminal behavior or goal. The entire program must_____toward the goal.	move, progress
3. If the frames are too few and too difficult, the chance of a correct response is_____.	small, reduced
4. Thus, a program consisting of many small_____which are not too difficult is desirable.	frames
5. Certain frames consist largely of prompts. These are easy to respond to because they simply give_____ the correct response.	away
6. These frames are meant merely as a demonstration of the kinds of techniques that can be used in writing an entire_____.	program
7. If this were an actual program, there would be many more_____.	frames
8. Most would borrow from previous frames to help you reach the desired_____behavior.	terminal

times in the program, a word might be requested which requires a synthesis of earlier concepts. From time to time frames may review previous material or require that it be used in new contexts. Programming, then, is not a sterile, mechanized technique, but offers a very wide range of possible responses. The teacher-programmer can approach his subject from a number of different directions with the basic requirement being essentially that the student move systematically toward the selected level of proficiency.

Table 1 is a very brief sample program[1] which employs some of the impor-

[1]These frames are intended to illustrate some programming techniques and are not geared to reach a particular goal beyond this. However, a program designed to teach programming appears to be quite practical.

tant concepts of sequencing. Hold a ruler over the words at the right and slide it down after each response to see if you are correct.

In constructing a program, a teacher goes through several operations. In selecting the desired terminal behavior, decisions have to be made regarding the depth of knowledge required; that is, how many principles, definitions, relationships, etc., have to be learned by the student. Once these decisions are reached, the information to be programmed may be arranged in an orderly manner convenient to the programmer. For example, terms may be written on cards which can be arranged in a meaningful order of presentation. Various terms and concepts are then repeated from time to time or used with related items to establish new relationships. As in most things, a thoughtful and careful plan will enhance the probability of writing a good program.

At this point in time, programming offers a great many possibilities for innovation and creative application. Indeed, it is difficult to imagine any body of objective knowledge which could not eventually be arranged in program form. Furthermore, as the techniques of programming are investigated within a scientific framework, it is quite possible that an entire technology of instructional programming will develop. Such a discipline might concern itself with the objective arrangement of materials in those particular sequences which would maximize learning. Not only will instructional programs play a large role in the future of education, but as one looks ahead there are many signs that programming may actually constitute a major portion of teacher education.

PROGRAMMING: AN INTEGRATED APPROACH

The classroom, as a primary part of the student's learning environment, should be designed to promote learning in a fairly wide range of topics and in a fairly wide range of ways. Changes in classroom format, and variety in both content and method appear to promote interest and involvement.

A sterile and doctrinaire approach to teaching deprives both teacher and student of the advantages of an integrated learning system. Such a system must be transmodal. That is, it must engage a student on intellectual, social, and emotional levels. A narrow, traditional approach, based largely on aversive practices and with little regard for programming, has proven neither objective, efficient, nor emotionally satisfying. The objective teacher, on the other hand, is not doctrinaire, not tied to rigid and closed explanations of education. She pulls together those methods which have been objectively shown to facilitate learning into an integrated system which becomes alive in the classroom. Such a system, of course, could not objectively exclude reinforcement, modeling, or programmed learning. But neither should it exclude other effective approaches with proven value.

The value of an integrated approach is that it takes into account the fact that a particular change in behavior may have been effected by not just one alteration of the student or the learning environment but several. Consequently, it may be fruitful to examine more complex methods, educational systems which include several distinct facets, and evaluate their relative effectiveness as units. For example, will a teacher employing modeling, reinforcement, and sequential (programmed) learning, in that order of priority, be more or less effective than one stressing programmed learning and imitative behavior? Many of our teaching problems may be resolved, then, when we determine the best *combination* of methods to enhance learning.

One step in that direction is reported by Dill and Gotts (1971). They observed boys and girls between 7- and 9-years-old who had serious problems in arithmetic and were at the bottom of the lowest third grade track in that subject. To begin with, all the children in the class were given self-concept scales pertaining to their arithmetic ability. They were also given objective tests on a weekly basis. The 24 children in the class were divided into six groups of four each, one from the most advanced group, two from the middle group, and one from the lowest group. Each of the groups elected leaders for the week and functioned in an informal manner, competing with other groups to solve arithmetic problems for prizes. The four target (lowest) children were additionally given systematic reinforcement for the first two weeks only. During the course of this study, the complexity of the problems was sequentially increased via programming. In other words, positive reinforcement, peer interaction, and programming were simultaneously employed in an integrated system.

The results were encouraging. The four target children gained steadily in their arithmetic ability until they paralleled the 20 more advanced students who had not been given extra reinforcement. The target students made significant gains in their arithmetic self-concept commensurate with their improved skills. On a more subjective note, the observers reported that the general atmosphere in the classroom was warm. Interestingly, a sociometric rating by the other students indicated that they now considered the original low-ability target children as "very smart". The researchers suggest that these "treatment effects must be attributed to this conjoint set of events . . ." rather than to a single event.

THE TEACHER AND THE MACHINE

Man tends to accept the present as a premise for what must happen in the future. His inability to see beyond his own conditioning often leads him to act as if significant change is beyond the scope of possibility. If one has learned anything from history, he must know that the only thing that can be predicted with certainty is the fact of change itself. Yet, even in the midst of so much change, some teachers still tend to conduct their classes in the same way they might have 50- or 100-years ago. The advances that have had such a profound influence on so many professions have somehow failed to gain significant acceptance in teaching. Objective teaching, however, promises to give a new impetus to the adoption of machines in the schools to facilitate teaching. It is safe to predict that the programmed teaching machine will become as standard a piece of equipment as the blackboard is in the classroom of today. Certainly a society which can produce cars and appliances by the millions can produce teaching machines, most of which are far simpler, at the same rate. It is the cost of not bringing advanced technology to bear upon the problems of education that is prohibitive. We cannot afford to allow education to lag while huge sums of money are spent on far more frivolous things.

To many, the term "teaching machine" strikes a certain note of fear. It is reasoned that if programmed teaching machines are used on a large scale, eventually teachers may be replaced. While this is possible in the distant future, it is no more likely that teachers will be replaced by machines than that any of us will be so relieved, irrespective of our work. And should this happen, there will be little need for people to work on a regular basis anyway.

Teaching machines, then, must be viewed in proper perspective. Like any machine, they are merely tools which permit man to perform more efficiently. They take over the more burdensome aspect of man's life so that he may be freer to do the things he deems important and enjoyable. They give the teacher more time to teach by taking over the grading of work and eliminating boring and repetitive drills. Teaching machines do not subordinate the role of the teacher, but merely remove the unnecessary obstacles which limit the amount of teaching a teacher can presently do. The systematic use of machines in the classroom enables the teacher to spend more time with individual students. He is able to focus on the improved use of materials and has much more time to devote to helping his students develop their individual interests. Resting assured that carefully programmed machines are increasing his students' academic proficiency, the teacher has a better opportunity to explore the new and creative possibilities within the learning environment.

THE TEACHING MACHINE

In 1926, S.L. Pressey published an article describing a machine he had designed which not only gave tests and scored answers, but actually taught material. The fact that this machine did not attract more attention than it did is somewhat surprising, especially in view of the fact that it could actually handle some of the routine drilling and testing tasks carried out by teachers. Roughly the size of a typewriter, Pressey's machine contained four keys which corresponded to the number of multiple choice answers available. Two of the keys could be used when true-false items were presented. By pressing a key, the student could turn up a new question. The only functions required of the scorer were putting the papers into the machine and later recording the number of correct answers. A counter clicked off correct answers, and for teaching purposes, a new question could not be presented until the former was answered correctly. Additional pieces of apparatus could be attached to enable tangible reinforcement, such as candy, to be delivered after a given number of correct answers.

While Pressey was a bit ahead of his time, B.F. Skinner, whose "operant conditioning" has been a major influence in education and psychology, has gained wider acceptance for his teaching machines. In 1954, Skinner published an article which provided dramatic evidence that programmed teaching could be successfully applied to a variety of subjects, including mathematics and spelling. Unlike Pressey's machine which required a multiple-choice or true-false response, Skinner's machine requires that the student actually compose his own answer through a slot in the machine. By moving a slide, the student places his answer under a transparent strip and simultaneously uncovers the correct response. If his response is correct, the student may move ahead to the next frame; if not, he may compose another answer. Incorrect responses may be recorded by entering a punch mark next to the wrong response.

As you can readily surmise from the above description, teaching machines need not be expensive, cumbersome monsters that require a room of their own, but may be small and inexpensive devices which sit neatly on the student's desk. What is of prime importance is not the machine, but the program placed in it by the teacher. Frames such as the samples given earlier are easily typed or otherwise produced and readily fed into the machine. In some machines the simple act of turning a knob moves the next frame into position to be answered. Some very inexpensive machines are available which take large numbers of standard writing sheets. About 8 or 10 average frames can be presented on a single sheet of paper and as a sheet is completed, it automatically returns to a compartment in the machine.

COMPUTERS AND LEARNING

The computer, once thought to be a mysterious kind of thinking machine used primarily by brilliant scientists engaged in highly technical research, will probably be as familiar to the classroom of tomorrow as the teacher himself. Due to major advances in production and cost sharing, the computer is already beginning to make a formal entrance into the classroom. As with any teaching machine, however, its role may be viewed as an assistant to the teacher, a device which significantly facilitates the presentation of programmed materials and gives instant feedback to the student selecting-from or composing answers. Perhaps the major contribution of this remarkable teaching machine is its ability to provide far more individualized instruction as a result of its potentially vast reservoir of relevant information, both content (e.g., facts, figures) and process (e.g., theories) oriented. By taking into account a student's history in given academic areas and by keeping records of his performance on the computer itself, the computer can actually present an academic program appropriate to the student's competence in that area. Of course, until someone can devise a computer program which enables the computer to write its own program, this crucial task will remain in the hands of the teacher or other program specialist. But the computer will be able to present such programs more effectively than earlier teaching machines and will enable far more flexible classroom use. The objective teacher, using information about a student's present level of functioning in given subjects, can make individual curriculum choices with a much greater degree of confidence than is presently possible.

Suppes (1966), discussing an ongoing research program at Stanford on the uses of computers in education, offers important insights into potential applications in the classroom. While the curricula adapted to computer presentation have been primarily at the elementary level, he points out that the computer is clearly applicable to secondary school and university education.

As described by Suppes, each computer terminal has a screen, often a cathode ray tube similar to a television screen, which facilitates presentation of visual stimuli such as questions and items to be filled in by the student. A typewriter key board is included so that a student can type his answers to questions, facilitating the actual composition of answers often so necessary in learning. For younger children, a "light pen" may be included which permits them to point directly to the screen without typing the answers. This allows even kindergarten children with very limited ability to use the computer. A sound component is also attached which enables the computer to present spoken messages as an aid to understanding problems and solutions.

The nature of the interaction between the student and the computer has been broken down into the following three categories: (1) drill and practice, (2) tutorial systems, (3) dialogue systems. The first category involves the repeated presentation of materials which may presently comprise much of the teacher's day. Computerized presentation of drill materials is conducted at each of several computer terminals which may be operated simultaneously. Students alternate in the use of the equipment and each student has a concentrated period of perhaps 5 or 10 minutes for drill exercises in such areas as reading or arithmetic. The level of difficulty of the curriculum is geared to the student's performance, but this is a far more precise breakdown than is usual in a traditional classroom. For example, fraction problems may be arranged according to subtle differences in denominators which are appropriate for a child's present skill level. After a student types in his name, he is presented an academic exercise. Incorrect answers receive feedback from the computer which types out WRONG and the student repeats the exercise. After the drill session, the computer provides the student with a summary of his work for both that and previous sessions. More comprehensive summaries of total class performance in specific areas (e.g., correct multiplication responses) are easily available to the teacher, facilitating her planning for the next day's curricula.

Tutorial programming, emphasizing to a greater extent concepts and process variables, permits systematic instruction in areas which may be time consuming to the teacher. Presentation of programmed material in this category is rather similar to the approach used in less sophisticated teaching machines, and the question of linear versus branching programs, as discussed earlier in this chapter, is still a relatively open one. Tutorial programming via computerization holds the possibility of improvements in individualized instruction since the computer can easily present material pertinent to the student's immediate academic needs as determined by his recorded performance in the area. This method has the further advantage of enabling the student to approach a problem from directions not always decipherable by less complex teaching machines. For example, in a program in mathematical logic, the student can select from a wide range of inferences in reaching a conclusion. The computer accepts any proof that is shown to be valid irrespective of its orthodoxy. It is apparent that this method of computer-use encourages the kind of individual creativity in problem solving which, paradoxically, may not always be achieved in traditional academic situations.

Dialogue systems are far less developed than drill and tutorial programs but may eventually permit highly flexible interaction between student and computer in which a student may actually ask questions of the computer or give verbal directions in solving a problem. This usage of computers in education is heavily dependent on improved technology but offers a wide range of future classroom application.

THE STUDENT AND THE TEACHING MACHINE

The teaching machine has infinitely more patience than even the most patient teacher. Furthermore, it provides immediate reinforcement for a correct response rather than forcing the student to wait several days or weeks to have his test scored and returned. The student, previously the passive recipient of information, now becomes an active partner in the educational process as he moves from frame to frame toward the final goal. Furthermore, he moves at his own pace rather than having to conform to the too-slow or too-fast pace of others. A skillfully written program will not only encourage progress, but it will also produce enthusiasm as the student, perhaps for the first time in his life, experiences one successful encounter with the material after another. At various points in the program the teacher might want to show films, have laboratory demonstrations, or take field trips to bring the programmed material into still clearer perspective. If one wishes to adhere to a grading system, a student's grade may rest on the number of frames completed, that is, how far he has gotten in the program. If his teacher feels so inclined, he may require the student to apply his knowledge to other areas via formal testing. He may prepare special laboratories and rooms in conjunction with written programs so that the student can pursue nonrequired subjects in accordance with his interest. Teaching machines, then, will enable students to acquire knowledge quickly and easily so that they may explore the limits of their ability, rather than the limits of their patience. The teacher need not wait until full mechanization is achieved to employ programming principles. By applying these techniques to the presentation of course materials, learning, and motivation will certainly be improved.

SUMMARY

In this chapter we introduced a new concept of development, one which emphasizes the building up of skill upon skill rather than focusing on rigid stages of development. This led naturally to a discussion of graded versus ungraded schools, and we pointed out that the ungraded school was more consistent with our current knowledge of human learning than the graded school.

We discussed the necessity of individualizing instruction to a greater degree than is presently practiced under the grade system of promotion.

The issue of ability grouping is still quite emotionally charged. We discussed some of the pros and cons. The objective teacher recognizes her responsibility to all of her students, not just the more advanced or less advanced students.

We covered many of the essential concepts of academic programming. The term *shaping* was defined—the process through which complex terminal behaviors are learned through a sequence of simpler responses which move toward the final goal. We described *backward chaining*, a technique which moves the learner back from the final step to the first, requiring him to complete more and more of the task by himself until he masters the entire sequence. From this, we progressed to formal academic programming and described the major elements of a good program. We warned against the pitfalls of both excessive reinforcement and insufficient reinforcement at various points in the program.

Linear and branching programs were contrasted and we then went into further detail about the actual construction of a program. We stated that a program actually consists of many *frames* which follow one another according to various criteria. The sequence may be arranged according to such factors as logical order or repetition.

Programming is going to play an increasingly important role in teaching, and we noted that an entire technology of programming seems to be developing. Eventually, experts may participate in the construction of academic programs, but for the time being it appears that the classroom teacher and his assistants will be very much involved in this area.

We argued against a narrow, doctrinaire approach and in favor of one which integrates two, three, or more effective methods such as reinforcement, modeling, and programming.

Academic programs can easily be presented on currently available machines. We described some of these, paying particular attention to the use of the computer as a teaching machine. Computerized instruction has many advantages and is especially useful because of the individualized teaching it can provide. Material can be tailored for a student depending on his present level of performance.

We made it clear that teaching machines were merely aids, permitting the teacher to spend more time understanding and helping individual students, but not displacing the teacher from his essential role.

REFERENCES

Baer, D. M. An age-irrelevant concept of development. Paper presented to the annual meeting of the American Psychological Association, New York, 1966.

Dill, N., & Gotts, E. E. Improvement of arithmetic self concept through combined positive reinforcement, peer interaction, and sequential curriculum. *Journal of School Psychology*, 1971, 9 (4), 462–471.

Hart, B. M., Reynolds, N. J., Baer, D. M., Browley, E. R., & Harris, F. R. Effect of contingent and noncontingent social reinforcement on the cooperative play of a preschool child. *Journal of Applied Behavior Analysis*, 1968, 1, 73–76.

Pressey, S. L. A simple apparatus which gives tests and scores—and teaches. *School and Society*, 1926, 23, 35–41.

Skinner, B. F. The science of learning and the art of teaching. *Harvard Educational Review*, 1954, 24, 86–97.

Suppes, P. The use of computers in education. *Scientific American*, 1966, 215, 207–220.

SUGGESTED READINGS

Birnbrauer, J., Bijou, S., Wolf, M., & Kidder, J. Programmed instruction in the classroom. In *Case studies in behavior modification* (L. Ullmann and L. Krasner, eds.). New York: Holt, Rinehart & Winston, 1966.

Haring, N., & Kinzelmann, H. The finer focus of therapeutic behavioral management. In *Educational therapy*. Seattle, Washington: Bernie Straub, 1966.

Lumsdaine, A. A., & Glaser, R. *Teaching machines and programmed learning.* Washington, D.C.: National Educational Association, 1960.

Skinner, B. F. *The technology of teaching.* New York: Appleton-Century-Crofts, 1968.

Spence, J. T. The distracting effects of material reinforcers in the discrimination learning of lower- and middle-class children. *Child Development*, 1970, 41, 103–111.

8
Ethical Considerations in Objective Teaching

The tendency for man to permit his technology to develop without examining the ethical implications of its development has contributed substantially to a wide range of human disasters including war, pollution, and starvation.

As the effectiveness of a particular scientific method or technology becomes apparent, it is essential to consider its application to mankind within an ethical framework. This consideration is especially necessary when one is dealing with a method which can affect human behavior, as can objective teaching. This chapter, then, is included as a guide to aid the reader in examining some of the ethical implications of objective teaching. By no means do we intend to suggest that we have covered the entire topic, as an analysis of the ethics of teaching would constitute volumes. Instead, the key topics to be discussed should serve as points of departure for the concerned and responsible reader.

The objective teacher recognizes his responsibility to promote change in his students' behavior. Education is inferred from behavior. If there is no observable change in a student's behavior, there is no justifiable claim that learning has occurred. Behavior, as it is used in this context, implies verbal and emotional responding as well as academic performance.

The decision to promote learning is, in fact, the decision to promote change in human behavior. The responsible teacher accepts the fact that he has made either explicit or implicit decisions as to the kind of changes he would like to promote in his students. He does not ignore the issue, deny that he is making such decisions, or attribute all of his decisions to regulations handed down by the school district.

As a behavior-change specialist, the teacher must come to grips with the underlying principles or preferences which influence his own teaching. Merely leaving them unexplored does not lessen their effect on his students.

While all teachers effect behavioral change, the objective teacher strives toward clarifying for himself and the community the direction of that change. He tries to recognize the role of his own particular biases and attempts to attain a sound ethical perspective to direct his teaching (behavior-changing) techniques.

The objective teacher knows that he has chosen a particular direction and method of change for a given student and knows also why he has made this specific choice. While the techniques of objective teaching have no implicit moral direction, we emphasize again the absolute necessity of ensuring that these behavioral techniques are employed only within a humanistic context.

EDUCATION VERSUS INDOCTRINATION

The importance of controlling school curricula has long been recognized by political demagogues and dictators. More recently this approach has been used by Hitler, the Communist Party, and even a surprisingly large number of school districts in the United States. All too often children are quietly encouraged to imitate derogatory statements about other economic, political, or even religious systems about which they have little or no information. Furthermore, the teacher who expresses points of view which differ from the larger society's may be subjected to subtle or not-so-subtle pressures to restrict his freedom of speech within the classroom. Should he believe strongly enough in his constitutionally guaranteed freedoms, he may actually be dismissed for a number of handy and misleading reasons. The school, then, reflects the biases of the larger culture and, in certain hands, the concept of education is perverted to indoctrination.

Incentive systems have often been used to control behavior, sometimes effectively and sometimes not. Objective teaching, as a careful, scientific refinement of the principles of human learning, could become a dangerous weapon in the hands of the would-be tyrant or dictator. It is incumbent upon those in the field of education to see that this is not permitted. A full understanding of acceptable and unacceptable educational goals is essential if objective teaching is to be used in an ethical manner.

EDUCATIONAL GOALS AND ETHICS

For matters of simplification, let us divide education into two basic areas: (1) factual content material and (2) logical processes. These, of course, are highly interrelated as factual content material is often derived through a logical process (e.g., the scientific method) and may frequently be described in terms of such a logical approach. On the other hand, implicit assumptions often determine the course of further reasoning. For example, our maps, communication systems, and transportation systems would be designed far differently if we still held the assumption that the earth was flat.

The interrelatedness of process and content variables suggests that adequate education must take both factors into account. Unfortunately, the schools have too long stressed the mere accumulation of content material which is then parroted back by more-or-less captive students. Students are often taught that one political or economic system is much better than another, but may only be given the most stereotyped and biased "explanations" as to why it is so. Of course, the failure to recognize the process variables in education, i.e., the systematic, well-reasoned approaches which contribute to real understanding, is not merely confined to the teaching of history, government, or economics. It also occurs in the teaching of mathematics and the physical and behavioral sciences. Students may be forced to memorize endless formulas which they do not understand and which could just as easily be looked up when necessary. Yet the crucial reasoning processes through which the formulas were derived are either totally neglected or explained so inadequately as to promote distaste, apprehension or, at best, boredom. However, since we are concerned here with the ethical considerations of objective teaching, our focus is largely upon those areas of content in which indoctrination poses a serious threat to the maintenance of a free society.

Education must be relevant to individual needs and yet take into account the structure of society. In other words, before one can intelligently design academic goals, he must achieve a clear understanding of the relationship between man and society. This question can by no means be pushed aside with platitudes and superficial explanations, but must be looked into in a free spirit of inquiry devoid of preconceptions and traditional myths. If compulsory education is to be maintained, what should students have to learn? Why? Does learning a particular skill merely maintain the society's expectations and traditions or does the skill actually enhance the quality of human life? The goals of society must reflect the individual goals of its members. A society which fails to meet the needs of the people provokes negative reactions such as apathy or civil disorder. In selecting academic curricula, it is crucial that courses be provided which help meet both individual and societal goals, courses which provoke interest by their very relevance to the needs of an individual living in a complex society. What, then, are the relevant needs of individuals? How can they best be met? How can education contribute?

In looking still more deeply at some of these questions, it is important to note a subtle though devastating assumption which has reduced significantly both the quality of education and of human life. This is the idea that a few highly capable and intelligent leaders can best decide the course of society and choose wisely for the entire population. Historically, this assumption was manifested in the reign of kings, certain religious figures, tyrants, and dictators. Once entrenched in power, the autocrat gradually recognizes that in order to maintain his dominant position, he must limit the opportunity for free inquiry which would ultimately result in the questioning of his authority.

Recognition of the inevitable outcome of education which permits free inquiry provokes constant fear of real education in many governments. Thus, they resort to political indoctrination or mundane training to sustain their own position through an uneducated populace.

Truly free education permits and even encourages open inquiry no matter where it will lead. It offers the greatest opportunity for enhancing progress and freedom; for true education permits alternative perspectives from which to view the society and provides the very basis for exploration and progressive innovation in both science and technology and human relationships. A highly educated and active population, not only in the narrow technological sense but in the broader humanistic sense as well, is the greatest bulwark against war, poverty, disease, and other conditions which impede human progress. Thus, any approach to teaching which limits free inquiry, and consequently limits human understanding, must be dismissed.

A major goal of education, then, is to provide an environment in which free inquiry can take place. Obviously, if content material is presented in a poorly programmed manner, so much time is wasted on learning content that other aspects of education are neglected. Objective teaching, by facilitating the presentation and learning of content material through systematic programming, reinforcement, and modeling, enables the student to learn content through an understanding of the process which developed it. He is then in a far better position to apply content to a wide range of areas. Objective teaching offers the teacher an opportunity to devote much more time to being an educator rather than a drill instructor. But it does not guarantee that all teachers will invariably use this time wisely. Thus, it is the responsibility of each teacher to become aware of his real responsibility to the youth he is teaching. He must ask himself repeatedly whether he fully understands the material he is presenting and the logical process on which it is based. He must continually push his own level of understanding beyond the superficial, particularly in the fields of government, economics, and social change, so that he may accelerate the process of inquiry which contributes to true education.

But by no means do we propose that the educator abandon his role as curriculum planner and devote himself only to nonspecific dialogue with his students. On the contrary, what we suggest is that the curricula be planned more objectively and less ritualistically. Krishnamurti (1963), certainly one of the most profound observers of man and society, discussing the role of the educator notes:

> Since we are concerned with the total development of the individual, the student may not be allowed in the beginning to choose his own subjects, because his choice

is likely to be based on passing moods and prejudices, or on finding the easiest thing to do; or he may choose according to the immediate demands of a particular need. . . . If the student is helped from the very beginning to look at life as a whole, with all its psychological, intellectual and emotional problems, he will not be frightened by it.

The educator at all levels must examine his own assumptions about human existence and determine, through sincere self-evaluation and open minded inquiry, whether his premises are based on reason or emotion, objectivity or conformity. Only after such a vital but painstaking self-examination will each educator be able to develop educational goals and curricula that are relevant to students and society alike; only then will he be teaching in a truly ethical manner.

THE ETHICS OF BEHAVIOR MODIFICATION

In addition to the question of educational goals as reflected in curriculum development, the general area of behavior modification in the classroom warrants examination from an ethical viewpoint. When one does not really have the means to change behavior predictably, as was often the case before the development of objective teaching, the question of the ethics of behavior modification is rarely pursued. Since systematic modification of student behavior is now a reality, specific decisions must be made regarding acceptable and unacceptable classroom behavior. When one considers the general capriciousness of many school regulations, the importance of looking at the problem rationally becomes evident.

It would appear that there is a general tendency for many adults to regard children and even late adolescents in a manner somewhat analogous to another class or caste. This treatment goes beyond the distinctions which must be made between adults and children which are necessary for the child's welfare. It is reflected in dual standards in which adults may be permitted many behaviors denied their children for their purported protection. In some schools, students may be compelled to follow rules and regulations which, if imposed upon adults, would probably lead to outright revolt. In certain classrooms students may be required to sit quietly with their hands on their desks for long periods of time or move from room to room or activity to activity in a rigid fashion akin to a lockstep. Usually these rules are justified on the basis of discipline training but, when examined closely, such rigid regulations are typically a result of overcrowded and large classes and of forcing the teacher to employ what he considers to be the most efficient means available to maintain behavior control. Since many rules and regulations are established by the classroom teacher, it is essential that he examine them from an ethical viewpoint. Are the regulations for the benefit of the students or really for the convenience of the teacher? What kind of student behavior really interferes with the learning opportunity of the rest of the class, and what student behavior is personally annoying but harmless? How much classroom freedom can be permitted without interfering with the rights of other students? Should silence be maintained at all times or should quiet communication among students be permitted? As the teacher begins to raise these and other questions, he may find that his students can function just as effectively and perhaps even more so in a relaxed classroom environment.

When disruptive behavior interferes with classroom functioning, the teacher may initiate a program emphasizing positive reinforcement of desirable behavior and extinction of undesirable responses. When such behavior modification is employed, the ethical questions frequently raised are quite similar to those arising in the therapeutic process. Kanfer (1968) has indicated three major aspects of the process of therapeutic behavior modification immediately relevant to changing behavior in the classroom:

1   methods of control
2   domain of the behavior to be controlled
3   discrepency between personal and cultural values

Objective teaching employs a more subtle form of behavioral influence than certain traditional techniques of behavior control relying on threat and overt punishment. Although the hazards of physical punishment as a means of effecting behavior change are clear, the approach is far better understood by the general public than the use of rewards. Reinforcement, then, may sometimes be regarded as a potential threat to an individual's control of his own behavior, particularly since, unlike punishment, it may occur without his immediate awareness. Thus the question of the ethics of reinforcement tends to be related to the old and familiar issue of free will. Put in another way, there may be more public acceptance of purposeful and direct behavior control through threat or even physical punishment because it is clear and overt than of covert behavior modification through positive reinforcement. An individual may feel more in control, that he has greater choice of response, when subjected to threat or punishment than when subjected to reward. This may very well be a cultural phenomenon peculiar to Western civilization. Since certain behaviors must be maintained in a school situation (e.g., peaceful interaction among students), the teacher may have to choose between two practical alternatives—reward of appropriate behavior, or punishment of inappropriate behavior. It would be difficult to suggest that coercion or punishment would be a more ethical approach by virtue of its being more overt. On the other hand, the covert use of rewards may appear dehumanizing even if the behavior which is reinforced is highly desirable.

This seeming dilemma, however, may be resolved when one looks closely at the nature of reinforcement. It is certainly possible to view positive reinforcement as positive feedback, a practical statement of appreciation of desirable behavior. Furthermore, there appears to be an increasing tendency to state outright to the student the contingencies of reinforcement. This tendency may be implicit in modeling (Chapter 6) and is certainly apparent in token, mark, and Premack systems. This more open-handed approach is an implicit feature of the increasingly popular contract system, particularly as certain studies which we have noted indicate that students seem to work harder when they themselves have a hand in drawing up the contract and setting their own contingencies. This is a primary goal of objective teaching; to foster the skills which will permit an individual greater choice and thus greater freedom. We are guided continually by the principle of enhancing self-direction. The increasing replacement of externally designed contingencies by self-designed contingencies gives man greater control of his own life.

This is supported by Glynn's (1970) finding that a self-determined reinforcement procedure was just as effective as an externally established one and in the Lovitt and Curtiss (1969) finding that students on self-instituted contingencies sometimes did better than those on teacher-set contingencies. Lovitt and Curtiss suggest that

> An individual who can control or manage his own behavior may be the person who has the ability to assess his own competencies, set his own behavioral objectives and specify a contingency system whereby he might obtain these objectives. Translated to a school situation, this would be an individual who knew his academic capabilities in terms of skill levels and rate of performance, could arrange a series of activities or steps to achieve a variety of self-imposed objectives and could grant himself reinforcers on a prearranged schedule to accomplish certain behavioral sequences. [p. 49]

With the exception of the technical language, this pattern of perseverance bears a striking similarity to William James's concept of will, the development of which he felt was a key educational goal. Gilmore (1971), examining James's potential contributions to modern education, noted James's definition of will as the "power of voluntary action." Sustained effort, according to James, is the pathway to success. The ability or inability to persevere in one's objective is what differentiates the outstanding from the mediocre. Gilmore argues that "helping a student to say with conviction 'I *will* do this,' or 'I will resist this temptation,' is at the heart of a practical education . . . ." The objective teacher goes still one step further by encouraging her students not merely to speak with conviction, but to act with conviction as well.

While thus far behavioral technology has been mainly used "on" people to direct their behavior from outside so that it conforms to certain preconceived standards, specific refinements of objective techniques seem to lend themselves directly to enhanced self-control. This provides each person who wishes to take advantage of it with additional means of revising his behavior in accordance with his personal choice. Specific applications of behavior-change techniques appear successful in combating smoking and other self-defeating behaviors. Now there is an incipient but growing tendency to apply behavioral technology to the thought process itself, via self-administration by the person applying it.

Irwin Sarason of the University of Washington psychology department, cited for his work in modeling in Chapter 6, is making important discoveries regarding cognitive processes. He found, for example (1973), that high-test anxious students did poorly in all given test conditions when compared to low-anxious subjects, with one important exception: this condition was one in which all subjects were allowed to observe a model who was working on a problem (an anagram) while simultaneously describing the reasoning processes involved and sometimes stating general principles. Under this condition the more anxious subjects actually outperformed their less anxious peers. This finding might suggest to some that a certain degree of anxiety can be closely associated with basic lack of skills or information. Since objective techniques lend themselves readily to the rapid transmission of information, it may well be that they serve a related function of reducing anxiety. This remains, however, a rather speculative area.

As early as 1965, L. E. Homme was giving very specific suggestions regarding the use of behavioral techniques to allow people greater self-direction. Not only did he outline ways of reducing smoking and overeating, but he pointed out basic ways in which simple reinforcement procedures could be self-applied to promote self-confidence and happiness. Homme considered these desirable mood states as related to desirable mental events. By teaching people to reinforce themselves for thinking happy thoughts, it may be possible to teach them happiness, Homme seems to suggest.

SOME FURTHER CONSIDERATIONS

While in therapy the domain of the changed behavior is typically intimate and personal, much change occurring in a school setting involves academic behavior. Objective teaching provides a framework for rapid and efficient learning, including the learning of those behaviors which are prerequisites for academic achievement. While the teacher can promote learning by fully appreciating his students' individuality and the environmental influences which shape their present behavior, he may not normally have the training which would permit him to treat complex psychological problems involving, for example, the child's total home situation. Thus, the teacher's major contribution to his students lies in providing a classroom environment conducive to individual learning of and inquiry into both content material and process factors. A genuine understanding of the individual and the environment in which he lives and learns may obviate problems which might otherwise ensue and permits appropriate referral to other professionals when their consultation is warranted.

In recent years a great deal of attention has been given to cultural differences between teacher and student. Frequently, middle-class oriented teachers find themselves teaching minority group students from vastly different cultural backgrounds. In an effort to be unbiased in his approach toward such a student, the teacher may attempt to learn as much as possible about the student's culture, some of the language, customs, etc. While this is desirable, the educator can avoid most difficulties by looking at his own culture in an objective and open way. Just as the therapist must understand his own prejudices and values to ensure that he does not inadvertently harm his client, the teacher who fails to recognize that many of his own values and ideas have been shaped by his culture will find it difficult to do justice to a student from a different culture. It is difficult for a teacher to avoid influencing his students' value systems. Since he will invariably be perceived as a model by many younger students, it is essential that he understand the directions in which he has been moved by the sheer weight of cultural conditioning. Egocentrism and ethnocentrism have no place in a classroom guided by the principles of unbiased open inquiry.

COMPULSORY EDUCATION

The entire concept of compulsory education is based on the idea that certain kinds of knowledge are required if one is to be capable of functioning in a complex society. In other words, it is necessary in the general welfare that everyone learn basic academic skills and have a certain range of information before entering society, unless, of course, he is physiologically incapable of mastering such knowledge. The underlying assumption here is that lack of certain abilities, such as reading or writing, would reduce one's capacity to get along and to contribute to society. Therefore, the poorly educated individual might even become dependent on other people or the state for his living. Furthermore, increasing technological demands would leave such an individual severely handicapped so far as obtaining most employment is concerned. Theoretically then, the student benefits from compulsory education in that it provides him with the rudimentary tools and general knowledge which are required for personal participation, and the society benefits in that there is a reservoir of its members with at least certain minimal skills to take over various occupational functions.

If we have identified these assumptions correctly, certain additional questions become evident: What about the precocious student who quickly masters all of the necessary academic skills—should he be compelled to remain in school until a given age? Should an individual who has not met certain requirements be permitted to leave school when he reaches a given age? What educational requirements can a society ethically make on its citizens?

New questions rise with the tide of popular concern. Should students be bused to school to achieve racial balance? What about religious balance? Ethnic balance? Socioeconomic balance? Can quality education be achieved within a racially segregated classroom or is learning to relate on an equal basis with members of different groups in the schools a prerequisite to total quality education?

Questions such as these will not be justly resolved in the heat of political debate or in the crossfire of uninformed opinion but in the minds and hearts of those who recognize that what we are is primarily what we have learned to be.

SUMMARY

The objective teacher is aware that learning is inferred from behavior and that promoting learning and changing behavior are inseparable processes. Thus the teacher is continually making decisions regarding what behavior is desirable and what is not. We call upon the teacher to come to grips with this responsibility rather than denying it or evading it. We have provided guidelines which may be helpful in dealing with these ethical considerations.

Since objective teaching methods rapidly increase the rate of learning, the would-be demogogue or dictator could use them effectively for propaganda purposes. Thus, it is essential that we understand the distinction between education and indoctrination. While objective teaching can promote the learning of specific curricula, the decision as to what is to be taught must be made within a comprehensive understanding of human life. We strongly advocate a classroom atmosphere in which there is a maximum opportunity for open inquiry no matter where it may lead, but at the same time we recognize that students must learn the academic skills which will permit their full participation in society.

Courses must be appropriate to the needs of the student in preparing him for life but must not be just another way of fitting him into the system. They must develop naturally out of a clear recognition of what is required to raise the quality of life in society.

We noted that reinforcement may be viewed as a feedback system, indicating to the student whether or not he is responding in a desirable way, but we pointed out that reinforcement must be limited to academic and related subjects and not used to promote narrow religious, political, or cultural ideologies.

Objective teaching is guided continually by the principle of enhancing a student's self-direction (freedom) by allowing him an increasing role in the setting of his own goals and outcomes. This, we learn, is consistent with William James's conception that education must build will, "the power of voluntary action."

We underlined the necessity for each teacher to recognize that he is a product of his culture and must be wary of viewing his students' behavior within his own value system. This is especially crucial in dealing with students from varied cultural backgrounds.

Complex educational questions such as the role of racial, religious, and ethnic balance in the schools must not be treated as merely political issues but as ethical and scientific issues as well.

REFERENCES

Gilmore, L. What teachers have to learn from William James. *Journal of Education*, 1971, **154** (2), 7–14.

Glynn, E. L. Classroom applications of self-determined reinforcement. *Journal of Applied Behavior Analysis*, 1970, **3** (2), 123–132.

Homme, L. E. Control of coverants, the operants of the mind. *The Psychological Record*, 1965, **15**, 501–511.

Kanfer, F. H. Issues and ethics in behavior manipulation. In *Operant procedures in remedial speech and language training* (H. H. Sloane, Jr. and B. D. MacAulay, eds.). Boston: Houghton Mifflin Co., 1968.

Krishnamurti, J. *Life ahead.* New York: Harper & Row, 1963.

Lovitt, T. C., & Curtiss, K. A. Academic response rate as a function of teacher and self imposed contingencies. *Journal of Applied Behavior Analysis*, 1969, **2** (1), 49–53.

Sarason, I. Test anxiety and cognitive modeling. *Journal of Personality and Social Psychology*, In Press.

SUGGESTED READING

Means, R. L. *The ethical imperative.* New York: Doubleday & Company, 1969.

Part II
Additional Applications of Objective Teaching and Behavior Modification

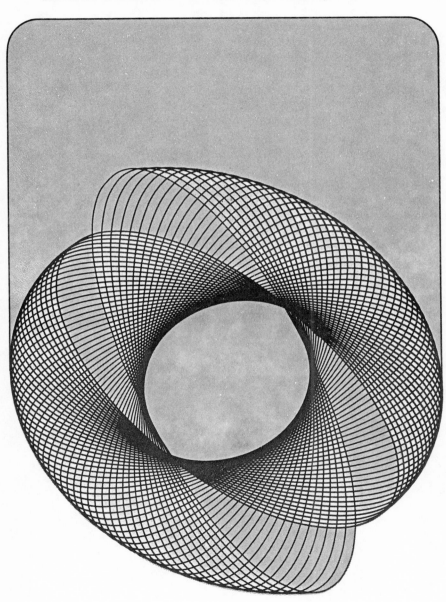

9
Application in the Normal Classroom

This chapter is devoted to that elusive youngster, the "normal" child. Elusive because there are so many conflicting definitions of what is normal and who is normal that the term loses much possibility of general meaning and finally becomes quite subjective. To one person it means a kind of statistical average so that the child with an IQ of 100 is normal. To another it means that the youngster is "mentally healthy," i.e., he has no behavioral aberrations that are indicative of illness. To yet another, he is a "good" child because he does all those things that are expected of him. In a Freudian sense, "normal" is an ideal of personality adjustment, a kind of utopian goal, for we are all "a little bit sick."

Here we wish to dodge these issues and say that the individual studies in this chapter that deal with normal children are really concerned with children who are placed in normal classrooms rather than in special-education classrooms. They are the kinds of children that teachers and parents mostly come in contact with. They do have problems, but then what child does not at some time or other. Perhaps that makes them particularly normal. Specialized educational systems that deal with the retarded, deprived, and emotionally disturbed will be reserved for the following chapters.

The studies which we will discuss deal with both individual students and groups of students. There will be class situations and tutoring situations. In some we will detail the data and in others, where the data might be redundant, we will simply present the results. In presenting these cases we have not intended to dramatize only successes, but have included some in which the results are in

131

doubt so as to illustrate both the positive aspects of behavior modification and some of the practical difficulties and problems that one can run into when he seeks to apply the techniques in the "real" world. Too often things that are practical in the laboratory are not in the classroom. The amount of data that a teacher can gather or the number of variables that he can practically control are limited. However, he can develop greater objectivity and gain better control over the results of his teaching. We feel that the following studies are instructive and hopefully will provide stimulation as to how you, the reader, may investigate similar problems and develop better and more creative ways of working with children. One result of using behavioral techniques is to be impressed with the true individuality of each child. What "works" with one need not work with another. But what reinforces the teacher is that the principles eventually prove themselves, even if the specific procedures must be varied for different children.

We have organized this section generally in terms of the kinds of behavior being modified. These represent a wide variety although there is some emphasis on academic behaviors. The intention is to give several examples of how various individual teachers have coped with a wide range of behavioral problems. Again we feel that we must warn the reader that it is not enough to simply copy what others have done. This is a fault with many of our existing educational methods. We must really treat each child as a totally unique individual. This is the root and substance of what we have termed *humanistic-behaviorism.*

In this section we do not use the actual names of the children reported and omit or distort some irrelevant background material. However, all the data are real and will be presented just as reported by various investigators.

A DISRUPTIVE SIXTH-GRADE BOY

Fred, an 11-year-old sixth grader, had been referred to a university clinic because he was a "problem in school." You may note immediately that this does not tell us much about him except that he was sufficiently aversive to enough people to warrant professional consultation. Often the thing that is done is to take the child to the experts for an evaluation, even if this merely results in confirmation that the child is somewhat disturbed or disturbing.

Fred was given a fairly typical battery of psychological tests and he came out perfectly "normal." His IQ on an individual test was 102; there was no test evidence of central nervous system impairment or serious emotional disturbance, and he behaved quite well during the testing, showing none of the problem behavior for which he had been referred.

We suggested earlier, and Fred is an excellent example of this, that many "problem" children who are quite disturbing in a classroom are often very docile and cooperative during testing. Often this is a function of receiving the undivided attention of another person, the attention which, unfortunately, is obtained in class only by being disruptive.

As a part of the clinic evaluation, we obtained a better description of Fred's deviant behavior from his parents and teachers. The description was rather general at that: "He does not participate in classroom discussions, seldom prepares his assignments, does not follow classroom instructions or work at his seat, and he daydreams and indulges in attention-getting and distracting activities while others are reciting." Then a little more specifically: "He speaks out-of-turn; he talks about irrelevant matters; he talks to his neighbors; he gets out of his seat; and he occasionally makes sudden loud outbursts which are quite disturbing." It was routinely necessary for the teacher to show him where the class was reading, repeat instructions, and correct him for annoying behavior.

Since we were unable to elicit any of this behavior in our educational laboratory, we decided to study Fred in his own classroom. Evidently the stimuli which served as cues for the deviant behavior were those associated with the classes he attended and were not generalized to all situations. By analyzing the factors associated with his disruptive classroom behavior, we hoped to discover means to modify that behavior so that he would become more acceptable to the teachers and improve his academic performance.

One of the authors assigned a graduate student to gather the data and then worked with her over several weeks in planning classroom interventions. What follows is a fairly detailed account of this procedure.

The first observations were in a 35-minute English class and in a 35-minute science class. The science teacher began the class by having the children read aloud from a text. She did this by calling on the pupils in order, row by row, starting at the opposite side of the room from where Fred sat. Under this system he was consistently about the twenty-fifth to be called upon to answer.

The observer noted that during this part of the class period Fred appeared to be busy at his seat with things other than science. He did not raise his hand or offer any responses to the general questions that the teacher put to the class as a whole. When his turn came to recite, he was completely unprepared. The teacher asked him to demonstrate a simple experiment from the text. He had not understood the instructions so they were repeated. Then, while standing before the class, he exhibited the behavior that was particularly annoying to the teacher. He shifted his weight from side to side, laughed, and looked at the class while raising his eyebrows in a humorous manner. His answers to questions were quite inappropriate, and the class reacted to these and his clowning by giggling.

However, after this demonstration something interesting happened. Fred began to get involved in the class. He listened to the discussions and even volunteered a comment that was appropriate to the subject. The teacher responded to this positively, remarking that he had made an interesting comment. Then, at the close of the science period, the class was instructed to clear their desks and get out the materials for the next class. Fred was the only one who did not comply with these instructions.

The next class was English and Fred was called upon within the first 5 minutes. He gave a correct answer and was praised for this. During the next 5 minutes he listened attentively, looked at the teacher, and raised his hand to volunteer 3 times. He was asked to recite the third time and was again praised for his class participation.

Then the class discussion turned to the criticism of oral and written reports. The teacher called on Fred to explain some aspects of a report that he had written. He seemed confused by her questions but read his report to the class. Then, during the discussion, his behavior became very much like what it had been in the previous class. He gave inappropriate answers and clowned while the class giggled. He acknowledged this attention by more clowning. However, when other reports were being discussed, Fred stopped his inappropriate behavior and became a constructive class participant. He volunteered comments twice and each time they were related to the subject. Each time the teacher acknowledged his contributions.

As we looked at this first general description of Fred's classroom behavior, we were struck by two things: (1) His behavior was not consistently deviant. True, he did more than his share of upsetting the classroom but he also participated several times (this finding is very typical and another reason why we need objective data to supplement teacher impression). (2) What seemed to be controlling his behavior was the attention he received, whether from his peers or from the teacher. Our impression from this general survey was that whatever behavior was attended to increased, whether appropriate or inappropriate. Therefore, we hypothesized that attention was reinforcing for Fred and that the natural reinforcers in the classroom were more frequently paired with inappropriate behavior, thus maintaining a fairly high level of this kind of responding.

We decided to try to increase appropriate class participation by managing reinforcement contingencies, since appropriate class participation was incompatible with the deviant behavior that he had been showing. While any attention seemed reinforcing for Fred, we felt it more desirable to try to work first with teacher attention before trying to control the class' attention (giggling) to his inappropriate behavior.

It must be noted that many of those who attempt to use behavioral techniques for the first time try to do too much at once. It is far better to pick one specific variable, modify that, and measure the consequences, than to try to do everything at once. Not only does this provide more precise information as to whether or not what the teacher is doing is positively affecting the child's behavior, but it often establishes a kind of "fall out" associated with definite positive behavioral change. It is surprising how often, particularly when a child has been disruptive, a modest change sets up a "benign circle" in which there are many more positive results than planned for. The teacher and pupil communicate better; there are more instances of positive interaction and less opportunity for negative interaction. The generalization of this "good feeling" has many happy consequences for teacher and child.

In order to test our hypothesis that the teacher attention was an important variable in Fred's classroom participation, we needed to get some baserate data and define just what it was that we were going to investigate. This was a little more complex than we first anticipated for we found that what we were really interested in was how often he participated in his science and English classes. We soon realized that "how often" was a function of the number of opportunities he had to respond, and we finally broke the data down in this way: we designated a response ratio (RR) as the unit of measurement. This was defined as the proportion of positive responses (PR) to the total number of response opportunities (RO) or, RR = PR/RO.

The figure used for response opportunities (RO) was derived as the total of all the situations in which Fred could have responded, either when the teacher called on him directly or when she called on the class as a whole and he could volunteer. Then the response opportunities were analyzed in terms of those times he actually responded (PR) or gave no response (NR) when he had the chance. Just to make it a bit more complicated, but also to allow us to look at the data a little more closely, we divided the positive responses into three kinds: (1) Fred raised his hand and was called on by the teacher; this we labeled *vc* for volunteering and being called on. (2) Fred raised his hand but was not called on; we labeled this *vnc* for volunteered but not called on. (3) Fred was called upon by the teacher and gave an appropriate response; we labeled this *cr* for called upon and responded. With these definitions we set out to get baserate measures in both the science and English classes.

Baserate data were obtained during one day by spending a half hour in each class. Usually it is desirable to get a longer sample of behavior, but because of the exigencies of time, we could not do this. Nevertheless, the data are interesting and very much in accord with what we had observed previously. The data are presented in Table 1.

Table 1

Kind of Response	Science Class	English Class
NR	8	11
PR	2	7
vc	0	3
vnc	1	4
cr	1	0
RO	10	18
RR	.20	.39

Table 2

Kind of Response	Science Class	English Class
NR	3	4
PR	3	4
vc	0	3
vnc	2	0
cr	1	1
RO	6	8
RR	.50	.50

During this time the teacher's behavior was very similar to what it had been in the early observation. The science teacher called on members of the class by row and started at a point at which Fred was far down the list. The English teacher called on him during the first 5 minutes. There was no inappropriate behavior during the English class but there were 2 instances of this during science. As one looks at the data here, he is struck by the marked difference in response between the two classes. Not only is the response ratio higher in the English class as compared to the science class, but the difference is in a somewhat unusual direction for a boy. At least one would generally predict that a boy would have a more positive response to science than English.

We hypothesized that early attention during class might be a significant aspect of the attention variable (Fred was called upon during the first 5 minutes in English but much later in science), so we instructed both teachers to give him a chance to recite within the first 5 minutes of the class and to reinforce immediately all positive responses by praising Fred. They were also instructed to ignore nonparticipation, lack of attention, or disturbing behavior.

The next observation was under the experimental conditions as previously outlined, that is, as close as the teachers could come to these conditions. It is very difficult to ignore a disruptive boy, especially if responding to him is habitual. However, the limited data as shown in Table 2 do indicate a substantial increase in response ratio in both classes.

The observer recorded six instances of "talking out of turn" in the science class with one instance of peer reinforcement (attention) for this undesirable behavior. However, there was much more reinforcement from the teacher, for she noticed and commented upon it three times. While positive class participation increased in science class, the disruptive behavior was also maintained.

Next, we decided to investigate a special problem with which one is often concerned when using an observer in the classroom. Does the observer have some sort of significant effect on the behavior being recorded and thus introduce an important variable? We asked the principal to take data during one session of the English class. Since she often observed in the classes we felt that no one would

Table 3

Kind of Response	Science Class	English Class
NR	3	6
PR	3	9
vc	0	3
vnc	2	5
cr	1	1
RO	6	15
RR	.50	.60

be particularly aware that she was observing one particular child. In addition, Fred had seen the graduate student at the university and we wondered if this had influenced his behavior. The data below, recorded by the principal, suggest that the two observers were not having a noticeable effect on Fred's behavior. For just the English class these figures were

NR	6
PR	7
RO	13
RR	.54

Two days after this observation, we made another behavioral count with the graduate student as the recorder. These data were fairly consistent with the previous count although showing a slight increase in the desired behavior in the English class (Table 3).

In addition to these data she also noted that the English teacher had reinforced Fred for an appropriate response by having him go to the board to demonstrate for the class. This presented an excellent opportunity to get peer reinforcement for appropriate academic behavior. On another occasion the teacher patted him on the head, adding positive physical contact to frequent verbal approval.

One week later, Fred's response rate dropped sharply in science. He made only one response out of eight opportunities. Again, the teacher had failed to call on him until after half the period had elapsed. Until this time he was inattentive and ignored classroom activities. Then the teacher, realizing that he was not "with the class," walked over and pointed out the page he should be on. Shortly after this, Fred volunteered and recited. However, despite an appropriate response he was not reinforced (praised) by the teacher. At this time Fred began talking out of turn. He was reinforced once by another child who reprimanded him loudly, and once by the teacher who indicated that he should not talk again. So he began whistling until he gained the teacher's attention. This was in the form of another reprimand.

Table 4

Kind of Response	Science Class	English Class
NR	8	5
PR	1	9
vc	1	2
vnc	0	4
cr	0	3
RO	9	14
RR	.11	.64

During the same observation there were no disruptive behaviors in the English class. The recorded data, showing a dramatic drop-off in science but a reasonable maintenance of appropriate behaviors in English, are shown in Table 4.

The observations that we have recorded here took place over a period of a month. We see in one class that Fred substantially increased his class participation and did not engage in disruptive behaviors. His teacher was pleased with his progress; she gave him a good amount of natural reinforcement (mostly verbal) and he responded accordingly. His response ratio increased from .39 to .64 and, with this much class participation, he had little time for disruptive behaviors.

In his science class, however, he not only failed to maintain his improved behavior, but actually ended up below his baseline as far as class participation was concerned, and he was still a disruptive influence in the class. The initial gains were not sustained in this changed environment. This certainly supports the thesis that we cannot manage classroom variables in an inconsistent fashion and yet expect to maintain consistent patterns of classroom behavior. While the science teacher was fairly consistent in reinforcing positive responses, she was quite inconsistent about ignoring undesirable behavior. The result was that she maintained both for most of the month although the last check showed a marked drop in appropriate behavior as well.

We had to leave at this point. The school year was over and, while it was clear that there had been some substantial gains, there was still much left to be done. Although the teacher had been very cooperative, there was just not enough time to follow through as consistently as would have been desirable. Certainly there would have been much more opportunity for continued gain for this little boy and his teachers if there had been a school-based person who was well versed in behavioral techniques. Such a person could have exercised more consistent follow-up, taking data over a more prolonged period and providing further feedback to the teachers. The following material illustrates in some detail what a school based person can do if given the opportunity.

PLANNING FOR SUCCESS
IN A JUNIOR HIGH CLASSROOM

Prospective teachers soon learn that planning classroom activities takes many hours outside the classroom. Experienced teachers who are successful make planning an integral part of their daily routine. Indeed, precise arrangement of classroom variables requires careful planning if the teacher is to be effective in implementing programs that will produce specific behavioral changes. Planning must become an ongoing procedure and should be based on data that determine the course of the teaching process so that the teacher maintains effective influence upon the learning at all times.

The next extended study illustrates the kind of planning that was necessary for successful behavioral change in a junior high school math class. True, this class was especially for "slow learners," whoever they might be, but the ideas presented here have broad generality whether for so-called slow learners or fast learners. Rate of learning, after all, appears to be heavily influenced by environmental factors such as degree of reinforcement.

In this classroom an effort was made to individualize instruction and to maximize the effectiveness of teaching for a group of youngsters who are sometimes forgotten. Forgotten not in the sense that they do not receive special attention, but rather in the sense that this attention brings little difference to bear on their basic problems. For purposes of illustration, the description includes an initial look at the classroom, with teaching errors and misconceptions included.

Mr. Smith was a junior high school math teacher. He was very efficient, always had his lesson plans up to date, and was noted among the students for being "hard" but fair, i.e., he required good work and lots of it but he was always ready to help a student who was having difficulty. Mr. Smith did not relish the role of disciplinarian but usually maintained good control in his classes. He liked to see students busy with their assignments and the only sounds usually heard in his classroom once he explained the work was his occasional discussion with a student, the quiet rustling of papers, and the restless movements of the early adolescent. Any significant deviation from this was met quickly and sternly. Yet, he was also quick to respond positively to students, for he was basically a very kind man who had considerable affection for them. For example, when he felt a class had been particularly well behaved and their work was progressing satisfactorily, he told them so and then, as a reward, canceled the formal lesson for the next day, using the period for mathematical games and puzzles that most of the students thoroughly enjoyed. If we were to analyze his contingency management from the point of view expressed in this book, we would say that he used a fairly heavy schedule of positive reinforcement and a fairly heavy schedule of negative reinforcement and punishment. Behavior did have consequences in his classes, sometimes good and sometimes bad, but rarely was a student ignored.

With this sort of approach and with a positive reputation among students and faculty, Mr. Smith rarely had discipline problems that he could not handle directly. His students were not seen at the office sitting in rows waiting to be "disciplined" by the assistant principal. Nor did they get sent to the counselor or the school psychologist.

Mr. Smith did not like the assistant principal much anyway. The man had been an excellent science teacher but was something less than an excellent administrator. He tended to alienate himself from the staff by a barrier of paper, and the current joke was that he needed nothing so much as a "memo-pause." Many times Mr. Smith mused on a system that rewards a good teacher by removing him from that which he does best (teaching) and placing him in a situation for which he has no talent (administration). Mr. Smith long since decided to avoid administration. He liked teaching and, while the salary left a bit to be desired, he was able to round out a comfortable income for his family by working as a painting contractor during the summer.

As to the counselor, Mr. Smith was ambivalent. The man had good training and had been a successful teacher, so he knew what went on in a classroom. However, he did seem to spend a lot of time drinking coffee with teachers and observing in classes when it seemed more proper and in keeping with his position to be seeing students in his office. He was well liked by most of the staff, particularly those who had been seeking his help with problems. The exception to this was Miss Jones, the new Spanish teacher, who referred about a third of her beginning class to him in the fall and then became very angry when he suggested that he would be happy to observe *in* her class and help her make any necessary changes in what she was doing. "It's as if he thought *I* were the problem, not these kids," noted Miss Jones. "If a counselor is any good (and there was no doubt as to her feelings on that score), he solves these problems in his office. I don't have time to be fooling around in the classroom. I'm here to *teach.*"

Mr. Smith listened to Miss Jones with some sympathy but, being a fair man, he felt that there probably was something to what the counselor had suggested. Anyone who would refer ten children in the first month of school must have been doing something wrong.

That fall, for the first time, the school was adopting an ability grouping plan for all classes. The previous spring all the sixth graders in the district were tested with a battery of achievement tests and these scores, along with IQ's, grades, and teacher recommendations, were used to form ability groups. The assistant principal was in charge of assigning students to groups. He delighted in all the paper work and the opportunity to be "scientific" with children. He developed a rather complicated system of weights for each of the variables (IQ, grades, test scores, and teacher recommendations) and produced six classifications of pupil ability. Rather unimaginatively, he named them 1, 2, 3, 4, 5, 6. The 1's were the top students and the 6's were at the bottom. A student might be a 1 in math but only a 3 in Spanish. So each student was fitted into slots for each class according to ability in that class. This, he believed, was truly individualizing instruction.

However, the counselor had been heard to mutter that he had never heard of any evidence that this sort of thing helped children learn. "It would be better to change *how* we taught, not *who* we taught." But most of the staff were enthusiastic (especially Miss Jones), and everyone hoped to be blessed with 1's and 2's. No one really looked forward to getting 6's.

Mr. Smith felt that in all fairness he should volunteer for a 6 since he was a good teacher, had had 10 years of experience, and could probably learn a few things that would be helpful to the less experienced teachers the next year. There was also just an element of wanting to get a bad thing out of the way first, but this was a very small factor.

At about that time the counselor began making statements to the effect that "as soon as we start categorizing youngsters, people begin thinking of them as categories rather than as individuals." And Mr. Smith agreed that he had heard a lot of things like, "He's only a 3 but I tell him if he works hard he can become a 2," or, "I told my class that they're supposed to be 2's but that if they don't shape up I'll send them back to 3's."

Classes of 6's were to be absolutely limited to 20 students, but Mr. Smith was only mildly surprised to find 24 in his class on the first day. This was better than the usual 35. The assistant principal apologized but said that the logistics of the situation were such that he had no choice. He had 24 math 6's and you couldn't expect to put them with 5's, could you? Mr. Smith supposed you probably couldn't. It wouldn't be fair . . . maybe. There seemed to be something wrong with this reasoning but he was too busy preparing for his new class to think it through at the moment.

He carefully went through the cumulative folders and found there were 16 boys and 8 girls; several had been retained somewhere along the way; IQ's varied puzzlingly from 80 to 133 but mostly they were in the 90's; math achievement was very low and quite varied. Further examination revealed that teacher comments were consistent in imputing to the students certain characteristics: "poor attitude," "lazy," "needs to be motivated" (this was the most popular statement). However, he noted wryly that all children "made progress" by the time of the spring comments. Their performance the first day in class indicated that they had evidently forgotten a tremendous amount over the summer.

The class of 6's got started reasonably well. The students were a bit subdued by being in a junior high for the first time and, since they came from several different elementary schools, it took a little time to get acquainted. They were appallingly poor in math and in so many different ways. When he analyzed their learning difficulties, Mr. Smith realized that he actually had 24 "groups" and soon found that he was spending twice as much time with them as with any of his other classes. However, he started to notice some learning taking place and this pleased him very much.

What did not please him was the behavior of three of the students, two boys and a girl. They had started the year just like the rest of the students but gradually things began to change. Work which had been improving began to deteriorate.

They generally did not finish their assignments and they usually made many errors, although he tried to help them as much as time allowed. Worse, though, was their noisy behavior in class. The girl had fits of giggling which disturbed everyone and often made it difficult to maintain order. One of the boys was a "sigher," and the other a "pencil rapper." All three talked too much.

At first they talked to each other, so he separated them. At this juncture they began bothering other youngsters. All the usual methods of control did not seem to work. He asked them to come in after school, and he talked with each child about his behavior and how he was expected to change. He paid strict attention to every infraction of the rules and punished them verbally in front of their classmates (a practice, by the way, he did not like and used only as a last resort).

Mr. Smith got the impression that he was spending most of his time disciplining these three students and very little time in teaching. He even began to think of sending them to the assistant principal, when he ran into the counselor in the teacher's room and, over a cup of coffee, asked his advice. The counselor asked if he could observe for a few days before making any recommendations. Mr. Smith readily agreed. For the next three days the counselor sat in the back of the room making notes and trying to be as unobtrusive as possible. Mr. Smith taught his class as he normally did and there was, indeed, an unpleasant tone in the class. Time that could have been put to instructional use was spent reprimanding students. The level of disruptive behavior was quite high for the class as a whole and not just for the three students that had been referred.

The next day the counselor showed his notes to Mr. Smith. They consisted of Tables 5 and 6.

Mr. Smith was a bit puzzled at first, but he was reassured by the numbers. He knew that he could eventually understand anything to do with mathematics. The counselor explained that in planning for changes in student behaviors, the first thing to do was decide what behaviors needed changing, and the second thing was to measure their incidence or rate. Mr. Smith had already decided on what needed changing (mainly noisy behavior) and had even selected 3 target children, Arnold, Betty, and Chuck. However, since there seemed to be a lot of

Table 5. BASERATE DATA

	Child Disruptive Behaviors			Teacher Responses (Disapproval)		
	Mon.	Tues.	Wed.		Mon.	Tues.	Wed.
Arnold	2	2	5		2	2	5
Betty	4	3	1		4	3	1
Chuck	3	5	2		2	5	3
Other	13	10	14		8	5	9
Total	22	20	22		16	15	18

Table 6. BASERATE DATA

| | Teacher Responses (Approving) | | |
	Mon.	Tues.	Wed.
Arnold	0	0	0
Betty	0	0	0
Chuck	0	0	0
Other	3	5	5
Total	3	5	5

disruptive behavior in this particular class, the counselor decided to expand his measurements a bit and keep data on the other 21 students as well.

What did the data show? That the three target children were indeed a disruptive influence but that many of the other children were also exhibiting poor control. For each class period there were about 21 instances of significant noisy behavior which, when combined with the general restlessness of the students, resulted in a rather unpleasant situation.

Mr. Smith agreed to that wholeheartedly. Then his eye caught the other data and he noticed they were labeled "teacher responses." He was a little disturbed by this, thinking the counselor's job was to work with students, not teachers. The counselor's explanation, however, made good sense: "In planning for behavioral change, one must also look for those variables that might be maintaining certain behaviors. The most powerful influence in the classroom is teacher behavior, particularly approving and disapproving behavior." So while measuring the disruptive behavior of the students, the counselor also measured the approving and disapproving behavior of Mr. Smith.

What did this show? That he had a fairly high rate of disapproval. This was certainly understandable under the circumstances. However, even Mr. Smith missed some of the disruptive behaviors. For example, he missed one of Chuck's belches on Monday but in a sense made up for it on Wednesday when he wrongly accused him of something another child had done. Mr. Smith remembered the boy's vociferous and outraged defense that only the frequently guilty can manage when they are temporarily innocent. He flushed slightly.

Table 6 showed his reinforcing behaviors which the counselor defined as "some approving verbal response to a student." True, there were not very many, but frequent disapproval is incompatible with frequent approval. It was difficult to do both when the students were so disruptive.

The question now arose as to whether there was a relationship between the student disruptive behaviors and teacher approval and disapproval. The counselor suggested that these students (he refused to call them 6's) had a long school history on a very thin schedule of approval or positive reinforcement. In other

Table 7

	Disruptive Behaviors	Teacher Disapproval	Teacher Approval
Arnold	3	2	1
Betty	1	0	3
Chuck	4	2	1
Other	5	1	20
TOTAL	13	5	25

words, they had had little success as students and most of the attention they received was for disruptive behavior of one kind or another. The youngsters were potential dropouts and eventual community problems. The goal as he saw it was to get them really "hooked" on school and learning. They had a lot of untapped potential. It might just be possible to do this if things were changed a bit. Would Mr. Smith be interested in a little experiment that might have some positive results?

Mr. Smith was intrigued—first, by the data which appealed to his ideas about precision and second, by the fact that there might be something that could really help these youngsters to become better students. So he agreed. With the counselor's help they set out to change Mr. Smith's behavior.

Mr. Smith was to increase his approval of desired student behavior (quietness) and completely ignore the usual disruptive behavior if he could. The latter would be the hardest, for he almost automatically responded to any noise that he thought was out of line. The counselor agreed to come into the class, keep data, and help Mr. Smith learn to keep his own data. Then they would determine if there were any effect on the behavior of the students that was achieved by changing Mr. Smith's style of responding.

The first week was very difficult. While he did increase his rate of approving behavior to about 25 per class, Mr. Smith had difficulty eliminating the disapproving behavior completely. This was especially true with Arnold, Betty, and Chuck. However, the counselor showed him data which indicated that by the end of the week there was already a noticeable change in the class. By Friday the data looked like in Table 7.

Starting the second week Mr. Smith began keeping his own data and conferred with the counselor only occasionally. This was simple enough to do. He made a small chart for each day like Table 7 and attached it to a clipboard that he used to carry papers. He found that marking the behaviors himself served to remind him of what he was supposed to be doing, and by the end of the third week he had almost eliminated verbal disapproval. By this point he was approving about 35 times per class. The disruptive behavior dropped to a level of about two per class. A fascinating side benefit was the increase in learning. Being a conscien-

Table 8. ACCURACY IN PERCENTAGES (MATH)

	Baserate	At One Month
Arnold	27	59
Betty	39	64
Chuck	33	58
Others	57	73

tious teacher, Mr. Smith kept detailed records on his student's academic performance. These were in percentage of accurate work, although he was planning to change to a rate of accurate work so as to have data on speed as well as accuracy. Table 8 shows some interesting changes from the period just prior to the "little experiment" to the end of the first month.

It seemed reasonable that since the students had more time for learning and were being consistently reinforced for their work, they were making fewer errors and doing more problems. Almost all of them finished the assignments now and Mr. Smith was beginning to lengthen them for some. He had a good system going in his class and was himself being heavily reinforced by a high rate of good student behavior and improved learning rates. So his approving behavior was maintained and his disapproving behavior was almost totally extinguished.

These procedures involved some time from the counselor and a teacher willing to experiment, but they brought about the desired changes in student behavior and the results were directly observable. Careful planning and data gathering eliminated the necessity for guesswork. Mr. Smith's new approach made a real difference and he knew it.

This example is easily extended to most classrooms. Any teacher with a little practice and, perhaps, some initial help in observation can make significant changes in student behaviors, whether these behaviors consist of learning rates or disruptive activities. Whether the behavior is changed in a step-by-step fashion as in learning multiplication facts or in a more direct fashion as in eliminating disruptive behavior, the utilization of these techniques results in academic gains and increased teaching efficiency.

A MIDDLE SCHOOL REMEDIAL READING CLASS

In the course of our work in the central city middle schools which we have discussed throughout the book, the primary purpose of the project was to increase attendance and decrease dropouts. There were, however, many subsidiary projects related to academic and nonacademic behaviors. One of these involved a class for students who were having difficulty with reading. The students were quite disruptive and it was very difficult to get them to settle down to work. They found many ways to "hassle" the teacher and it usually took 10 or 15 minutes of a class period before they would begin to work. The class was relatively small, about 10 students each period, and there were 2 aides. But things did not go smoothly.

Our first task was to find some means to get the students motivated to start work on time. Each was on an individualized program which entailed his getting out personal folders and following the instructions written by the teacher. We suggested to the teacher, after observing a particularly disorganized session, that she try the following: at the beginning of the class the next day, if a student was in his seat when the bell rang and was ready to go to work, she should reward him with a lunch token and say something like: "this is for being ready to work on time." We had previously determined that lunch tokens had high value for these students since they could readily be converted into cash. The teacher followed the instructions admirably and, fortunately, the next day there was a student ready to begin work. He was a bit surprised at the reward and lost no time in showing it off to his peers. The following day all the students were quietly sitting in their seats at the bell and waiting expectantly for the reward. The teacher, who was a little dubious about behavioral techniques, said: "The good fairy doesn't come every day." This immediately established a variable schedule of reinforcement. However, we persuaded her to reward the class often enough to maintain the behavior and soon the class was getting to work without hassling or being hassled.

This group was also put on a reinforcement system for academic behavior and were (see Chapter 4) making good gains academically as well as doing quite well behaviorally. They continued to need extrinsic reinforcement, however. Before too long, a new problem entered the situation. The students became distrustful of the teacher rather arbitrarily handing out rewards. These youngsters were used to seeing the world and the people in it as adversaries and they were quick to respond to anything they thought was unfair. At this point one of the teachers had an excellent idea. This was to provide the students with a chance to draw from a box tokens that would name the reward for the particular academic or nonacademic behavior. We placed in the box slips of paper on which were written the particular rewards. These varied all the way from one or more "points" that could be accumulated and traded in for tangibles, to such things as "lunch tokens," "hamburger tokens," "record albums," or (and this was the top prize) a ticket to the local NBA basketball game.

The students accepted this as fair and enjoyed the game. They did not object to the fact that we controlled what went into the box and thus could "thin" the schedule. Taking a chance was very much a part of their lives. Our only problem was convincing the administration that we were not running some sort of gambling casino! As previously stated, we gradually increased the amount of work necessary before the student could draw from the box and we developed a variable ratio schedule so that they could not predict just what academic task would be rewarded. This was satisfactory to them as long as they had a chance at the big prize. By the end of the semester we were getting 3 or 4 times as much academic behavior from these youngsters for the same rewards that were used at the beginning. We also had many more opportunities for the teacher to respond positively to students rather than in a negative manner.

A HIGH SCHOOL REMEDIAL HISTORY CLASS

It is often very difficult or impossible to tell what classroom variable is affecting the behavior of students. We may change so many things or introduce them in such a way as not to be able to assess their effect. In such cases we proceed more on faith than on knowledge. The research oriented behavioral psychologist, gazing out from his laboratory in which it is possible to control many variables, is often apprehensive about some of our less well-controlled techniques in the classroom. There is undoubtedly some justification in this if the desired outcome is very precise knowledge about the effect of a particular stimulus. Granted, we cannot run the classroom exactly like a controlled experiment. Yet, there is one technique familiar to all behavioral psychologists that is very useful to the teacher if he is willing to experiment just a little—that is to introduce a variable, measure its effects, and then remove it to see if the dependent behavior returns to the original level. For example, one might start marking the spelling papers so that only "right" answers were checked and note if this made a difference in the spelling scores. Then one could return to marking only the wrong answers. If the first condition increased accuracy rate and the second decreased it back to the baserate or near it, we could assume that this variable (the manner in which the papers were marked) did indeed affect the scores.

Something like that was done in the little study reported next. The teacher conducted a reasonable check on his techniques by reversing one variable and noting the results. Any teacher can do this either with reinforcement contingencies or with some management of the eliciting or other stimuli (e.g., cues and prompts). In this case the latter variable was systematically modified.

The setting was a summer class of high school juniors. They were taking the course in U.S. history either because they had failed it during the regular year (11 of them) or they had not been able to take it because of illness (2 of them). While the structure of the course followed the regular curriculum pretty closely, the entire year's work had to be covered in only 8 weeks so there was not much time for class discussion. The class met for 2 periods a day, 5 days a week. They used a standard text and the course was mostly devoted to lectures by the teacher and tests twice weekly to check the amount of learning.

The teacher wished to experiment with some ideas he had for the class and we decided to try to introduce some changes in a reasonably systematic way to see if they made a difference in the degree of learning. Our criterion of learning was accuracy percent on the twice weekly quizzes. These were averaged together since we were interested in group change. Data were also kept on individuals, of course, but they need not concern us here.

The teacher established a baseline of 67% for the quizzes under "normal" class conditions. These consisted of the students' listening to lectures, taking notes, and reading the text. There was very little chance for discussion.

Then he introduced two new ideas to his class. He allowed the students to read the text for 10 minutes at the beginning of class in order to have some specific time for a general look at the day's materials, and he gave the students a 10-minute group study time just prior to the quiz. During the latter they could ask each other questions or work in any way that they felt might help. The next quiz grade was 78 which seemed to be a fairly good gain. However, which factor was more important, the reading time or the study time? He decided to check this by dropping the study time and the quiz scores dropped to 71. Then he reintroduced the study time and the scores went back up to 77. Here he had some hint of a possibility that the group study time did have a positive effect on the scores since they went up and down as he introduced or removed the variable. On the next quiz under the same conditions the scores went up again slightly to 80. Following that there was a drop to 74. However, one variable that he could not control was the specific subject matter. Undoubtedly some material was more interesting to the students than other.

As a final change, he decided to mark the papers immediately and return them to the students before they left for the day with only the correct answers marked. The test score after this rose to 84. Unfortunately, there was not enough time left to determine if this change was "real" or chance. This is often the way of life in the classroom. Just as things get exciting, the semester comes to an end. However, every teacher can do as the teacher in this example—check his ideas in a planned manner to gain a better grasp of the factors affecting the learning process. Then we can continue to employ the superior techniques and refine our methods from one situation to another. Teaching is much more exciting this way and this itself may be one of the most important of all the variables.

DISRUPTIVE CLASSES

One of the most trying aspects of teaching for the beginner is getting and maintaining "discipline." Some teachers seem to have the knack and others do not. We feel that there is considerable evidence now at all grade levels that the teacher who responds positively to appropriate behavior and tends to ignore that which is inappropriate will have well-behaved classes. There are always exceptions when there are children who have specific problems. However, the model we suggest tends to make the teacher a nicer person from the point of view of students, one who only becomes punitive or negative for unusual offenses and who generally, in the contemporary parlance, "keeps his cool."

Sonic (1969), a third grade teacher in a Michigan school district, reports on her attempt to get children to change subjects quickly and quietly. She found that her students, when changing from something like arithmetic to English, characteristically talked to their neighbors, got out of their seats, wandered around a good deal and even got involved in minor fights. She reasoned that if she could get the students to cut down the time between subjects she could eliminate much of the undesirable behavior. She set as her goal a change that took less than 3 minutes.

During a baseline period she behaved as she customarily did at these times. She asked them to be quiet, asked them to stay in their seats, and reprimanded individual children for bad behavior. Teacher attention went to the disruptive behaviors and she was controlling her class through negative means. It was taking the children about 4 minutes to settle down. During her experimental phase, she gave social reinforcement to those children who quickly got ready and ignored those who did not. The time for change dropped to about 1 minute. To check her results, she did a reversal and the time increased close to the baseline conditions. Then she returned once again to the experimental conditions and the class continued to change subjects quickly and relatively quietly. Thus, merely by changing the manner in which she responded to her class this teacher effectively changed her class' behavior and improved their discipline.

Akin to this, at the junior high or middle school level we worked with teachers to help them change the way in which they responded to students. The teachers had agreed that they wanted to behave more positively towards their students but they didn't want a lot of pressure and discussion about this. Since this was a special project and we had the staff available, we were able to get data on the teachers' interactions with their students at random times over several months. We simply shared this data with them and this was enough to bring about positive change. By the end of the year they were doing much less reprimanding and much more praising.

Sometimes classes get completely out of hand and it may be necessary to use some sort of extrinsic reinforcement system paired with praise so that a positive change may be initiated. A good system in this situation is to get the class to agree to some common goal (a party, a trip, etc.) and then set the criteria so that there is strong peer reinforcement as well as teacher praise for moving toward this goal. For example, many teachers use an interval timer and tell the children that if everyone is busy at his task when the timer goes off the class will have taken one step toward the goal. A party might require 30 steps and these could even be portrayed graphically on the board. Then the timer is set so as not to be visible to the children. The first few intervals are quite short and the tangible reinforcement is seeing movement towards the desired goal. There are also peer reinforcers operating as the children become excited about a common achievement. Gradually the schedule is "thinned," i.e., the youngsters have to work longer for the reward and the teacher has a variable interval schedule of reinforcement in the class. A colleague of ours reports that in a school where she serves as a consultant psychologist this technique not only worked quite well in an unusually disruptive fifth-grade class but that other teachers in the building began dropping in to praise the formerly disruptive children for their good behavior. This acted as a powerful reinforcer and soon the children no longer needed the extrinsic contrived reinforcement.

At the junior high school we found that most youngsters would work to earn certain special excursions. However, here we generally placed the contingencies on an individual basis. That is, each student had an opportunity to earn the ski trip or the movie by earning academic or social points. Thus no student could, by his behavior, deny the others the reward, and all had an equal opportunity to earn it.

SOME ACADEMIC RESPONSES

We are endeavoring in this chapter to give a wide variety of "little experiments" in order to illustrate the way in which teachers have selected behaviors and modified them. Let us turn our attention now to some other academic responses. These have been selected with no particular goals in mind other than to give the reader some feeling for the broad spectrum of behaviors that are amenable to planned environmental alteration. As further examples of these academic responses, let us first take a look at a task requiring drawing a human figure and how an art teacher systematically improved the drawings of an 11-year-old girl.

This little girl was a beginning fifth grader who had been retained one grade because she missed too much school by reason of illness. The teacher noted that she seemed to feel very unsure of herself and tended to avoid academic-type work by keeping a steady conversation going. This apparently enabled her to avoid demonstrating her abilities (or lack of them). Many children learn this technique early and it will work if the teacher is particularly prone to enjoy talking. Thus the child reinforces the teacher by his conversation and the teacher reinforces the talking by allowing the child to use this as a means of avoiding a situation that could lead to an unflattering evaluation—another product of aversive controls.

In this situation, however, the teacher was not put off by the talk and insisted that the little girl draw a human figure. The figure was quite primitive and much below the expected quality for a girl of this age. However, the teacher did not disapprove; she accepted the drawing without comment. Using a scale for measuring specific attributes of human drawings, the teacher found that the student had included only 15 of these attributes out of a total of 51. On this particular scale (developed by Florence Goodenough) the 15 points were what we would expect of the average child of about 6½ years. This score of 15 became the baseline from which change would be measured. It was obtained under conditions of no approval.

Since there was prior evidence that social approval was reinforcing for this girl, the established plan was to approve of as much of her drawing and verbal behavior related to drawing as possible while simultaneously attempting to keep disapproval at a minimum and at zero if possible. For example, when the little girl remarked, "The cheeks and the chin are rounded shapes," the teacher responded by saying, "Good! You noticed more shapes."

In addition to developing a heavy reinforcement schedule, the teacher introduced some instructional behavior but not directly related to drawing. For example, she showed the student a carved mask and asked her to notice where the artist had placed the various parts of the face. She had the youngster slide her hands down the side of her head and body and note what this felt like in terms of shape. The counts for the child's drawing behavior and the three categories of teacher behavior, approving, disapproving, and instructional, are in Table 9. Note that the girl made a dramatic change the first session under contingency and instructional management. Part of this may represent what she could already do, but we cannot know this because she would not emit the behavior under the usual circumstances.

At the end of the sixth session (each was about 45 minutes and spaced about 4 days apart) the girl had achieved the terminal behavior, producing drawings that scored at the 11-year-old level. Like much of the work in the classroom, there was an immediate improvement, then some regression, and then continued improvement. The teacher felt that if she had continued this process, she probably would have made slight gains or maintained the quality of the work but with much less need for reinforcement or instruction. Already the latter had fallen off to near zero. Also the additional drawing characteristics needed to gain a still

Table 9

Sessions	Points On Child's Drawings	Teacher Approval	Teacher Disapproval	Instructional
1, 2 (baseline)	15			
3	31	13	0	14
4	19	36	1	5
5	30	45	0	6
6	33	30	1	2

higher score were more difficult and themselves might have required a significant change in instructional techniques. The important point is that this youngster did improve remarkably, although the data do not indicate if this was due to the increased amount of approval and decreased disapproval, the instructional behavior, or what is most likely, a combination of all three.

The most important thing about the technique was that the teacher became very aware of her own behavior. She ended the project by remarking, "I can see that as I increased the very pleasant job of reinforcing her, her behavior rose and I was not required to do as much instructing."

IMPROVED ARITHMETIC SKILLS

The next case under consideration concerns a beginning fifth-grade girl who seemed to have some difficulty with arithmetic. She was referred for help on this problem and the first task was to discover in just what she needed assistance. "Arithmetic" covers a lot of territory. Her own suggestion was that she did not know much about multiplication. Consequently, the tutoring team decided to try her on various aspects of multiplication facts. In a general test taking about 7 minutes and covering a random sampling of multiplication problems, the girl obtained a score of 39 correct and only 4 wrong. On another set which was deemed to be slightly more difficult, she scored 28 correct and 6 wrong in 10 minutes.

At this point the tutors analyzed the kinds of errors that the student was making and determined that they involved multiplication facts dealing with 7's, 8's, and 9's. Now things were a little more specific. Next a baseline was obtained. She was given a series of multiplication problems using flash cards without instruction or any teacher response. She attempted 18 problems in 5 minutes, with 13 being correct and five incorrect. The goal established for this student was

Table 10

Session	Multiplication Facts	Teacher Approval	Teacher Disapproval	Instructional
baseline	13 right 5 wrong	0	0	0
1	33 right 3 wrong	10	0	7
2	64 right 0 wrong	15	0	7
3	94 right 0 wrong	25	0	8

to significantly increase her rate of responding to multiplication facts using 7's, 8's, and 9's while keeping the error rate at a minimum, hopefully zero. Before each session there was an instructional period of 5 minutes in which the teacher tried to maintain a fairly consistent level of instruction. The variable of initial interest to us was how this student would respond to praise. Thus, praise was increased while instructional behavior remained constant.

From Table 10 it is readily evident that she improved her specific skills on multiplication facts very quickly. For a girl who "hated" arithmetic this seemed quite remarkable. Furthermore, there was one reinforcement contingency we had not counted on. After receiving praise for a formerly disliked task and then immediately seeing that she was improving, our student was further motivated to "top" her previous score. She was able to accomplish this without any sacrifice of accuracy.

As is usual with these kind of data, the cold figures do not tell the entire story. With very little investment of time, these tutors (one recording data while the other taught) helped a child to overcome a specific difficulty and helped her to become excited about her ability to learn. We do not know if this will generalize to other situations but would be inclined to feel that it might not. However, what was accomplished here by keying in on a specific problem and maintaining a positive learning atmosphere could certainly be accomplished in other settings with other instructional materials. Frankly, we would be hesitant to say that this little girl ended these brief sessions by liking arithmetic. That would be asking quite a bit. However, she was well on the road to improved mathematical ability and, given some more time, through her own success and the praise of adults we can safely predict a far more positive attitude toward the subject.

A slightly different approach to a similar task was taken by another team. The goal here was to improve a child's response rate in the use of multiplication facts while trying to maintain his accuracy rate. The boy was 11-years-old and beginning the sixth grade. He had no particular problems with arithmetic except that he was a little slow. As with many rote-type facts, it is frequently useful to the child if he can make them an almost automatic part of his academic repertoire without having to particularly "think" them through. Then material like multiplication facts become handy tools that are quickly available for many situations.

This student, Jimmy, was instructed to do as many of the multiplication problems as he could while maintaining accuracy. The problems were presented on a mimeographed form and his task was to write the answer to each one. Then the behavioral data for him consisted of the number of problems he completed and the number that were correct during a 10 minute test period.

The team recorded four kinds of teacher behavior: (1) approving, (2) disapproving, (3) instructional, and (4) other. The latter involved watching or sitting quietly without interacting with the student. Teacher behavior was recorded during a 10 minute instructional period. The assumption was that teacher approv-

Table 11

Session	Problems Completed	Number Correct	Percent Approving	Percent Disapproving	Percent Instructional	Percent Other
Baseline	134	129	0	0	0	0
1	168	156	5.5	1.4	91.6	1.4
2	198	194	15.1	0	75	9.9
3	210	207	19	0	81	0
4	210	208	0	0	59	41

ing behavior would act as a reinforcer for increasing the academic response rate. The data are presented in Table 11.

Note that for the first three sessions there was a steady decline in instructional behavior and a steady increase in approving behavior. During these sessions Jimmy quickly improved his rate of responding to a point at which the teachers thought it to be quite adequate. There was only an opportunity for one more session with this youngster (session 4) so we decided to see whether or not dropping approving behavior to zero would have an immediate effect on the rate and accuracy of his responses. It did not have an immediately deleterious effect in that he did not regress, but he made no further progress.

While it is possible that Jimmy had reached some sort of limit for this type of academic response, continued approval might have increased his rate still further. At least he had reached the point at which the teachers were satisfied. Again the actual time spent on this particular aspect of his academic behavior was brief. This sort of drill is a routine part of most classrooms. The difference here was the systematic attempt to increase reinforcement and thus quickly help the student to achieve the academic goal. Once the goal is achieved, the teacher can maintain it through intermittent reinforcement, a schedule that is much more natural to the usual classroom.

While we have made a particular point of emphasizing the use of natural reinforcers in the classroom, there are occasions in which these are not adequate and it is necessary to bring in something more tangible. The idea, as you will recall from Chapter 4, is to pair the tangible reinforcers with teacher praise and attention so that the latter gradually "take over" and maintain the desired behavior. The following case describes how a tutoring team helped a child from a disadvantaged area to quickly improve two behaviors so that the youngster became a much more effective learner. This was accomplished during just one week of a summer program, although the little boy continued in tutoring for several weeks after these data were taken.

Billy was a hyperactive boy He was 10-years-old and would be entering the fifth grade in the fall. He liked to do almost anything other than school work and was particularly adept at asking questions about things that had no relationship to academic tasks. He found it very difficult to sit still and seemed to be the kind of youngster who could distract a teacher much of the time, leading her to believe that there was no way of controlling him except by "sitting on him." He was somewhat deficient in arithmetic but in his case the main difficulty was with subtraction, and particularly the process of regrouping while solving subtraction problems.

This team decided to try to modify two of Billy's behaviors since they seemed interrelated. They would try to get him to ask only relevant questions and they would try to increase the accuracy of his use of the regrouping method. The former would help him to concentrate more on the material at hand and the latter would get him over a particular hurdle that was giving him trouble.

The teachers took data on five separate 5-minute instructional periods and found that he was interrupting with irrelevancies about twice in each 5-minute period. This was somewhat surprising because it seemed that he was doing even more than this amount of interrupting. The team felt, however, that even this was detrimental to learning. He did not seem to respond much to praise, perhaps because he was accustomed to receiving a lot of teacher attention for disruptive behavior. Thus, they told him that he would receive a nickel each time he did not interrupt a teaching session with irrelevant questions. However, he could interrupt for relevant questions. His irrelevant interruptions immediately dropped to zero and none recurred during the remainder of the week. The teachers gradually thinned the schedule of reinforcement. First, he was rewarded after 5 minutes of relevant behavior, then 10, then 15. Still there was no turning back. He asked only relevant questions and he stuck to the task at hand.

Incidentally, people often question the use of this kind of reward saying, on the one hand, that the child should do what he is told without some specific "bribe," but on the other, that he is incorrigible and will not do what he is told. The significant point here is that if his behavior cannot be modified through the usual application of social reinforcers and contingency management, and if it is clearly desirable for the child's welfare that he change, then we should use what we have available to help the child bring this behavior under natural self-control. There is nothing intrinsically evil about the systematic use of positive reinforcement as compared to natural social reinforcement (see Chapter 8 on ethics). However, since for most people it is more desirable to use social rather than tangible reinforcers, we urge that whenever the tangibles are used that they be paired with the social. There are obviously some behaviors (e.g., work) that, under the present circumstances, need to be rewarded with a tangible outcome (money). However, even in these cases improved work efficiency would occur if the employer paired a paycheck with social reinforcement (e.g., "You're doing a fine job, Charlie.").

Concurrent with the first task of stopping the irrelevant behavior, these teachers took a baseline on Billy's accuracy on subtraction problems requiring regrouping. This turned out to be 33%; he was able to do only about a third of the problems correctly. Then followed a 10-minute instructional period in which the teacher used a heavy schedule of approving behaviors. Bill's accuracy climbed to 45% on the next test. Another instructional period under social reinforcement maintained this accuracy but did not increase it. Billy still got about 45% of the problems correct.

At this point, since the tangible reward had worked so well on the other behavior, the teachers decided to try it again. This time they used an edible in the form of small pieces of candy. Billy was informed that if his accuracy improved, he would receive candy as a reward. On the next test his percentage correct was 75, on the next one it was 85%, and the final test reached 100% correct. In 5 instructional sessions totaling about 1 hour, he learned to use the regrouping process without error. The teachers then began to thin the tangible reinforcements but maintained a high level of social reinforcements so as to get him, hopefully, to maintain his improved level of performance when he returned to the classroom. Unfortunately there are no data on this. We have said from time to time that one cannot expect the behavior that has been learned under these special conditions to transfer back totally to the classroom unless the teacher there in some degree continues the program started by the special teachers. In Billy's case this would be to reinforce socially the desired academic and social behaviors. However, if he were still seen as basically disruptive by his teachers and they reinforced this kind of behavior by attending to it, we would expect disruptive behavior to return in full force rather rapidly. Though we make this point frequently in this book, it is still one of the most difficult concepts to grasp. Student behaviors are stimuli for our responses and we are trained to respond to disruptive behavior much more than any other. This appears to be the result of the immediate diminution in disruptive behavior, even though the long-term outcome is to maintain or increase the undesired behavior.

READING

This next study focuses on the ability to pronounce correctly words from a graded word list. The student was a 10-year-old girl entering the fifth grade. She had come for help in arithmetic and reading claiming she was "dumb" in both. She clearly was not, but had evidently acquired this self-evaluation as a protective device. Since she could hardly accuse the teacher of not having taught her adequately, she blamed herself for her deficiency. While one person helped her with her arithmetic until she was about 90% accurate on problems at her grade level, another helped her with word pronunciation. Let us take a look at this case in some detail since one of our predictions—what would be reinforcing for this girl—did not work out at first and had to be modified.

The teacher administered three informal reading tests. These involved spelling, oral reading, and word pronunciation. The word pronunciation test contained a sample of several words at 9 levels of difficulty, ranging from grades 3 through 12. Some of these would obviously be very easy for her and others quite difficult. However, the word lists were arranged in order of increasing difficulty so that as the youngster learned, she increased not only the rate of correct pronunciations but also the level of difficulty of the words she could pronounce. This should be kept in mind as we examine the data.

Under baseline conditions, with no reinforcement and no instruction, the student pronounced 32 words correctly in 10 minutes. She did not seem particularly motivated, however, despite the fact that she had asked for help in these skill areas. Then two procedures were instituted by the teacher, one involving instruction and the other testing.

In the instructional period (15 minutes) the teacher gave the student a booklet containing the entire collection of over 700 words and 24 lists. The teacher pointed out phonetic structures and pronunciations. The student was then asked to practice pronouncing the lists and was given prompts by the teacher. This was also an opportunity for giving verbal praise, which we thought would be reinforcing, in order to get the youngster to practice harder during the instructional sessions. We measured the effect of this by the number of lists that the girl attempted during her practice period.

The test situation consisted of her reading single words from lists of increasing difficulty, and her score was the number of correct pronunciations. Reinforcement here consisted of a token for each correct pronunciation. These tokens were to be traded for a high probability behavior, in this case they could buy rides at an amusement park at a cost of about 25 tokens per ride.

After the first session the teacher felt that the girl was not really responding to praise during the instructional period. She dawdled during this time and seemed inclined to resist the situation. This is certainly a normal reaction for a youngster who is asked to do a task which has become aversive. Therefore, the teacher introduced tokens into this part of the modification procedure by giving the girl a token for each word list attempted during the instructional period. The

Table 12. CORRECT PRONUNCIATION AS A FUNCTION OF TEACHER BEHAVIOR

Sessions	Correct Pronunciations	Attempted Lists	Approving	Disapproving	Instructional
baseline	32	0	0	0	0
1	43	6	20	11	9
2	53	12	25	1	12
3	72	19	42	0	21

data in Table 12 warrant close attention. Note that the student behavior, correct pronunciation of words, is that associated with the test period. The "attempting behavior" and the teacher behaviors are those associated with the instructional period.

When we remember that the increasing number of correct pronunciations involved increasing difficulty, the results are quite good. This student improved rapidly with a total instructional and test time of about 2 hours.

The other data are interesting also. Teacher disapproving behavior dropped rapidly once it became evident through record keeping. The tokens for attempting lists were introduced at the second instruction period and the number attempted doubled. This introduced an interesting variable related to teacher behavior. For now, with the student attempting more materials, the teacher had more opportunity for both instruction and verbal approval. Each of those behaviors increased with the amount of work that the student did. Then the amount of work that the student did increased. The benign circle here results in what we would be tempted to call increased motivation. Let us examine this notion.

Most teachers are interested in increasing a pupil's motivation to do the assigned tasks. This is usually thought of as some sort of inner drive (and it may well be), but the only manifestation of its operation is overt behavior. If the student increases his rate of responding to some academic task, as did our girl in the above example, we have some behavioral basis for saying she increased her motivation. Here she increased her "attempting behavior" and the teacher wisely reinforced this as a means of helping her to increase her correct academic responses. The teacher felt that the student was not particularly motivated until the reinforcements were changed, at which point her attempting responses increased.

We urge that the *index of motivation* should be a behavioral check rather than a verbal one. Many teachers ask students something like this: "What's the matter, Leroy, don't you want to learn to read?" And Leroy dutifully answers that learning to read is very important for him. However, his behavior frequently does not change. He continues to dawdle, daydream, and do other things besides reading. If we make the mistake of accepting just his verbal behavior and ignoring his attempting or study behavior, we may think we have a motivated child when we do not. Then things can become rather confusing as the child reiterates his motivation (after all, teacher is reinforcing this verbal behavior), but does not respond to the tasks. And we may find ourselves eliciting and reinforcing more and more irrelevant verbal behavior when we might better be eliciting and reinforcing the appropriate academic behavior. This leads naturally into the next section in which we will look at verbal behavior and some instances in which it is very important in its own right and worthy of reinforcement.

EIGHTH GRADERS AND AMERICAN HISTORY

Silverman and Miller (1971) worked with an eighth-grade teacher to improve learning in American History for 160 students in the teacher's five classes, a fairly typical load in our contemporary schools! The teacher covered a chapter of the text each week and gave out 40 short essay questions on each chapter for the students to study. The exam consisted of 25 of these questions chosen at random. A score of 20 was necessary to get a passing grade. The tests were constructed and graded by another teacher who knew nothing about the project.

The experimenters tested two variables in various combinations with these students. One was to provide each student with a "buddy." These were selected by previous grades with high students paired with the low students and average students paired with each other. The second, was to provide preferred or high-strength activities. After two weeks of baseline in which the teacher followed his normal routine of lectures, films and Friday tests, the students were told who their buddies were and were informed that as soon as *both* passed the test, which could be taken anytime during the week, they could go to the back of the room and work at any of the activities for the balance of the week. The data on 100 of the students in three of the classes showed that slightly over half the class were passing the test during baseline conditions and all under the new conditions. The researchers tried various combinations of conditions, such as buddies alone without a reward and buddies with advanced work. All seemed to help but the most powerful was the combination of the buddy system and a preferred behavior. Their conclusion is, we believe, worth quoting in full:

> The results of this study show that the use of a combination of preferred activities as reinforcers and a buddy system (where reinforcement is contingent upon both members of the pair reaching a pre-defined level of performance) can increase the learning of junior high students. Equally important is the fact that the program required no funds, no extra teachers, no programmed materials and no cut in class size. On a subjective basis, the classroom teacher indicated that lateness and absence decreased during the weeks when reinforcement was in effect. Also, in those weeks, less time was spent in discipline and more time spent in helping students on a one-to-one basis, so that the teacher's work was more enjoyable.

It is this kind of creative use of a behavioral approach, where "good" things happen as a result of learning and students learn to help each other that is particularly appealing to us.

VERBAL BEHAVIOR

Verbal behavior is one of the most fascinating areas of human behavior. It is our primary means of communication because, as we heard someone remark once, "We carry the apparatus with us constantly. It's easy to use, readily available, and needs refueling only occasionally."

Of course, there is a good deal more to it than this. Holz and Azrin (1966) correctly point out, "Verbal behavior is taken as an index of mental life of which all behavior is a manifestation." So, if we want to know something about a person, what he is thinking or what his attitudes are, we need only ask. Then, assuming that his responses are honest, we will get statements that are accurate reflections of inner states. The puzzling or perhaps not so puzzling fact is that there is often a remarkable discrepancy between what people say and what they do. This seems to be true even under those conditions in which the person is not trying to be deceitful but is giving his ideas honestly. A child may long and loudly proclaim his willingness to be good and then, a few moments later, be in the thick of it again. An adult may long and loudly proclaim his liberal attitudes toward minority groups but refuse to sell his house to a member of one for clearly economic reasons. In other words, there is no perfect juxtaposition of verbal and nonverbal behavior. We might well remember the aphorism that has been ascribed to American Indians in referring to their dealings with the White conquerors: "What you do speaks so loudly, I can't hear what you say." The teacher might well make this a standard part of his way of observing child behavior. What the youngster does is a better index of whether he has learned or is willing to learn than what he says.

We would speculate that one reason for this is that there are different eliciting stimuli and reinforcements for verbal behavior than for nonverbal behavior. The child responds one way to the teacher verbally because that is expected and reinforced, and he responds another way to other individuals (e.g. peers) because that is reinforced by their approval. These may be in conflict. Unless the youngster has learned to carry along with him some self-administered verbal cues, he may behave quite differently from teacher expectations.

We tend to make the assumption that anyone can be pretty well controlled or his behavior changed by verbal means. Yet the evidence for this is far from conclusive. A very practical question related to this is whether the child who is misbehaving should be sent to the counselor or principal for counseling or discipline, or be treated in the classroom? We have argued that the best place to change behavior is under those same conditions in which it occurs. There are others who argue that the best way would be to work through some form of verbal mediation such as counseling or psychotherapy. There are certainly many who believe that "talking out" a problem is an efficient and successful method of dealing with problem behavior, although the evidence is rather sketchy. The interested reader might refer to the introduction of Krasner & Ullmann (1966) for a detailed discussion of this. It suffices here to say that there is a great deal we do not know about changing behavior through verbal mediation.

We do know, however, that it is not very efficient to substitute a verbal goal for a behavioral goal in teaching. We have detailed our ideas about this in Chapter 3 and will not reiterate them here, except to suggest that a written test is probably a fairly good measure of what the child can write about a subject, but a rather poor measure of potential behavior in that area.

But what about verbalizations themselves? Do they follow the same kind of learning model (eliciting stimuli and reinforcement contingencies) as other behaviors? Holz & Azrin (1966) suggest that the answer is yes. They warn, however, that a major difficulty with research of this type is that it is often very difficult to study verbal behavior in and of itself without allowing some reference to an inner state to creep into the study.

Teachers are often interested in verbal behavior, not just in terms of what the student communicates but of how he communicates as well. Frequently the teacher encounters children who are shy and retiring and who do not communicate verbally with either other children or the teacher, or who do so only occasionally. The case of a little boy who talks quite well at home with his mother but will not communicate with anyone at school was recently brought to our attention. Why this is so is difficult to explain. But the psychologist is currently working to generalize the behavior from home to school by using behavioral techniques. There is no problem here of building correct speech, but there is one of determining what will elicit the behavior in school so that the youngster can have normal communication with his classmates and his teacher.

When the problem involves correction of speech we would certainly recommend that the speech therapist be consulted. However, when it becomes necessary to just encourage the student to talk more, the teacher may accomplish this through means similar to those discussed throughout the book. First, find what stimuli prompt the behavior (e.g., modeling techniques) or an adequate approximation of it, then reinforce it by whatever means have been determined to be useful with the particular student. Let us take a look at two cases in which the task was to increase the verbal behavior of children, since this was a necessary precondition for adequate participation in the class.

The first case involved a 12-year-old girl who was entering the seventh grade. She came from a fairly large family in which one of her primary chores was caring for her younger brothers and sisters. She had several hobby interests, particularly some associated with the outdoors, and she came for help in reading and science during a summer tutoring program.

During the initial meeting with her, the teachers were struck by her reticence to talk about her reading. They had asked her to read a story and then discuss it. She gave no spontaneous speech and offered only very brief responsive speech. It was clear that if this girl was to function adequately in her classes it would be necessary for her to become more verbal (i.e., to discuss things more and to volunteer ideas more). Thus, they decided to use reading and science as vehicles to help her increase her verbal skills.

Baseline data were taken on all verbal responses on two separate fifteen-minute intervals on consecutive days. The average number of verbalizations during these times was 17, all of them responsive. There was an average of 1.53 words per verbalization and no spontaneous remarks at all.

The teachers then began to search for ways to reinforce her verbalizations. Consumables did not work and excessive praise only seemed to embarrass the girl. They finally decided to use attention to her interests, encouragement, praise, tangibles, and interesting activities which seemed most appropriate for an adolescent girl. This rather "massive" reinforcement was difficult to measure. However, let us look at the verbal behavior data in Table 13 and then at some aspects of the contingency management. Each session consisted of two 15-minute periods.

From an experimental point of view, the drawback to this study is that the specific kinds of reinforcers are inadequately defined. However, from the point of view of helping the girl to a more fluent speech, the results are very encouraging. There is a dramatic drop in her performance at the seventh session when the teachers assumed a neutral role as much as possible. Then in the next session the behavior picks up again as the teachers returned to a heavy schedule of reinforcement. Although they did not keep further data, the teachers continued to work with this girl for several weeks and continued to help her on both the subject matter and her verbal fluency. One would be tempted to say here that what these teachers provided was a warm, accepting environment for this girl, and there is no doubt about that. They also demonstrated that her verbal participation was contingent on this kind of environment. We could only hope that those conditions would prevail when she returned to her regular class.

This student could certainly do the required work if only she could learn to participate. She, like many students, felt inadequate (and had been told that she was inadequate) and was treated in this manner in the class. It was not her ability

Table 13

Session	Average No. of Responses	Average No. of Words per Response	Average No. of Spontaneous Verbalizations
1,2 (base)	17	1.53	0
3	14	2.1	0
4	19.7	4.9	3
5	14.5	3.1	4
6	9.3	7.2	6
7	2.5	2.0	1
8	16.7	2.8	4

to learn that was inadequate, it was her inability to express herself in the social context of the classroom that was the key to her problem. Someone had mistaken this nonverbal child for one with a learning disability. And once that label was attached, it was difficult to remove.

The schools are highly oriented toward the development of verbal skills and, while we do not quarrel with this as being necessary in our contemporary society in which communication is crucial, we do wish to keep making the distinction between having the skill and displaying it. Another case that came to our attention recently is atypical only in the rather extreme nature of the problem.

A first grade teacher referred a girl to the school psychologist for an evaluation of "mental retardation." She described the girl as a sweet child who sat all day in the back of the class without doing anything. She hardly responded when spoken to and seemed content to just sit and gaze out the window or look at what the other children were doing. She was not a behavior problem in the usual sense of the word, but neither was she accomplishing anything.

The psychologist visited the class and agreed that the general description of the girl's behavior was correct. However, she also noticed that the teacher did not require the participation of the youngster. She was merely given some crayons and paper and left to her own devices. The drawings she produced were fairly good, but she did not involve herself in reading classes or other activities.

The psychologist took time to get acquainted with the student and found her very shy but responsive. The youngster consented to go to another room in which they would do an individual test of intelligence. By taking time to let the child proceed at her own pace, the test was finished in about double the usual length of time. However, the results indicated an IQ of 125, and this was a highly verbal test. Further investigation revealed that the child came from a culturally deprived home environment. The test score might have even been an underestimation since she had not had the opportunity to learn some of the things required by the test.

A little more coaxing and close work with the teacher and this child was soon involved in normal classroom activity. The point here is that the nonverbal behavior had been erroneously regarded as an index of retardation when it was really based on lack of social skill and the nonverbal nature of the child's home. Since verbal behavior is so important in the school, there is often a tendency to label a child on the basis of this factor alone rather than determining whether the verbal behavior itself could be improved. This youngster was obviously not retarded, nor was the junior high school girl discussed above a slow learner. They both had problems in expressing themselves, but not in learning the usual classroom skills.

Another brief example and we will leave verbal behavior. The child was seven and entering the second grade. She had been referred for help in her reading skills but when these were analyzed, there seemed to be no particular difficulty. In fact, she read quite well for her age and grade level. However, she lacked social skill and, we suspected, would not do too well when called on by the teacher to read in front of the class. We concluded that the best way to help her in the short time available was to give her an opportunity to use more responsive and spontaneous speech so that she would become more confident in talking with others.

Baseline conditions showed no spontaneous speech and very little responsive verbalization. During a 10-minute period she replied only three times to prompts directed at her. There were no approving, disapproving, or instructional behaviors during this time.

Since this student liked to draw with crayons, the teacher decided to use her drawings as a means of eliciting verbal behavior, and the crayons as a reinforcer. She was informed that every time she spoke without being asked she would receive a gold star and then, at the end of the 10 minutes, each gold star could be traded in for two crayons of her choice. Table 14 gives the data. They reflect a slight change in the reinforcement that resulted in substantial change in the response rate.

For the first two sessions, the gold stars were given at the end of the 10-minute period and then traded in for crayons. Beginning with the third session, the gold stars were given immediately after each spontaneous utterance. Note how rapidly they increased. Up to this time there had been a fairly heavy schedule of teacher approval, but this was thinned considerably with the new way of alloting the stars. While spontaneous speech did not stay up for the next session (although it was higher than in any of the earlier ones), responsive speech continued at a high rate. This was an interesting bit of "fall out" from the conditions since responsive speech was not being directly reinforced. It may well have been indirectly rewarded by the general approval for speech. Crayons were probably no longer necessary, or the student may have become somewhat satiated in her desire for them. However, the social reinforcement potential of the teachers was improved by being paired with tangibles.

We do not argue that all "shy" children should be brought willy-nilly into the center of the classroom social whirl. We do suggest that when shyness, as exemplified by low verbal participation, is detrimental to further necessary learning, then the first task is to help the child become less shy and more participating.

Table 14

Session	Spontaneous Speech	Responsive Speech	Approval	Disapproval	Instructional
baseline	0	3	0	0	0
1	3	7	12	0	9
2	0	15	21	0	3
3	17	30	4	0	0
4	5	29	5	0	0

What we are saying here is analogous to teaching the child to attend or lengthen his attention span. If nonattending or intermittent attending is seriously interferring with learning, then increasing attention is a first step in the modification procedure. The criterion for the teacher becomes the desired terminal behavior and the steps that are necessary to achieve this. It is not our intent to argue, however, that the teaching of blind conformity to social norms is a desirable activity. The desirability of the activity must be determined by how it relates to the educational goals within an ethical framework.

SOME MISCELLANEOUS BEHAVIORS

Thumbsucking

When young children come to kindergarten they often bring with them behaviors that are rather infantile and which do not "fit" in the classroom. Sometimes these behaviors reappear when the child starts school because they are associated with anxiety producing situations, and school is an anxious time for many children. One such behavior is thumbsucking including "fingers-in-the-mouth" over a protracted period of time. This brief study demonstrates how a kindergarten teacher cured one child of this habit in 10 days by simply controlling attending behavior. The interesting thing was that though she had "cured" the child at school, he still sucked his thumb at home until his parents instigated similar procedures.

The boy was just five and was barely of legal age to enter kindergarten. He was the oldest of three children and thus the first to leave the home. His mother was a bit anxious about his going to school but tried not to show it too much. However, when she brought him to school (she would not allow him to walk with the other children for fear of automobiles), she tended to hover around the class for a few minutes to determine if he would be all right. During this time the teacher greeted the other children and tried to ease this mother gently out of the room so that her son could settle down to playing and getting acquainted with the other children.

At this point he started to suck his thumb rather consistently both at home and at school. His mother reported that he had not done this for almost a year and that she was afraid the other children would laugh at him and call him a baby. When this occurred, however, he sucked it more and more. Though his mother was constantly pulling his hand down from his mouth, he was constantly putting it back in. His behavior did not seem to be a deliberate defiance of his mother's wishes, rather it was a kind of reflexive action which occurred when he was doing other things.

At school he sucked his thumb primarily when his teacher was reading or when there was some quiet activity. If he could be kept busy with trucks and blocks where two hands were necessary, he seemed to get along quite well. Aside from this problem, he was a normal little boy, had the usual beginning kindergarten difficulties, but was adjusting to the situation satisfactorily.

After about 2 weeks of school the other children began to tease him to some extent. The teacher insisted that they stop and they complied. The teasing had no appreciable effect on the behavior except possibly to increase it.

At this time the teacher wished to try some behavioral techniques but realized that she did not have any data. She had many impressions but nothing specific. She obtained a baseline of thumbsucking over 2 consecutive days by keeping a stopwatch with her and trying to time the total amount of time he kept his thumb in his mouth. This was a fairly crude measure since she missed some thumbsucking, but the time did accumulate on the watch and she did not have to record each instance separately.

She found that the youngster had an average time of 56 minutes of thumbsucking for two hours of class. Up to this time she had been trying to ignore it but had not been fully successful. During this baseline she found that she admonished him for his thumbsucking four times the first day and five the second. Consequently, she decided to institute rigorous self-control and not call attention to his thumbsucking. Instead, she would smile, hug, or approve in any way appropriate at those times in which he did not have his thumb in his mouth. As one would predict by now, this worked very nicely and at the end of eight more class days he was hardly ever seen with his thumb in his mouth. The teacher kept a chart which is reproduced in Table 15.

The question mark on the eighth day was meant to convey that the teacher had not detected any instances of the undesirable behavior. He did occasionally suck his thumb briefly after this but she continued to ignore it, and at this time he has not done so in several weeks.

Constructive Play

As our final example in this section, we will examine a case concerning a child's constructive play. This is a broad category of behavior, but most teachers

Table 15

Day	Time in Mouth (min)	Number of Times I Approved (Nonthumbsucking)	Number of Times I Disapproved (Thumbsucking)
1	58	4	1
2	42	10	0
3	44	8	1
4	32	14	0
5	19	12	0
6	3	15	0
7	5	10	0
8	?(0)	13	0

have a good idea of what they expect children to do on the playground or in the classroom during a play period. In general, they prefer activities that are healthful, educational, and socially acceptable. This is sometimes difficult with young children in new situations to achieve because they do not know what is expected, and may engage in almost any activity.

The study reported here was actually conducted by a teacher at home in order to show a neighbor how to get her 3½-year-old boy to play more constructively. He was constantly "in his mother's hair" and she was desperate for some advice.

The teacher observed the little boy for several days and concurred that he did have difficulty sticking to a task. So she set out to teach him to stay with one kind of activity over an extended period of time. She took him to her house where she had a great variety of toys (blocks, puzzles, beads, pegboards, etc.) which usually appeal to children of this age. Then, to get a baseline of constructive play, she allowed him three separate half hours of free play with these toys. He averaged just over 6 minutes of play for the three baseline sessions. He also exhibited a strong tendency to throw things about and be generally disruptive.

At the beginning of the fourth session (the first experimental session), the teacher sat down with him and told him that he would get candy for playing properly with the toys. This resulted in an immediate improvement in his play behavior. The teacher not only gave him candy for appropriate play behavior but, of course, strongly praised him as well. The data for the 14 half-hour sessions are given in Table 16.

While candy reinforcement had been given on an intermittent schedule during the play, the youngster gradually became less dependent on it and even

Table 16

Session	Constructive Play (min)	Candy Reinforcement	
1	5	no	
2	8	no	
3	6	no	baseline
4	19	yes	
5	23	yes	
6	25	yes	
7	24	yes	
8	24	yes	
9	11	no	
10	15	no	
11	26	yes	
12	23	yes	
13	28	yes	
14	24	yes	

tended to ignore it. Thus, while records were not kept as to the exact amount, there was much less candy given near the end of this procedure than during the early session. Yet his appropriate behavior was being maintained, largely by the social reinforcement given by the teacher. Furthermore, the intrinsic reinforcement of play became apparent. This child, as others, was able to do many constructive things with the toys when provided a contingent environment within which to function.

CLASSROOM MANAGEMENT

While many teachers see the value of using behavioral strategies with an individual child they frequently balk at the idea of managing an entire classroom with such techniques. They envisage piles of data charts, and inordinate amounts of time spent in observation, recording, and collating. They see hours spent in planning strategies and then checking these strategies and they wonder when they will have time to teach.

We are quite sympathetic with this point of view, having worked with scores of teachers on behavior modification projects. They sometimes complain that they "can't see the child for the data" and this is a very astute observation. Children are far more than numbers we use to describe them or marks we place on graph paper and too much involvement in this kind of activity will obscure our vision rather than sharpen it. Yet objectivity requires objective information. Just how much in any given situation is variable so we have no ready answers that will meet all needs. However, in this section we will discuss several ways to manage large classes with, hopefully, minimum distraction from teaching. In fact, when classrooms are properly managed and become self-managing the teacher is much freer to teach than if she is constantly involved in control. While vast amounts of data are necessary for research and publication much less are needed for every day classroom management. We suspect that the researcher in his zeal for science has asked for too much and thus alienated some teachers. When a principle is found to be valid only occasional checks will be necessary to see if it is still functioning properly. Thus, while we will suggest some observation and data collecting here, we do not expect the results to meet the standards of a major journal even though we do expect the teacher to be able to make significant changes in his classroom. Many references to group management are scattered throughout this book but we felt it would be useful to the teacher to have the essential strategies gathered in one place in order to facilitate application. So we hope the reader will forgive some redundancy in the interest of utility.

Rules

In and of themselves, rules are not of much value in managing a classroom. However, they do set the structure of the class behavior and provide the occasions for applying contingencies. They also provide cues for the internalization of certain behaviors so that the youngster can gradually come to rely more on himself and less on the imposed structure. Thus the structure they apply is much more important in the elementary grades than in high school. In the latter there seems to be more emphasis on schoolwide codes of conduct than on specific rules for each classroom. One might argue that rules are a necessary but not a sufficient condition for good classroom management. They become important in the broader context of how they are used. For example, they can be used to determine whether the teacher is being fair or whether a child should be rewarded or punished. But if the rules are consistently ignored they become worse than useless.

We feel that there are three elements that are critical in establishing rules. First they should be few in number, short, and clearly stated. Thus there is the implication that children are pretty much able to manage their own affairs (this is a good self-fulfilling prophecy) and a few readily understood rules are all that is necessary. The teacher does not have a large number of infractions to monitor and all will know when she is being fair. Second, we feel that rules should be positively stated whenever possible. This makes for a better classroom "climate" and takes the emphasis off punishment and/or negative reinforcement. It is better to state, for example, when talking is permitted rather than when it is forbidden. *Positive rules tend to elicit desired behaviors.* Then these behaviors can be reinforced by the teacher or by peers. Third, the students should be involved in making and, where necessary, interpreting the rules. This insures that the rules are clearly understood and agreed to. There can be little or no problem of "fairness" of interpretation. Most ambiguities can be handled at this stage and the mechanism for future difficulties is clearly defined. Most important concerns reinforcement for following the rules. It is much more likely that the teacher will obtain peer (student) contingencies for proper behavior when they were involved in making the rules. When someone transgresses it is "our" rules that are being flouted not just teachers'. And finally, involving the students is an excellent way to enhance intrinsic motivation. We feel much better about following guidelines we have agreed to than those imposed. We recently observed this process in a fifth grade classroom where a new student was being introduced to the rules. He sat with the teacher and a group of other students. Each rule was gone over carefully with both the teacher and the students explaining its purpose. After the explanation he was asked to give the rule in his own words until it was clear he understood it and the consequences. This was all done in a friendly manner and we couldn't help but feel that the new student felt much more at home afterwards. He knew the structure of the class and he knew his peers were involved and approved.

Reinforcers

We have already discussed reinforcement in detail in Chapter 4. Here we will emphasize those generally available in the usual classroom.

If there were a single theme in this book or an idea that we think would be most valuable to the prospective or working teacher it is that the teacher is the most powerful reinforcer in the classroom. Teacher attention in the form of approval or disapproval exercises control over much of the behavior of students and sets the "climate" in the room. This has been demonstrated so frequently in research and practice that we will not belabor the point. A teacher who will increase the amount of approval for appropriate behavior and decrease the amount of disapproval for inappropriate behavior will have a happier class and will feel much better about teaching. The process of looking for "good" behavior to approve seems to change how one feels about the class. The students respond better and the teacher responds to them in more positive ways. This is a good example of the benign circle.

However, it may be useful to get some help in starting the "circle." One good method is for the teacher to enlist the aid of someone to take data. This could be a teacher aide, a parent, the principal, or even a student in the class. We have found students to be very accurate data collectors when the process is carefully described and there are no ambiguities. In fact, they seem to enjoy the task and are often much more motivated than adults. The usual procedures should be followed. (See Chapter 2.) First a baseline of approval and disapproval behaviors is obtained and then the teacher increases the amount of approval and decreases the amount of disapproval. For the skeptic it is also a good idea to take concurrent measures of student disruptive behaviors. Data are collected as long as necessary and then occasionaly thereafter just to keep the teacher "honest." On several occasions we have found that simply sharing the data with teachers is enough of an incentive to bring about change. However, it might help to get some extrinsic reinforcement. We know of one situation in which a teacher with the help of a school psychologist made some dramatic changes in her own behavior and in the behavior of the class. Other teachers in the building and the administrators popped in occasionaly to compliment the group. This made both the class and the teacher feel very good.

To be a particularly effective dispenser of approval the teacher also needs to be active. Reinforcers work best when they are immediate so that the teacher who is near a child who has done something meriting approval can respond quickly and with both verbal and nonverbal approval. Some children who do not respond too well to words may respond very quickly to hugs and pats. Thus when children are doing "seat-work" it is very desirable for the teacher to circulate not only to help when problems occur but to be a constant source of reinforcement. The presence of the teacher also acts as a cue for appropriate behavior and discourages inappropriate behavior. Active teachers tell us that they may get a little more tired than some of their more sedentary colleagues but they do have an incentive to keep in good physical condition!

Peers are another very powerful source of reinforcement. Many a disruptive child is reinforced by attention from other students. The job for the teacher, then, is to so manage the classroom that peer approval and disapproval follow the pattern that she has set for herself.

One method is to have the class working for a common goal such as a party or an outing and to make attainment of this goal contingent on appropriate behaviors over a period of time. This may be controlled through a token system or somewhat more casually through a time sample. In this latter situation the teacher uses a simple timer and places it on her desk so that the face is not visible to the students. She sets the timer and when it goes off checks to see if the students are engaged in the previously agreed upon behavior (e.g., in seat and studying). If the class is functioning appropriately, the entire group gains points towards the desired reward. If one or two people are not, there are no points. Assuming the potential reward is highly desirable there is a lot of peer pressure for appropriate behavior. This is maintained over many days by having some visible method of showing the progress of the class. One teacher we heard was going to have a "fudge" party. So each time the class was behaving properly when the timer went off she marked a part of the word "FUDGE" on the board. The class could see just how well they were doing. Other teachers have used variations of the thermometer mock-up so popular in community campaigns. It is usual to start out with fairly frequent opportunities for reinforcement and then gradually lengthen the time. This brings more and more behavior under control. We also urge that the teacher use a good deal of praise in this process so that her praise comes to take the place of the contrived reinforcement. In this method, then, the teacher has the children reinforcing each other, some contrived extrinsic reinforcers, and her own social reinforcers. In addition to all of this it is a lot of fun!

A variation of this technique is for the teacher to give the entire class some special treat when she feels that they have been doing particularly well. There is no prior consultation with the class but it is a good idea to inform them carefully of just what it was that made the teacher respond so well. This should be done on a variable schedule so as not to be expected and should not be used too often. Even special treats can become boring (satiation of reinforcement) if they are repeated too often.

Almost every classroom contains a child or two who is a leader and a model for the other children. He or she is frequently imitated and this can be a source of pleasure or frustration for the teacher. However, leaders respond to reinforcers in addition to those from peers and can be very helpful in setting behavior standards for the class. The knowledgeable teacher when observing one of these youngsters modeling appropriate behavior will call it to the attention of the rest of the class (and reinforce it) by saying something like, "Mary. I like the way you are. . . ." Mary usually responds with a smile and other children hasten to imitate. Pairing a socially isolated child with a popular one on some classroom task that will bring them into contact with many other children is also a useful way to help the isolate to become more accepted. Being frequently seen in the company of a leader helps the isolate to appear more worthwhile to his peers and puts him in a position to receive some of the reinforcement that goes to the popular child. Quite frequently popular children are very secure in their position and even like to be of some help to others. This should be reinforced by the teacher.

Another excellent source of reinforcement and class control is the teacher aide. While it may be necessary to have such a person do some of the bookkeeping chores in order to free the teacher for more important duties, teacher aides can also, with a little training, become excellent managers of contingencies They can gather data when necessary and take much of the burden off the teacher for information gathering. If one is fortunate enough to have an aide in the room it is much easier to plan management strategies. We have seen aides do everything from gather the milk money, take attendance, and ditto work sheets to tutor individual children. We feel that if they are accepted as paraprofessionals and helped to learn classroom procedures they can be of tremendous help. Most of the teachers we have worked with who have had aides in their classrooms have had no difficulty planning and implementing behavioral strategies.

Thus far in this section we have been concerned primarily with the use of social reinforcers. We intentionally stress these throughout the book since we feel that it is through the medium of social reinforcement and the modelling of appropriate behaviors by the teacher that the student learns to use self-reinforcement or intrinsic motivation. However, part of the management of a classroom is to provide other kinds of reinforcers so as to help motivate those children who are not yet responding to the normal social reinforcers and who are not self-motivated. At least they do not respond with reference to school oriented tasks. Many so-called unmotivated youngsters have many things they do and do well. We just don't happen to require those behaviors in school. "Hustling" is a very highly developed social behavior in some areas but we tend to look upon it as inappropriate for school.

One of the best kinds of reinforcers for most children is to use a normally high-strength behavior to reinforce a low-strength behavior. (See Premack Principle in Chapter 4.) This requires some adjustment in the room in order to provide areas where the students can congregate for reading, games, and other activities. The activities selected for reinforcers cannot be very loud or they will disturb the other students. So fairly quiet games such as chess and checkers are appropriate where ping pong would not be. Some teachers use the gym or recreation room for their more boisterous students.

A reading center is almost always popular especially if it contains an overstuffed chair or two or an old davenport. We have even seen such centers equipped with T.V. and radio but with headsets so as not to disturb the nonlistener; also a coffee table covered with favorite reading material. Students are often eager to help decorate and furnish such an area and this provides another opportunity for a class project which is fun and beneficial to all. All such areas that we have seen emphasize comfort and convenience.

Just organizing the classroom to take advantage of high strength behaviors is not enough. The teacher also needs to develop a system to dispense these reinforcers. This may vary in structure from a casual "When you have finished doing your arithmetic correctly, you may play or read until time for social studies," to a carefully monitored token system. This depends on just how structured the teacher feels she needs to make the class, and that probably depends on the kinds of problems she has with the students. Our bias is to impose the minimum structure to get the job done. But this is a judgement that each teacher will have to make.

Token Economy

The token economy is a special means of dispensing reinforcers in a very systematic way. While some of our colleagues feel that this system should be widely adopted we feel that it should be used in cases of extreme difficulty and then dropped for the normal social reinforcers when feasible. Actually, the tokens or points could be gradually "faded" until the normal reinforcers took over.

It takes considerable planning to set up a token or point system but once in operation it can run rather smoothly. The important thing is to devise a system of payoffs for specific academic and nonacademic behaviors. These should be clearly stated and rigidly adhered to. The student earns points which he may then at some agreed upon time trade in for free time or specific things. This is an excellent way to teach a child to delay gratification. While he gets his points immediately and, in most systems may trade them in immediately, he can get better (higher priced) items or more free time if he will collect his points and trade them in at a later time. It is important to have many desirable back-up reinforcers so that if a youngster satiates on one he can move to another.

We have seen some token economies operate like a store where at designated times the student can buy goods or activities. Others are more flexible so that any time a student has enough points he may trade them in. The management of such a system almost requires an aide although student help is also useful. In fact, we have seen a system whereby the student helpers earned tokens in order to be helpers!

We feel that one of the primary benefits of the token economy is to train the teacher in giving reinforcement. She is compelled to respond positively to a student when he emits the desired behavior. Thus social reinforcement is paired with the contrived reinforcer and, hopefully, the teacher learns to become a more reinforcing individual.

In this section we have attempted to provide a brief overview of general classroom management using behavioral principles. The teacher may choose to function in a fairly casual way or in a very structured token economy. Which is best must be decided in the situation in which it will be operative. However, it is not difficult to manage the classroom in this manner. It takes some planning and, if complex, some help. We would suggest beginning gradually. Add only those elements that are necessary to reach the desired behaviors. We believe that most classes will respond to a high rate of approval and a low rate of disapproval. Some will need this coupled with some managing of reinforcers in the form of high-strength behaviors. And a very few will need the more complex token systems and contrived reinforcers.

THREE FINAL IDEAS

There are no end of ideas that creative people can produce when they are imbued with an objective approach to the classroom tempered by a strong human warmth toward their students. We are constantly impressed and delighted with teacher creativity. Here are just three more examples that might intrigue the reader and get him to thinking along divergent lines.

On a recent trip to Los Angeles one of us was talking with a group of educators when a somewhat elderly but very spry first grade teacher gave us this tip. She had a telephone installed in her classroom at her own expense. There were no funds for such nonsense in the school budget. The phone was to be used by her students to talk to their parents when they had done something that merited special attention. It was quite a privilege and quite a thrill for these little youngsters to be able to call home and tell mommy or daddy about some special accomplishment. Of course, not only was there reinforcement for the youngsters in this but there was also excellent public relations for the school. Too often schools contact parents only when a child has misbehaved or is doing poorly academically. Here there was almost immediate contact for desirable behavior. We think the school ought to at least pay the phone bill!

Many teachers invent games of one kind or another to increase motivation. One math teacher we knew started her classes with a puzzle and there was a special reward for finishing it within 3 minutes after the class started. She frequently used mixed words with mathematical connotations and the students had to unscramble these in the prescribed time. An example would be "munrea-tro." This was an excellent device for getting children in their seats and working. Another math teacher invented a game called MATHGO which was played much like Bingo. One student read off the problems and the players each had cards with answers in rows and columns. The one who correctly covered a row or column first yelled "mathgo," and his reward was to read out the next set of problems. This made the learning of basic addition and subtraction facts fun. We see nothing wrong with that!

Finally, one of our teacher's aides obtained excellent results in improving the reading skills of her students by a simple game in which each student read a passage and the other students at the table (usually three or four) obtained points towards prizes for correctly detecting errors in their classmate's reading. The student with the greatest number of points for the week won a special prize (e.g., a record album or a ticket to the skating rink). Not only did this focus the attention of the would be critics, but the reader, not wishing to yield points to his competitors, worked hard to avoid making errors.

SUMMARY

It is difficult to summarize what has been offered here as each of these cases is meant to serve as an example of the principles we have been suggesting in earlier chapters. These were not the "tight" research designs of the laboratory but the looser, more flexible experiments of the teacher. We do not always end up knowing the precise variable which made the difference for each child, but we do see a definite improvement in behavior. We have presented these "little experiments" to show the teacher that the classroom can indeed be seen as a laboratory, but one with the immediate goal of helping children learn appropriate social and academic behaviors. These cases, then, are practical applications rather than basic research. They are down-to-earth examples of what a teacher may accomplish in the normal classroom through the methodology of objective teaching and behavior modification.

REFERENCES

Holz, W. C., & Azrin, N. H. Conditioning human verbal behavior. In *Operant behavior: Areas of research and application* (W.K. Honig, ed.). New York: Meredith Publishing Co., 1966.

Krasner, L., & Ullmann, L. P. *Case studies in behavior modification.* New York: Holt, Rinehart & Winston, 1966.

Silverman, S. H., & Miller, F. D. The use of the Premack principal and a "buddy" system in a "normal" eighth grade class. *School Application of Learning Theory*, 1971, **IV** (1), 14–19.

Sonic, C. The use of positive social reinforcement to help a third grade class change subjects quickly and quietly. *School Application of Learning Theory*, 1969, **I** (2), 9–14.

SUGGESTED READINGS

Bolstad, O. D., & Johnson, S. M. Self-regulation in the modification of disruptive classroom behavior. *Journal of Applied Behavior Analysis*, 1972, **5**, 443–454.

Brophy, J. E. Fostering intrinsic motivation to learn. *Journal of School Psychology*, 1972, **10**, 243–251.

Grieger, R. M. Behavior modification with a total class: A case report. *Journal of School Psychology*, 1970, **8**, 103–106.

Kirby, F. D., & Shields, F. Modification of arithmetic response rate and attending behavior in a seventh grade student. *Journal of Applied Behavior Analysis,* 1972, 5, 79–84.

Lounin, J., Friesen, W., & Norton, A. Managing emotionally disturbed children in regular classrooms. *Journal of Educational Psychology,* 1966, 57, 1–13.

MacDonald, W. S. *Battle in the classroom.* New York and London: Intext Educational Publishers, 1971.

Staats, A. , Linley, J., Linke, K., & Wolf, M. M. Reinforcement variables in the control of unit reading responses. *Journal of Experimental Analysis of Behavior,* 1964, 7, 139–149.

10
Retarded Behavior

Hidden away behind gates of iron and ignorance which surround these public institutions are tens of thousands of people who have been legally classified as retarded. This population includes men and women, girls and boys, of every racial, religious, ethnic, and socioeconomic group in our society. A small percentage of these people are as physically disabled as they are intellectually impaired. Hydrocephalus, a condition in which an excess of cerebrospinal fluid accumulates within the skull, leaves its victims both intellectually retarded and physically handicapped. Down's syndrome, more commonly known as mongolism, involves both genetically influenced physical abnormalities and moderate intellectual disability.

Yet most of those residing in these public institutions for the retarded have no observable physical disability. Many are active, friendly, and, if a pragmatic adaptation to an inescapable environment may be reflective of intelligence, they are intelligent as well. Some of these people show extremely deviant patterns of interaction with their physical and social environments. Others are in obvious emotional pain, anxious and disturbed by the barren anonymity of their surroundings. A few rock endlessly back and forth in their chairs in the understaffed dayrooms; still fewer emit unusual sounds. Many chatter among themselves or work in the residence halls, usually without pay or with token reimbursement, cleaning or helping prepare meals. A few live in halfway houses where they are trained for their eventual return to the community. Others will live out the remainder of their lives in the same building.

177

In a few of these institutions, too few, the problem is seen as primarily an educational one; in most, it is a custodial one. Tens of thousands of people, who with intensive educational programs could leave the institutions and contribute socially and economically to society, are instead confined to a lifetime sentence of boredom, deprivation, and neglect.

We believe that with greater public commitment and funding such institutions could be transformed from negative learning environments, teaching bizarre though institutionally adaptive behavior patterns, into positive learning environments, using objective teaching methods to promote the return to the community of thousands still confined. It is the cost of *not* meeting the educational needs of those we have classified retarded that is prohibitive.

LABELING

Naming something does not necessarily describe or explain it. Yet there are those who still confuse denotation with explanation and analysis. They assume that by using such terms as "mental retardation," "minimal brain dysfunction," or "intellectual deficiency," they provide information which is of real use to the teacher. This practice not only fails to help children with learning gaps, but it actually establishes low expectations which are frequently harmful to further learning. It is growing increasingly apparent that environmental deprivation plays a major role in much faulty learning. Objective teaching offers a total educational framework within which this deprivation can be remedied.

Educators, psychologists, psychiatrists, and other professionals increasingly acknowledge the necessity to abandon diagnostic labels, but they nevertheless continue to use them. It appears that before the practice can be eradicated, it is necessary to spell out more precisely than ever the harmful effects it has had on those so labeled.

It is generally accepted that only 15 to 25% of the total cases of retardation have known genetic or other organic bases (such as brain damage or malformation), while the remaining 75 to 85% have not been successfully accounted for within a clear category of organic impairment. Yet the widely used term mental retardation, which is frequently part of the diagnostic label of cases in which there is no known etiology, still carries connotations of organic causation. No doubt, medical and related research will reveal some additional genetic factors and diseases which may reduce the rate of learning, but to continue to assume that these are responsible for all existing cases of retardation, or even most of them, will limit progress in educational and behavioral research and application. Before physiological limits on behavioral repertoire can be accepted as valid, they must be defined and demonstrated. At present, there appears to be an imbalance of research expenditures in favor of medical and genetic research in retardation, while educational and behavioral research is generally inadequately funded. This is still more peculiar in view of the growing evidence that environmental factors have an enormous influence on learning.

INTERFERING BEHAVIORS AND RETARDATION

The concept of undesirable behavior interfering with the development of desirable behavior is especially applicable to retardation. It is even possible to argue that interfering behaviors actually play a major role in many patterns of retarded behavior as well as in childhood autism, a pattern often characterized by poor language development, stereotyped behavior, short attention span, and poor social relations. Such behaviors, inadvertently strengthened at home by parents and older siblings, may obtain so much reinforcement for a child that more complex behavior does not develop. Positive reinforcement frequently takes the form of adult attention and as the maladaptive behavior gains in strength, such behavior reduces the probability of the emission of more adaptive behavior and its reinforcement.

Hyperactive behavior, discussed earlier in the book, can frequently interfere with social and academic learning to a marked degree. Often described as short attention span, an excessive rate of behavior diffusion (e.g., moving from object to object or activity to activity in an apparently haphazard manner) is frequently the leading factor in a child's diagnosis of mental retardation or autism. A child who is moving through his environment rapidly and continually is far less able to attend to relevant cues and does not make appropriate academic responses. This behavior is typically reinforced at home by the attention of an anxious mother. She may follow the child around the house hour after hour alternately scolding him and giving him various toys in an effort to divert his attention from destructive or annoying activity. In school, the teacher may pick up where mother left off and increase the rate still further. Such a case is clearly demonstrated in a study by Eileen Allen and her associates (1967). The child, a 4½-year-old boy enrolled in a special preschool program, showed very poor attending behavior and was extremely hyperactive. Judging that adult attention served as a positive reinforcer for such behavior, the teachers gave attention and approval contingent upon the boy's continuously remaining with a single activity for at least a minute. He received social reinforcement as long as he remained with the activity. The teachers systematically extinguished hyperactive behavior by withholding attention for activity changes. A marked reduction in hyperactive behavior and activity changes occurred in just 7 days. Attending behavior, so crucial to academic achievement, was clearly established.

INTELLIGENCE TESTS

The diagnosis of mental retardation is frequently, though not always, based on a score achieved on one of the standardized tests purported to measure "intelligence." The very concept of measuring intelligence is highly misleading as it gives the impression that intelligence is some sort of substance which exists and is subject to measurement. The mistake of "reifying intelligence as some mystical substance," is noted by Wesman (1968). Challenging common misconceptions about intelligence, Wesman defines the concept as ". . . the sum total of all the learning experiences he [an individual] has uniquely had up to any moment in time." Standard tests, whatever else they claim to do, essentially provide information about what behavior an individual is presently capable of, and what behavior he is not. True, given a constant environment, present behavior may well predict future behavior, but there is no necessity to keep the environment constant. However, in its broad sense, objective teaching is concerned with the systematic rearrangement of the environment to maximally facilitate learning.

A further misconception is that an individual's test score reflects his potential. This is a presumptuous approach and one which can be especially detrimental to the child who achieves a low score. Thinking of this kind is most clearly visible in certain institutions for the retarded in which residents are grouped according to test scores. When a child scores low, he may be assumed to have little potential for learning. Thus, he is placed in an environment in which little functional learning is possible. When a psychometrist retests him on the same or similar tests some years later, his repeated low score is used to support the notion that he really did have little potential to begin with. As you can clearly see, this is circular reasoning of the most naive variety.

The degree to which a teacher's expectations of a particular child may actually influence the way he treats the child was examined in a study by Rosenthal and Jacobson (1968), a study which has since been seriously challenged on methodological grounds. An IQ test, heavily emphasizing "verbal" and "reasoning" ability, was administered to each child in an elementary school. About 20% of the students, randomly selected within their classes, were placed in the experimental condition. Their teachers were told that they had shown outstanding ability on the IQ test and could certainly be expected to blossom within the school year.

At the end of 8 months, all the children were retested and their scores were compared to their earlier IQ test scores. The researchers reported that those children whose teachers had been told they would blossom did exactly that. They showed a significantly greater gain on the test than those children whose teachers had not been given such feedback. Furthermore, the younger the child, the more he tended to be affected by his teacher's expectancies.

Unfortunately, these findings could not be replicated by Soule (1972) on a population of severely retarded residents of a state institution. These residents, who ranged from 8 to 16 years of age, were tested on the Peabody Picture Vocabulary Test as well as other tests of intelligence and objective ratings of behavior. Once tested, they were assigned randomly to either an experimental or control group. The cottage parents were then told that certain children (experimental group) had been selected by the psychology department as seeming to "have the potential for higher performance than they are presently showing." In addition, the psychologist made weekly visits to the cottages of these "selected" residents to stress their high potential. A post test several weeks later, using the same instruments as in the pretest, showed no significant change in IQ test and objective rating scores of the experimental group as compared to the control group.

While it is possible that the cottage parents, those responsible for the day-in, day-out care of the residents, were simply not convinced by the psychologists, the findings of this study point again to the unpredictability of the bias effect.

Even if no bias effect whatsoever were to be detected in further research, a highly unlikely occurrence, there is another reason why it may be useful to eliminate or at least reduce the use of the general intelligence score. Unlike objective measures of specific skills in particular relevant tasks, the low IQ score carries a serious stigma which may serve to limit the "retarded" student's social contacts as well as his educational opportunities. This is seen at its extreme within the locked gates of the public institution for the retarded.

Objective baserates of performance do not carry the stigma of the low IQ score. Though they may indicate that a child has a long way to go academically, objective baserates do not prevent a child from getting there. For this reason, and for the others outlined in Chapter 2, specific measures of relevant behavior, where possible, should generally be used in favor of broader tests whose outcomes are open to misinterpretation and which may result in academic discrimination by relegation to an inferior learning environment.

Although objective teaching has made significant breakthroughs, we are far from being in a position to know just how much any individual is ultimately capable of learning. It is important to remember, then, that intelligence is merely a hypothetical concept which is used to account for behavior which has functional value in the culture. When one measures intelligence, he is merely measuring certain kinds of desirable behavior. When he begins to attribute present academic performance to an immutable kind of native intelligence, he leaves the domain of objective teaching.

All of this is not to say that behavior need not be evaluated. It is mainly to suggest that standardized evaluations of behavior, most of which are essentially very general measures of responding, should never lead one to believe that he has greater predictive knowledge than he really does. If you are interested in evaluating a student's ability to do arithmetic, spelling, history, etc., design items which provide precise cues or models of what is desired and record his specific performance. If he does poorly in some area, or even all areas, prepare specific instructional programs to remedy his educational deficiencies rather than attribute his inability to perform to low intelligence, mental retardation, etc. Finally, the tests or rating scales used to evaluate behavior must be relevant to educational goals, relevant in terms of both the kinds of behavior evaluated and the degree of difficulty of the items. Traditional intelligence tests are particularly irrelevant on both counts when used to evaluate obviously retarded behavior. Deprived and institutionalized children score particularly poorly on such tests because they, as other behaviorally retarded children, have not had the kinds of experiences which are prerequisites to correct responding on test items. In addition, test items call for far more complex responses than they are presently capable of emitting. Unlike specific baserate scores, IQ test scores do not generally provide information relevant to programming for the child, a major requirement in objective teaching.

OBJECTIVE ASSESSMENT OF RETARDED BEHAVIOR

We endorse the view that, with the exception of certain cases in which physiological dysfunction can be clearly shown or strongly inferred from physiological data (e.g., microcephaly, neurologically validated brain damage, etc.), it is counterproductive to deal with individuals as if they were confined to their current low level of performance forever. Because the term "mental retardation" has come to imply a generalized limitation on intellectual potential across all or most skill categories, it may well promote a self-fulfilling prophecy of inferior performance. Consequently we favor the term "retarded behavior." This term, we feel, best reflects our point of view that by overcoming specific disabilities rather than dealing with as abstract a concept as IQ, we can effect greater positive change.

Retarded *behavior* can be improved through objective teaching; the retarded *person*, however, once labeled as such, tends to remain socially and intellectually stigmatized for a lifetime.

Recent evidence suggests that even IQ tests, once thought by many to be relatively immune to the effects of the learning environment, may be heavily influenced by it. Witmer and his colleagues (1971) randomly divided third- and fourth- grade children into three groups, an approval group, a disapproval group, and a neutral group. Each child in the approval group was given verbal approval (e.g., "Fine," or "That was good.") after the first response following each subtest and between subtests of the Wechsler Intelligence Scale for Children (WISC). Each child in the disapproval group was admonished (e.g., "That wasn't so good," or "I thought you could do better than that.") at these same times during the test. The neutral group was given the test according to nonbiased, standardized instructions. Estimated differences of as many as 11 IQ points, favoring the approval group over the disapproval group, suggest that even rather blandly delivered positive reinforcement can affect IQ test results. On the basis of this finding, one can reasonably hypothesize that real, marked differences in the personalities of test givers might be manifested in the scores attained by those they test. We have not attempted to research this area, but a review of reported research on this topic should prove useful.

Still another researcher (Edlund, 1972) showed that tangible positive outcomes (M&M candies) following each correct response on the Stanford-Binet IQ test produced an "appreciable, statistically significant difference" in IQ scores favoring those children who had been reinforced over those who had not.

The motivational factor in behavior has been somewhat obscured in recent years due to the reluctance of overly orthodox behaviorists to deal with such cognitive notions as expectancy of outcome. A more integrated approach, such as we advocate in objective teaching, will help us to cover greater ground more effectively than a narrow point of view. For example, we note the serious questions posed by these two studies just cited, and by the Edlund study in particular. The IQ test is supposed to measure skills already within the child's behavioral repertoire but is not designed to teach new skills. Consequently, the improvement in these children's IQ scores with the introduction of positive outcomes points not to an increase in the rate of learning (with the remotely possible exception of improvement in test taking skill per se) but to an increase in the rate of emitting behavior already learned. The improvement of a specified behavior, without the child's having had a significant opportunity to master that behavior or acquire new information, better fits a motivational explanation than a description of new learning. This is not unlike the frequent scene in old time detective movies in which the detective offers money to help "refresh the memory" of his prospective informant. The role of reinforcement in increasing motivation per se deserves considerable attention from researchers.

What is occurring in these studies is apparently a process in which change in expectancy of outcome via the introduction of positive reinforcement promotes emission of behaviors already present in the child's behavioral repertoire. This variable, expectancy of outcome, should gradually emerge as an essential factor in teaching.

The objective measurement of retarded behavior requires an instrument which is sensitive in detecting present skill levels and changes in them without being overly dogmatic in accounting for specific ways to attain positive change. This method of measurement appears to be making inroads against traditional intelligence tests for several reasons. Among these are the relative ease with which objective behavior ratings can be obtained by nonprofessional, briefly trained personnel in institutions for the retarded, and the greater usefulness of these kinds of measures as compared with IQ scores when it comes to planning a remedial program. Furthermore, because it usually does not involve an IQ score, there is far less stigmatization in an objective behavior rating.

In 1966, one of the authors was given the difficult task of assessing the skill levels of all one thousand residents in a state institution for the retarded. The use of standard IQ tests in the short time allotted would have been impossible, nor would the results have been particularly useful. Consequently, he devised a rudimentary objective behavior rating scale in just a few days. Over the years, with the able assistance of other staff at Fircrest School, Seattle Washington, the scale evolved rapidly. A state-wide group of psychologists and other professionals made important contributions to its final development. Now, the Washington Assessment and Training Scale (WATS) offers an objective method of evaluating the behavior of people with retarded behavior without the IQ stigma, the production of relatively inapplicable data, or the unnecessary use of professional staff time. This instrument measures a wide spectrum of skills ranging from basic self-help abilities (e.g., dressing) to complex academic tasks. The scale generates a "behaviorgram" which graphically displays a person's skills in all measures of behavior. Interjudge reliability is reported as above .90, and this is encouraging. But what is most encouraging is that this instrument, and others like it, are gaining increasing usage in the evaluation of retarded behavior.

SPECIAL EDUCATION

The behaviorally retarded child, with rare exception, has not been adequately assimilated into the public school system. Frequently, an arbitrary cutoff point such as a score of less than 70 on an IQ test determines who will be accepted and who will not. The authors feel that it is the responsibility of the educational system to take into account the academic needs of all children, irrespective of their present levels of academic performance. This can be largely accomplished through the establishment of ungraded schools as discussed earlier, wherein a child may be provided with a program commensurate with his present skill, rather than his present age. Unfortunately, the typical responses to the needs of those with special educational difficulties have so far been relatively meager. Haring and Lovitt (1967) noted four usual patterns of adjustment to this problem by the school: (1) providing the same curriculum, but reducing the rate of presentation, (2) establishing separate curricular procedures—in other words, treating the special education class as a discrete unit, (3) requiring that teachers meet certain educational requirements, such as having courses in the characteristics and particular origins of retardation, and (4) increasing the ratio of teachers to students and altering the classroom environment in other ways.

With few exceptions, these approaches have been relatively ineffective when not combined with a reward program in which reinforcement is contingent upon desired classroom performance. Such a program was reported by Haring and Kunzelmann (1966) who described the Experimental Education Unit (E.E.U.) of the University of Washington. An excellent example of objective teaching in action, the E.E.U. employs carefully programmed materials, automated teaching aids, and a well-designed contingency plan in which reinforcement tends to take the form of preferred activities. The Unit emphasizes the Premack principle, as discussed in Chapter 4. Low-strength classroom behaviors, such as attending to academic material or completing work, are reinforced by high-strength activities, often involving games, toys, and manipulation of other equipment.

The Unit is actually divided into high- and low-strength areas, and access to the high strength area is typically contingent upon completion of a particular task or a portion thereof. To increase the desirability of the high-strength area, both the ages and interests of the students are taken into account. Thus, highly favored record albums, miniature racing cars, and various science and craft objects are maintained in the junior high classroom while the room for preprimary level students contains clay, simple musical instruments, and a great variety of large toys which the children can manipulate as soon as they gain the privilege through appropriate responding. The students receive points which serve a dual process: they provide immediate reinforcement for the student and facilitate recording. Entrance into the high-strength area is contingent upon earning the required number of points.

Automated teaching aids help in transmitting and recording responses for each child. An event recorder, a device which records several separate events simultaneously by means of pens and movable rolls of paper, receives information from trained observers posted in observation booths. Pocket-size automated devices allow the teachers to relay instantly information to be recorded. Careful daily records are kept for each student so that his performance can be charted and his rate of progress on various tasks carefully examined. A child's daily record might include, in abbreviated form, the number of successful responses on programs in mathematics, reading, or language arts.

Academic programming, as discussed in Chapter 9, takes a central place in the E.E.U. Goals are set depending upon a child's baserate on various skills, and the task is broken down into small successive steps. At a given time, one child may be attempting to make simple form or color discriminations while a more advanced pupil in another room moves through his program in composition.

The E.E.U. has greatly expanded its range and depth of services in recent years, and has been a productive research center as well. Thousands of teachers and education students have had contact with the E.E.U., which has consistently disseminated new and important information concerning the direct application of many methods used in objective teaching.

TOKEN SYSTEMS IN SPECIAL EDUCATION

Token systems, you will recall, involve the dispensing of tokens as reinforcers for desirable behavior. In special education, students may earn such tokens by displaying appropriate classroom behavior or by successfully responding in academic areas. For example, a correct answer on a simple addition problem may earn a token or, depending on the progress of the student, several correct answers may be required before he is reinforced. Tokens are sometimes used as an intermediate step in moving from a tangible reward system in which food and candy are given to a mark system in which check marks are placed on a sheet which, when completely filled with marks, may be cashed in. It is obvious that this approach bears striking similarity to our currency system in which negotiable certificates or notes are earned instead of tangible products. Marks are very convenient records of progress and take on particular value as the student can see them accumulating on his sheet for his correct responses. They are far easier to dispense than tangible reinforcers, and it is usual to set up a kind of store in which students can select from a number of items or activities according to the number of marks or mark sheets they have earned.

Tokens and marks acquire their reinforcing qualities through association with tangible reinforcers. First, the teacher places a token such as a poker chip in the student's hand, immediately removes it and replaces it with a piece of food or candy saying something like, "Let's trade." Gradually, the teacher begins to require that the student hold on to the token for a second or two before allowing him to trade. This process may continue to the point at which the student holds the tokens he has earned for correct responding until the end of the session before he is permitted to cash them in for items or activities. The teacher introduces marks in a similar manner. Each mark is displayed to the student as he earns it (along with praise) and when his sheet is complete, it is placed in his hand and quickly replaced with a tangible reinforcer. A phrase such as, "Now that your page is filled, we'll trade," is used consistently. Just as with tokens, the student is gradually required to hold on to the sheet and trade it without assistance. This is usually learned quite easily. Eventually mark pages may be cashed in at the end of the session or, with more advanced students, saved for a more expensive item or activity.

Whether tokens or mark sheets are used, it is always desirable to maintain a wide variety of items and activities at different "prices" because of great variation in individual preference. Marks are especially useful in that they are amenable to use with an intermittent schedule of reinforcement such as a fixed-ratio schedule. At first, a mark sheet may contain only one or two boxes for marks and, consequently, one or two correct responses result in a full mark sheet. As the student acquires increasingly greater proficiency in a given task, a 4 : 1 reinforcement schedule may be quickly achieved by using four mark boxes per sheet, then six (6 : 1), and so on. Eventually, a student may be required to obtain as many as 32 or more marks before the sheet is filled and ready to be traded in for preferred items or activities.

It is not unusual for a question to be raised as to whether or not tangible or token reinforcement is really necessary to change behavior effectively and whether or not such reinforcement is applicable to special education. The effectiveness of reinforcement is, of course, well substantiated in the studies presented throughout this book, but how important is token reinforcement in modifying retarded behavior?

Birnbrauer et al. (1968), using data from a special classroom for retarded students, show rather conclusively the significance of token reinforcement. The teacher employed a mark system in which the students earned marks for correct responses in academic subjects such as arithmetic and writing, and earned extra marks if their performance was completely free of errors. All programmed material was carefully prepared by the staff who also did the recording. In addition to marks, the students were given knowledge of results regarding the accuracy of their performance. Mark sheets, which were kept in individual mark books, constituted different values enabling greater trade-in flexibility. A mark book, for example, might contain two 2¢ sheets and one 5¢ sheet, depending on the number of squares on the page. Under this program of token reinforcement via marks, student performance on academic tasks markedly improved, and youngsters began to display academic achievements normally thought impossible.

To test the actual role of the mark system in the increased learning of these students, the staff began a 21-day period of nonreinforcement. Marks were no longer given for correct responding for the 15 students involved. The contrast in the performances of most students between the usual mark reinforcement program and the nonreinforcement period was striking. While only five showed no significant change in performance, the remaining 10 students clearly deteriorated in their classroom behavior and work output. Six of these 10 showed a significant increase in errors and a decline in previous progress while the remaining four showed an increase in errors, a decline in study time, and a marked increase in disruptive behavior. One of the most capable students, for example, regressed from an average of 5% errors to a poor 66% error rate. Another student again began to display disruptive patterns of behavior which had previously been overcome when the token system was initiated.

In another study employing token reinforcement in a special education situation, Perline and Levinsky (1968) successfully eliminated a great deal of interfering behavior in a preschool classroom. Four children with severely retarded behavior, 8 to 10 years of age, were the subjects for the research. Interfering behaviors, which occurred at a high rate, were seriously impeding the learning of preacademic skills which were prerequisites for admission to the institution school. The researchers divided these interfering behaviors into the following five categories:

1   aggression toward peers
2   taking possession of objects belonging to others
3   aggression toward teachers
4   rising from chair
5   throwing objects

They collected baseline data over 5 days, 1 hour in the morning and 1 in the afternoon. Then they instituted a token system during the usual 2-hour morning and 2-hour afternoon sessions. Poker chip tokens were awarded on an intermittent basis for appropriate behavior which competed with the categories above. These could be traded for desired objects. As a result of the token system, all subjects showed a marked reduction in interfering behaviors. The greatest decrease occurred in aggression toward peers, a behavior which had previously been a major source of disruption in the classroom.

In the years since the first edition of this book, several additional comprehensive programs emphasizing positive outcomes via token systems have been developed. As we noted earlier, the use of student instituted contingencies is a relatively new method which offers promise in promoting greater self-direction. The contract system, developed essentially by Homme (1969), may be useful in cases of less severe overall retardation and has immediate application in most other teaching situations. Modeling, too, is a useful procedure in overcoming retarded behavior.

Broden et al. (1970) instituted a comprehensive program employing positive outcomes and a token system. They successfully eliminated most disruptive behaviors and increased the academic achievement of students with previously severe behavior problems and marked academic retardation.

A wide range of programs using token systems have been reported by Axelrod (1971). These were highly effective in improving learning disabilities. There are a number of natural reinforcers in the home (e.g., allowance, T.V. time) and at school (e.g., free time, access to special equipment) which the teacher can easily use to overcome retarded behavior once thought hopelessly immune to change.

SUMMARY

The diagnosis of "mental retardation" frequently sets into action a self-fulfilling prophecy in which the individual so labeled is excluded from an opportunity to remedy his educational deficits. Tens of thousands of these people are confined in public institutions which are not designed to provide the intensive learning environment required to return them to the community. Thus, we reject the excessive use of this label in favor of a precise description of behavior in relevant academic and social areas. Specific baserate measures of such behavior provide much more useful information than a broad performance measure such as the IQ test. The Washington Assessment and Training Scale (WATS) is an example of this method which is gaining wide usage. The term *retarded behavior* was introduced to define that behavior in which an individual reveals significant deficiencies in learning.

We cited studies indicating that even the IQ score, once thought so immutable, can be changed through positive expectancies and positive outcomes.

Retarded behavior appears less clearly a function of organic deficiency than was once believed, and there is increasing evidence to support the enormous role of environmental factors in producing retarded behavior. There is now growing emphasis on interfering behaviors which compete with adaptive behaviors and reduce overall development.

Since much retarded behavior is closely related to environmental deficiencies, the education of such individuals must be comprehensive and systematic. Deficits must be objectively assessed, and objective teaching procedures must be focussed on areas of greatest academic need. In short, a highly contingent environment must be developed.

We discussed some comprehensive environments designed to overcome retarded behavior. They included Premack systems, careful and detailed programming and individualization of materials to meet specific student needs. Token systems were also regarded to be highly functional in such programs as they increase objectivity and allow for meaningful reinforcement. Self-instituted contingencies appear useful in providing self-direction for those with retarded behavior.

REFERENCES

Allen, K. E., Henke, L. B., Harris, F. R., Baer, D. M., & Reynolds, N. J. Control of hyperactivity by social reinforcement of attending behavior. *Journal of Educational Psychology*, 1967, 58, 231–237.

Axelrod, S. Token reinforcement programs in special classes. *Exceptional Children*, 1971, 37, 371–379.

Birnbrauer, J. S., Wolf, M. M., Kidder, J. D., & Tague, C. E. Classroom behavior of retarded pupils with token reinforcement. In *Operant procedures in remedial speech and language training* (H. S. Sloane, Jr. and B. D. MacAulay, eds.). Boston: Houghton Mifflin Co., 1968.

Broden, M., Hall, R. V., Dunlap, A., & Clark, R. Effects of teacher attention and a token reinforcement system in a junior high school special education class. *Exceptional Children*, 1970, 36, 341–349.

Edlund, C. V. The effect on the behavior of children as reflected in the IQ scores when reinforced after each correct response. *Journal of Applied Behavior Analysis*, 1972, 5 (3), 317–319.

Haring, N. G., & Kunzelmann, H. P. The finer focus of therapeutic behavioral management. *Educational Therapy*, 1, *Special Child Publications*. Seattle, Washington: Bernie Straub, Publisher, 1966.

Haring, N. G., & Lovitt, T. C. Operant methodology and educational technology in special education. In *Methods in special education*. (N. G. Haring and R. Schiefelbüsch eds.). New York: McGraw-Hill, 1967.

Homme, L. E. *How to use contingency contracting in the classroom.* Champaign, Illinois: Research Press, 1969.

Perline, I. H., & Levinsky, D. Controlling maladaptive classroom behavior in the severely retarded. *American Journal of Mental Deficiency*, 1968, **73**, 74–78.

Rosenthal, R., & Jacobson, L. Teachers' expectancies as determinants of pupils' I.Q. gains. In *Studies in educational psychology* (R. C. Kuhlen, ed.). Waltham, Mass: Ginn/Blaisdell Publishing Co., 1968.

Soule, D. Teacher bias effects with severely retarded children. *American Journal of Mental Deficiency*, 1972, **72** (2), 208–211.

Wesman, A. G. Intelligent testing. *American Psychologist*, 1968, **23**, 267–274.

Witmer, J. M., Bornstein, A. V., & Dunham, R. M. The effects of verbal approval and disapproval upon the performance of third and fourth grade children on four subtests of the Wechsler intelligence scale for children. *Journal of School Psychology*, 1971, **9**, (3), 347–356.

SUGGESTED READINGS

Bijou, S., & Orlando, R. Rapid development of multiple schedule performances with retarded children. In *Case studies in behavior modification* (L. Ullmann and L. Krasner, eds.). New York: Holt, Rinehart & Winston, 1966.

Brison, D. A non-talking child in kindergarten: An application of behavior therapy. *Journal of School Psychology*, 1966, **4**, 65–69.

Galloway, C., & Galloway, K. C. Parent groups with a focus on precise behavior management. *Institute on Mental Retardation and Intellectual Development, Nashville, Tennessee: Peabody College for Teachers*, 1970, **VII**,(1).

Martin, G. L., & Powers, R. B. Attention span: an operant conditioning analysis. *Exceptional Children*, 1967, **33** 565–570.

Patterson, G. R., Jones, R., Whittier, J., & Wright, M. A behavior modification technique for the hyperactive child. *Behavior Research and Therapy*, 1965, **2**, 217–226.

11
The Socially Deprived Student

We state again, and with even greater insistence than before, that the economic factors which influence the social structure continue to have an especially cruel effect on the children of the Black, other minorities, and on the poor in general. For the very deprivation which afflicts the adult members of the family sets the stage for the deprivation of their children. This continuing poverty, fostered in large measure by unemployment, low wages, inflation, and inadequate training opportunities, drives the wedge between two societies ever further. The division can never be healed until active economic measures are taken to ensure decent jobs at decent wages for all who are willing and able to work. Equal educational opportunities are not enough, what is needed is *an opportunity for all people to become equally educated,* and the two are not the same.

The concept of equal educational opportunities for all assumes that most children will be equally capable of taking advantage of such opportunities. This assumption reflects a failure to consider the real environmental deprivation that occurs as a result of poverty and the effect of this deprivation on the ability of a child to benefit from the average school curriculum. It will be recalled from Chapter 7 that there is growing evidence which supports the stepwise development of skills. Academic skills do not generally emerge until the prerequisite responses are learned, and the economically deprived child is frequently forced to live in an environment which deprives him of an opportunity to learn necessary preacademic behavior. Elementary school curricula tend to be geared toward the performance of middle-class children living in relatively comfortable surroundings. The children of the poor, however, are frequently forced to live in barren, noisy, and overcrowded conditions in which they do not receive the stimulation and consistent reinforcement necessary for positive learning. Unemployed, frequently absent, or overworked parents, consequently depressed, anxious, apathetic, or alcoholic, may serve as primary models for their children's behavior. Thus, the economic deprivation of the family tends to contribute to the broader social deprivation of the child. The socially deprived child suffers in a great many ways. Here however, we will focus upon the educational aspects of social deprivation and the role of objective teaching in overcoming these academic deficits.

What we are saying, then, is that the socially deprived student enters school with already existing deficits. These deficits involve both specific tasks and motivational factors related to the history of past reinforcement. For such a student, equal opportunity to use available educational resources is not enough simply because the presently available educational resources themselves are insufficient to overcome the effects of social deprivation. He requires an educational environment which allows him to develop academic skills at a level equal to his middle-class peers. It is only fair for the socially deprived student to be given extra educational benefits, just as it is only right for his deprived parents to secure a fair share of society's resources.

While programs such as Head Start are encouraging, they must be intensified and extended beyond the preschool years. Academic gains, once made, should not be allowed to be diluted through years of later academic neglect.

CULTURAL CONFLICT

Not only does the socially deprived child enter school with preacademic deficiencies, but he frequently brings with him culturally learned responses which interfere with his functioning in a middle-class oriented classroom. Whether he is Black, Chicano, native American, or a member of any other excluded minority, he must often unlearn things he has learned before he can learn what is required of him in school. Language difficulties are especially hard to overcome since there have not been adequate programs to teach English to foreign-speaking students. Ethnocentricity, the peculiar tendency to assume that all other cultures are inferior to one's own, leads to misinterpretation of the behavior of the minority student on the part of the teacher and fellow students. Resulting discriminatory treatment creates profound damage to the minority student's estimate of his competence and worth. The combined handicaps of social deprivation and cultural conflict pose a challenging problem that can not be ignored if the continuous separation of people through simple misunderstanding and systematic exclusion is to be stopped.

INADEQUATE REINFORCEMENT AND SEQUENCING

The socially deprived child does not receive the degree of positive reinforcement necessary to develop and maintain the kinds of behavior required even by children just entering school. He may be frequently neglected due to economic necessity, left home alone while his mother is earning the family income or supplementing it by working outside. Of course, this tends to cut off access to social reinforcement so necessary for learning. In addition, the socially deprived child frequently has to compete with numerous brothers and sisters for attention, and many of his responses, though appropriate, are extinguished and lost through lack of positive reinforcement. Often large family size contributes to other difficulties and parents have a hard time keeping up with the activities of the various children. Thus, attention and other reinforcement is frequently given inconsistently and indiscriminately, tending to create patterns of behavior which are both interfering and difficult to extinguish. For example, children may learn that they receive additional parental attention or other reinforcement by teasing or annoying their brothers and sisters, and this pattern is easily generalized to a classroom situation.

When parents are tired and overburdened, they will often offer candy or other reinforcers to their children in an effort to get them to calm down. Of course, this only strengthens the disruptive behavior and places additional stress on already harried parents. Furthermore, since many economically deprived parents have neither the time nor the knowledge to arrange and maintain systematic contingencies for their children, the deprived child shows great inconsistencies in his behavior. This is a direct result of a disruption in sequencing, the lack of a stepwise progression to a desirable goal. Middle-class parents may go into great detail in planning their child's environment so as to promote learning. They tend to have a fair degree of information about just what their children can do. This planning results in reinforcement of more or less appropriate behavior, behavior which is neither far above nor far below the child's ability. The socially deprived child, unlike the middle-class child, has his environment arranged as much by circumstances of the moment as anything else, since environmental stability is often dependent on economic stability.

DISPLACED-ROLE MODELS

The Sarason and Ganzer study (1971) helps elevate the part played by the role model to its rightful place. Children scan the learning environment for adult figures to imitate and emulate. The socially deprived student, seeing the despair and frustration in his parents' lives, or rarely seeing his parents at all, is frequently forced to search elsewhere for a role model whose behavior he perceives as promoting success and satisfaction. In the ghetto, suggest Sarason and Ganzer, the role models may be those adults who have achieved visible symbols of success via socially deviant behavior such as crime. The socially deprived student can all too easily learn that the road to crime is the main road to success.

The frequent absence of socially functional role models among the families and neighborhoods of the socially deprived makes the teacher's job all the more demanding. All too often the ghetto teacher may be an unexciting model for the students he teaches. If he is perceived as prejudiced, he is displaced, ridiculed, or even attacked by his students. If what he teaches is irrelevant and unreinforcing, he will be ignored and induce classroom disruption. Because no one teacher can serve as an ideal role model for all of his students, he should not hesitate to invite into his classroom other minority adults, such as lawyers, physicians, scientists, entertainers, sports figures, business people, and working people who can serve as socially adaptive models. By raising his students' aspirations, and by encouraging movement in these new directions through reinforcement and good programming, the teacher of socially deprived students can expect accelerated progress in his classroom.

EFFECTS OF PUNISHMENT

In addition to inadequate reinforcement and sequencing, the deprived child may also be subjected to erratically dispensed punishment which is often the result of overcrowding and generally poor housing. This increases the chance for conflict between parent and child. Severe punishment tends to suppress the behavior proceeding it. Often the deprived child is punished for behavior which is important for later learning in school. In a small, crowded apartment or house, speech, so crucial to academic performance, can be severely limited if punishment occurs whenever the child explores his verbal repertoire. Avoidance patterns also develop in the face of punishment and the deprived child may begin to limit his range of behavior in accordance with the degree of threat. Objective teaching, through its reliance on positive reinforcement, introduces the deprived child to a wide range of experiences which allow him to overcome the handicaps imposed by a history of arbitrary punishment.

MOTIVATIONAL DEFICITS

The socially deprived student, then, brings to school a more limited and erratic pattern of behavior than the middle-class child. His disruptive behaviors, frequently learned at home, often may be increased since they permit him to escape academic subjects for which he is inadequately prepared. In addition, his teacher may find that he does not respond to usual social reinforcement so important to the middle-class student.

It is of great importance that the teacher understand the factors which limit the socially deprived student's functioning in the classroom so that he may design an environment which both fills in basic learning gaps and establishes positive attitudes toward learning. The teacher has to take into account motivational differences between the deprived and nondeprived student. He will then be better equipped to deal with the unique motivational tendencies of the socially deprived child.

The deprived child, unlike his middle-class counterpart, enters school with a history deficient in successful experiences due to the factors mentioned: inadequate reinforcement, inconsistent sequencing, inadvertent reinforcement of interfering behaviors, displaced-role models, and excess punishment. This history is essentially one of failure, and the teacher who approaches the already deprived and unsuccessful student with threat of further failure will begin the process which may ultimately lead to early dropping out.

Gruen and Zigler (1968) offer valuable experimental evidence of class based differences in motivation. While these researchers compared groups of retarded, lower-class, and middle-class children, here we will consider only the comparison between the lower-class (deprived) and middle-class children. Sixty children served as subjects in each group, and each group was further divided into a variety of subgroups assigned to various experimental conditions. The children were permitted to play certain games in which they experienced different kinds of outcomes. Finally, the criterion task was introduced which was a simple three choice discrimination problem. For each subject, only one of the three choices (knobs) was "correct" and received partial reinforcement. Selection of the other two knobs by the subject went unreinforced. The major question concerning the experimenters was essentially which group would settle for less—how much patterning (left-middle-right) would occur among the children in each group in their effort to find a higher paying option, and which group, deprived or middle-class, would tend to ensure at least partial reinforcement by picking the constant but low-paying option without much shifting. Since the children in each group had been matched for general ability level, this was not a factor. The results were clear: the deprived (lower-class) children showed the greater amount of maximizing; that is, consistent responding to the "correct" but low-paying stimulus. The middle-class children tended to shoot the works; they showed significantly more shifting as they tried to find a higher paying option than the "correct" one. The experimenters interpret these findings as indicating that middle-class children have a greater expectancy of success than deprived children. They conclude:

> In the middle-class child this expectancy [of success] is relatively high and therefore he is unwilling to settle for that degree of success provided by the maximization

response. On the other hand . . . lower-class children have a lower expectancy of success and are therefore more willing to give up the patterning response in favor of the maximizing response.

Since the children were matched on general ability level, the crucial variable was socioeconomic. The deprived children came from low-rental housing projects and the mean income of their families was under $3000 per year. The middle-class children were selected from higher rent areas and their fathers tended to be in white collar and professional categories. In other words, the environmental factors in their family living arrangements tended to reduce the aspiration of the deprived children. Unfortunately, the public tendency to view school as a competitive situation reduces still further the ability of the deprived child to function in school. Failure at home is compounded by failure in school and whatever motivation may have initially survived is often further suppressed. Finally, since a history of success appears to increase the tendency to try new approaches and a history of failure appears to reduce innovation, middle-class children are frequently more creative in their approach to new problems. Deprived children, in an effort to avoid further failure and to maximize the probability of even minor success, often persevere on rigid, unadaptive modes of problem solving. The introduction of success in a school situation can counteract much of the failure experienced at home and increase the creativity of the socially deprived student.

INCREASING MOTIVATION THROUGH REINFORCEMENT

Specific applications of positive reinforcement have proven to be of particular value to the socially deprived child. Working with adolescent dropouts, Homme (1966) employed the Premack principle in a rather inventive way. A "contract" was drawn up between teachers and students which outlined the desired high-strength activity (e.g., a coffee break) that could be earned for specific amounts of low-strength responding (e.g., spelling). In the course of the day, the students moved from low-strength to high-strength activities so that the work became gradually less aversive and more reinforcing as the day progressed. Not only did Homme's approach result in an increase in desirable social behavior, but in just six weeks the mean academic gain was about half a grade level. Furthermore, not one of the dropouts dropped out of the program when the contract arrangement was instituted, a remarkable achievement in itself.

The study by MacDonald et al. (1970) discussed in Chapter 5 involved not only the teachers but mediators from the community as well. Working together, they successfully carried out a contract system which reduced the truancy rate of socioeconomically deprived ninth-grade students. Of particular interest is the fact that the contracts, "deals" as they were referred to, were carefully integrated into the students lives not merely at school but in their neighborhoods as well.

For example, one student was permitted access to the local pool hall contingent upon school attendance. A control group of counselors, having more contacts with the students but using no "deals," showed significantly less ability to reduce absenteeism. These researchers are to be commended for their realization that community involvement is an important feature in an effective learning environment.

Between 1969 and 1971 we served as consultants and behavior specialists in Seattle's predominantly Black central area under a federally financed dropout prevention program. The program gave us an opportunity to apply a wide range of objective teaching methods to the education of socially deprived adolescents in the seventh, eighth, and ninth grades. In addition to other reinforcement approaches, we found that a contract system was especially effective not only in substantially reducing disruptive behavior which interfered with academic achievement, but in reducing absenteeism as well. In the second year of the study the contract system, along with other reinforcement methods, enabled us to reduce the rate of truancy 18.4% as compared to a matched control group in a traditional teaching setting.

The severely deprived adolescent who is not afforded an opportunity to succeed in school due to an inadequately planned academic program tends to avoid the school situation. He may either escape physically or engage in daydreaming while his middle-class classmates move ahead. Furthermore, there is a relationship between poor academic performance and delinquency which might reasonably be considered to contain some "causal" elements. The inability to derive social reinforcement through academic accomplishment may very well move the socially deprived adolescent to try other spheres of action which gain him such reinforcement through peer approval. While comprehensive social action is required to remedy the conditions which frequently set the stage for school failure, establishing an opportunity for academic success in school may serve to decrease delinquent behavior outside school. When we consider the total opportunities open to an individual to obtain reinforcement and relate these to socioeconomic class, it is quite clear that the student from a deprived home environment has little chance of being reinforced in a strongly middle-class school environment. Consequently, he may then move outside the classroom for most of his reinforcement and may turn to delinquent activity because of the prospect of immediate gain. The introduction of extensive opportunities for reinforcement into the classroom may reverse this process. This approach was successfully employed by Staats and Butterfield (1965) in their work with a 14-year-old Mexican-American boy.

The youngster's history was replete with problems of delinquency including truancy, running away, and burglary. He had received failing grades in all subjects and was considered to be "incorrigible." His disruptive classroom behavior led him to be disliked by many of his teachers and he was even considered to be retarded by some. When he entered the reinforcement program, he was reading at approximately the second-grade level, and the program focused mainly on increasing his reading skills. A published reading program was employed in which each story was presented in terms of vocabulary words, oral reading, and comprehension-oriented materials. Three types of tokens, valued at various fractions of a penny, were dispensed by the researchers for correct responding. The tokens could be cashed in for items the boy liked.

In the vocabulary section of each story, correct pronunciation of words printed on cards led to reinforcement. After the vocabulary section for the story was completed, the boy was then required to read paragraphs. If he completed a paragraph without errors, he received a high value token; if he had to repeat it before getting it fully correct, he received a midvalue token. After completing all the paragraphs in a given story, he moved on to the comprehension section. Here tokens were dispensed at irregular intervals as long as the boy attended to the materials. The boy then wrote his answers to questions about the story in a space provided. Correct and perfectly spelled answers earned him a high value token while incorrectly spelled or incorrect answers which were later corrected earned him a midvalue token. There were occasional rechecks of certain vocabulary words to ascertain the degree of retention.

The results were quite dramatic. The boy's attention span progressively increased and his retention of words improved considerably. His reading ability increased from the second-grade level to a better than fourth-grade level, and his general behavior clearly improved. Not only did he pass other courses for the first time, but he actually passed all of his courses. This accomplishment is particularly significant in view of the fact that the entire training period was only about 4½ months and at a cost of only $20.31 in cash value of tokens. Since the boy had to emit more and more correct reading responses to get reinforced as the training progressed, he was, in effect, gradually weaned away from external reward and apparently began to read for the sake of reading. Sustained performance in the absence of concrete reinforcement is required in most schools and thus the youngster was far better equipped to return to a normal classroom environment. The researchers also noted that the specific nature of the reading program enables a person with only a high school education and reading ability to administer it. The real manpower shortage in education precludes much intensive personalized teaching at this time, and programs such as these can easily be carried out by teacher's assistants or even volunteers. Advanced students may be encouraged to assist their less skillfull classmates. This pyramid system may not only help socially deprived children to learn more, but it may alter traditional concepts of the virtues of keen academic competition. Increased cooperation among students is an ingredient of a good learning environment.

In an effort to explore still further the effects of expectancy and delivery of positive outcomes, Chadwick and Day (1971) established a token system in which tokens earned for academic performance could be cashed in for food, various other items, or field trips. The students were 30 Blacks and Chicanos from deprived, low income homes, between the ages of 8 and 12. The results were impressive: on all three indicators of performance employed, work time, rate of output and accuracy, there were substantial improvements. The California Achievement Test indicated an average .42 year improvement in grade placement as a result of the 11-week program.

One of the most comprehensive applications of reinforcement and other methods of objective teaching to the socially deprived child is discussed by Risley (1968). Though cited briefly in Chapter 4, it is important enough to warrant in-depth study. The Juniper Gardens Project, operated in conjunction with the University of Kansas, is a direct attempt to overcome the effects of social deprivation. Actually, two programs are carried out simultaneously: the Turner House program for the so-called hard-core group and the Parent-Teacher Preschool for the group termed upwardly mobile.

The Turner House program focuses on 4-year-olds from families in which there are a great many problems including extremely poor housing, alcoholism, unemployment, neglect, etc. The parents, sometimes for a fee, get the children ready for preschool each day but do not participate in the program themselves. Upon arrival, many of the children are given breakfast and also have an opportunity to receive additional food (milk, cookies, etc.) as rewards for appropriate behavior later. This latter technique pairs tangible (food) and social reinforcement (teacher praise, smiles) largely because these children do not always respond for social reinforcement alone due to their environmental history. Since the basic purpose of the program is to fill in educational gaps in preparation for public school attendance, learning to respond for social reinforcement is important as it is the major form of reward used in public schools. In addition, the children lack many of the rudimentary social amenities, such as saying "good morning" to the teacher. Learning some of these kinds of socially desired behaviors may increase the chance of a child's being more warmly accepted later by his public school teacher.

Using a modified Premack technique, the teachers set up requirements for the use of such highly sought items as tricycles and toys. Children were permitted to use an object only after naming or describing it or completing a similar task. Furthermore, a "switching operation" was initiated in an effort to cut down the great amount of movement around the classroom by the children, as frequent movement interfered with learning. Parts of the classroom were designated according to their function, such as the block corner, and the children were permitted to move from area to area only after completing a required task (matching pegs in a pegboard). Problem solving on the pegboard greatly increased and the children also tended to spend longer sustained periods in the various areas. A simple pegboard problem increased the amount of time spent in a given area from 10 to 26 minutes.[1]

[1]The reduction in student switching from one area to another by means of requiring the student to complete a task before making his switch is further elaborated upon in a study by Jacobson et al. (1969).

The researchers developed an especially creative approach to encourage the children to use much more description and detail in answering questions put to them by their teachers. Since children know many more words than they use, Risley attempted to expand the repertoire of spoken responses. A baserate was established over 13 days, and it was found that the average answer to certain frequently repeated questions was about one-and-a-half words. By using various kinds of prompts arranged in a logical sequence, the teachers were able to coax more and more complete answers and descriptions from the children. For example, when a boy answered that he had seen "a doggie" on the way to school, his teacher pursued the question further with, "what kind of doggie?" As the child expanded his answer to a "German Shepherd doggie," he was reinforced. Logical prompts of this kind were presented in such a manner as to encourage the child to "chain" his responses together. In other words, the teachers made reinforcement contingent upon answers of gradually increasing length including connected sentences. Significant increases in length of response were found. The children also generalized their new skill to additional questions, answering more elaborately and descriptively. Average answers to new questions were more than five times longer than the answers they had given during pretraining questioning (baserate). Since academic education is so heavily verbal in orientation, this new narrative ability could certainly be expected to contribute to improved performance in school.

Teaching the children to imitate was also an important aspect of the Juniper Gardens Project. As has been noted earlier, imitation or modeling plays an especially important role in the development of language, and the socially deprived child almost invariably presents language problems. Using an approach similar to that of Baer et al., the teacher first reinforced the children for approximating gross motor movements, facial movements, and finally spoken sounds. At various points in the modeling program, the children were tested to determine the degree of imitative learning they had acquired. In about a year the children learned to imitate well enough to repeat short novel sentences prompted by the teacher. The next step, of course, is to increase the length of the imitated sentences still further.

The Parent-Teacher Preschool program directly involved the mothers of deprived children. They were given daily instruction in how to provide their children with the necessary preacademic skills to permit them to function in public school. While the parents and children in this program were generally more motivated than those in the hard-core Turner House program, Risley points out that inexpensive incentives were sometimes given to the parents for their participation in the Preschool.

In addition to usual preschool activities, the parents were taught to administer programmed materials to their children in such areas as counting and color naming. Since the techniques were as new to the parents as to the children, it was quite typical for the mothers to make mistakes in teaching their children.

For example, they would often present a task far above their child's ability level and then threaten or scold him in an effort to get him to respond correctly. To overcome this the mothers were given instructions which they were to read before presenting materials to their children. The instructions told them what to do (e.g., hold up an object), how to ask the question, and what responses to reinforce. Two innovations helped the mothers acquire still more expertise in the technique of objective teaching. First, they were assigned to teach children other than their own. Second, they were given feedback (a red light) whenever they dispensed social reinforcement in the form of praise. These were effective in increasing the amount of praise that was given and coercive methods were drastically reduced. After the mothers worked with other children, they were reassigned to their own. Though they transferred their improved techniques to the teaching of their own children, the mothers seemed to interact somewhat differently with their own than with other children. Nevertheless, the program was instrumental in giving the mothers the kind of teaching skills necessary to train their children in important areas of academic preparation.

COMPENSATORY EDUCATION

Despite effective innovations in compensatory education such as those just described, a paper was published in the Harvard Educational Review (Jensen, 1969) which cast a dark but hopefully temporary shadow over much of our promising new vista. A central concept of the article was "heritability" which, broadly defined by Jensen, simply means that portion of the differences among a population on a given trait (e.g., intelligence) attributable to hereditary (genetic) factors. While Jensen noted (1969) that high heritability (i.e., a strong genetic influence) may not necessarily be unchangeable, he nevertheless defended the position (1972) that:

> . . . the probability is very small that two individuals whose IQs differ by, say 20 or more points have the same genotypes [inherited organic structures] for intelligence or that the one with the lower IQ has the higher genetic value.

The basis of an individual's intellectual handicap, and Black handicaps in particular, implies Jensen, may be the lower "genetic value" of intelligence he possesses, genetic value meaning the strength of the inherited factor. Furthermore, he argues, it should not be any more surprising to find genetically influenced differences between races in intelligence than in body structure or susceptibility to various diseases.

Finally, Jensen concludes, even if major environmental factors could be found which improved intelligence, the overall average IQ of the entire population would change without affecting the relative position of a given genetic (racial) group. In other words, even if improved educational techniques could raise overall IQ, according to this point of view, certain racial groups, handicapped by the anchor of their genetically inferior intelligence, would sink to the bottom of the population. And, despite his token assertions that environmental changes may ameliorate certain learning difficulties, he nevertheless seems to believe that ". . . compensatory education has been tried and it apparently has failed [1969, p. 2]."

Anastasi (1972), after questioning Jensen's position on theoretical grounds, states:

> To draw conclusions regarding such group differences from probabilities estimated from intragroup heritability ratios is logically equivalent to diagnosing a child's brain damage in terms of the base rate, with no attempt to obtain a case history or other pertinent data about the individual.

A truly objective approach to this question of the primary influences on "intelligent" behavior requires that we suspend our personal biases and examine Jensen's assertions on their own merit. Briefly, let us analyze some of Jensen's contentions.

First, Jensen's definitions of Caucasian and Negro are unclear. There is sufficient genotypic overlapping to raise serious questions about the meaning of his findings. There are few Blacks in this country who do not have some Caucasian ancestry, and many people who are phenotypically Caucasian have some Black ancestry. Genotypic admixture is a fact of life and will likely alter the entire genetic picture in generations to come, weakening still further the already shakey ground upon which a racial analysis of intelligence uneasily rests.

Second, recent studies cited in the previous chapter indicate that IQ scores themselves are amenable to change through reinforcement. If even simple reinforcement can alter the level of performance on the IQ test itself, it is reasonable to imagine that massive systematic reinforcement administered within the total learning environment would improve the behavior measured by IQ tests still more.

We find no evidence to refute our assumption that academic deficiencies among Blacks and other minorities reflect deficiences in the learning environment promoted by socioeconomic factors.

Third, an enlightening study by Vane (1971) revealed that when subtle socioeconomic background factors were taken into account, correlated differences in IQ scores could be detected. The 120 Black children studied were either in Head Start or prekindergarten programs, or in a control group. Warner's index of status characteristics (ISC), which took into account such factors as parents' occupation, type of house, etc., successfully separated the children into upper-lower class and lower-lower class. "On the Boehm Test of Concept Formation, the upper-lower class control group children scored significantly higher than the lower-lower class control group children [p. 395]." In addition, Vane suggests that "the results indicated that the common practice of grouping all disadvantaged children in one category (lower class) masks differences in socioeconomic background that affect the children's school performance."

While the advocate of racial differences in intelligence might argue differently, we feel that if subtle environmental differences are so closely related to intellectual performance, and if changes in the learning environment promote rapid gains, an environmental rather than a hereditary interpretation fits the data best.

Finally, we find Jensen's cynical view of the effectiveness of compensatory education so premature as to defy our comprehension. New research almost unanimously supports the concept of compensatory education as an effective means of promoting gain in academic performance. Projects such as Head Start, Juniper Gardens, and others are continually refuting Jensen's position that compensatory education has failed. If anything, compensatory education within the framework of objective teaching is still in its infancy. But the child is doing well and growing stronger, nourished by the solid success of its initial effectiveness.

The effects of busing, which will be discussed shortly, point again to the fact that environmental changes appear to enable socially deprived children to make academic gains upon and not merely stay in the same relative position as their middle-class peers.

In light of these findings, we argue that Jensen's attempt to find the answer to disparities in intellectual performances between Blacks and Whites through vague genetic concepts will continue to prove ineffective. We invite Dr. Jensen to join us in exploring the potential of objective teaching and compensatory education in overcoming the effects of early environmental deficiency. This, we believe, will obviate the meaningless search for genetic limits upon intelligence which has strengthened neither education nor racial harmony.

BUSING

The prematurity of Jensen's condemnation of compensatory education is rivaled by Armor's (1972) view that the busing of school children to achieve racial balance has not promoted significant academic gain. In a recent article (Goodall, 1972), T. F. Pettigrew effectively challenges Armor's conclusions and points out numerous defects in Armor's analysis. To begin with, Pettigrew reveals that in Armor's own study some of the students classified as bused were not, and some classified as not bused actually were. In one case attitude scales were completed in school, in another at home without provision for differential scoring to take into account possible "help" that these students might have received from parents anxious to ensure that their children's attitudinal responses corresponded to their own. Furthermore, Pettigrew argues that samples from which Armor drew his conclusions were selectively picked and consequently the results were biased. Armor, Pettigrew points out, failed to take into account the results of busing as reported in seven other cities. These showed statistically significant gains in math and/or reading by Black children that were bused, and frequently these gains tended to close the preexisting academic gaps between Black and White children. There is also evidence of academic gains for the White children in the integrated schools.

Pettigrew further suggests that "the [Armor] article establishes unrealistically high standards by which to judge the success of the racial desegregation of schools." For example, in Armor's study, the achievement gains of Black students had to be statistically significantly greater than White gains for the desegregation of the school to be considered successful. "But such a standard," insists Pettigrew, "ignores the possibility that both racial groups can make meaningful educational advances in interracial schools."

In addition to the methodological questions of how one evaluates the effects of busing to achieve racial desegregation upon academic achievement, there is another basic question which seems to have been ignored: the definition of education. If one accepts a narrow definition, education may be considered a simple process of learning academic and other specific practical skills. But if education is defined more broadly, that is as a process by which students become prepared to meet not merely intellectual but emotional and social challenges as well, than it is very difficult to conceive of segregated schools as providing a good quality learning environment. Whatever one's definition, however, we feel that the issue of busing must be removed from the emotional and political contexts in which it has been so inappropriately placed. The busing of school children to achieve racial integration is fundamentally an educational question which must be addressed objectively and in a spirit of good will toward *all* children.

SUMMARY

In this chapter we pointed out the close relationship between economic deprivation and inadequate school performance. The concept of equal educational opportunities is not sufficient to deal with learning deficits arising directly from an impoverished environment. We emphasized that what is needed is an opportunity for all to become equally educated. This implies that those with environmental handicaps should receive additional educational resources so that they can derive full benefit from public education facilities.

The effects of environmental deprivation upon academic performance were examined closely. Cultural competition, primarily affecting racial and ethnic minorities, is often a serious educational handicap. Children from impoverished homes have frequently failed to receive adequate reinforcement for desirable behavior because of large family size and absent parents. These same factors impede the systematic sequencing of learning experiences for socially deprived children, and inconsistency results in extremely spotty learning. The absence of adequate role models may deny the socially deprived student an adequate adult figure to emulate and to pattern his own behavior after.

Excessive punishment produces side effects which reduce desirable as well as undesirable responses. Basic preacademic skills are often lacking as the socially deprived child enters school.

Motivational deficits also present a problem, since the socially deprived child may not respond for the same social reinforcement which motivates the middle-class child. Furthermore, the child from an impoverished background tends to have lower expectancies than the middle-class child and is willing to settle for a lower level of academic performance.

Reinforcement is particularly applicable to the socially deprived child, increasing both motivation and rate of learning. Token systems and monetary reinforcement programs have been quite successful.

We described a comprehensive project for socially deprived children which employed a wide variety of objective teaching techniques. It included parent training geared to generalize reinforcement procedures back in the home. One of the more difficult problems to overcome was insufficient verbal responding by the children. The teachers were able to deal with this by a systematic probing technique which resulted in much lengthier narrations by the children. Teenage students also benefit from objective teaching, and contracts between student and teacher have substantially increased learning. Especially effective are those contracts which involve people from the student's neighborhood as well as his teachers.

In view of the marked success of compensatory education employing objective teaching methods, we took issue both with Jensen's premature rejection of compensatory education and his genetic analysis of intelligence. We also took to task the emotional and biased views regarding busing for racial integration and urged that busing be treated as an educational rather than a political issue.

REFERENCES

Anastasi, A. Interpretation of heritability: A rejoinder. *American Psychologist*, 1972, 27 (10), 975.

Armor, D. J. The evidence on busing. *The Public Interest*, Summer, 1972.

Chadwick, B. A., & Day, R. G. Systematic reinforcement: Academic performance of underachieving students. *Journal of Applied Behavior Analysis*, 1971, 4 (4), 311–319.

Goodall, K. The Anti-busing paper—wayward and wrong. *Psychology Today*, 1972, 6 (6) 42–44.

Gruen, G., & Zigler, E. Expectancy of success and the probability learning of middle-class, lower-class, and retarded children. *Journal of Abnormal Psychology,* 1968, **73** 343–352.

Homme, L. Human motivation and the environment. In *The learning environment: relationships to behavior modification and implications for special education* (R. Whelan, ed). Lawrence, Kansas: University of Kansas Publications, 1966.

Jacobson, J. M., Bushell, D., Jr., & Risley, T. Switching requirements in a head start classroom. *Journal of Applied Behavior Analysis,* 1969, **2** (1), 43–47.

Jensen, A. R. I.Q. and scholastic achievement. *Harvard Educational Review,* 1969, **39** (1), 1–24.

Jensen, A. R. Interpretation of heritability. *American Psychologist,* 1972, **27** (10), 973–975.

MacDonald, W. S., Gallimore, R., & MacDonald, G. Contingency counseling by school personnel: An economical model of intervention. *Journal of Applied Behavior Analysis,* 1970, **3** (3), 175–182.

Risley, T. Learning and lollypops. *Psychology Today,* 1968, **1** (8), 28–31, 62–65.

Sarason, I. G., & Ganzer, V. J. *Modeling: An approach to the rehabilitation of juvenile offenders.* Final report to Dept. of H.E.W. for partially supporting grant No. 15-P-55303, June, 1971.

Staats, A. W., & Butterfield, W. H. Treatment of nonreading in a culturally deprived juvenile delinquent: An application of reinforcement principles. *Child Development,* 1965, **32,** 925–942.

Vane, J. R. Importance of considering background factors when evaluating the effects of compensatory education programs designed for young children. *Journal of School Psychology,* 1971, **9** (4), 393–398.

SUGGESTED READINGS

Exceptional Children, 1970, **37** (2) Entire Issue.

Sweet, R. C., & Ringness, T. A. Variations in the intelligence test performance in referred boys of differing racial and socioeconomic backgrounds as a function of feedback or monetary reinforcement. *Journal of School Psychology,* 1971, **9** (4), 399–409.

12
Severely Deviant Behavior: The Emotionally Disturbed Child

There is now ample evidence to suggest that the very procedures which have proven so effective in changing disruptive patterns of behavior in the classroom can be used with comparable effectiveness in altering the severely deviant modes of responding that characterize many emotionally disturbed children. In fact, the same fundamental change occurring in the educational system is also apparent in the agencies and institutions which serve the emotionally disturbed child. Objective teaching regards much of the severely deviant behavior of the emotionally disturbed child as an extreme example of behavior patterns which are commonly seen in the classroom. In this chapter we will present a representative sample of such behavior modification approaches. While it would be somewhat unusual for cases as severe as those to be presented to occur in the average classroom, they nevertheless provide further understanding of the essential principles discussed throughout the book. The material in this chapter, then, should prove a useful addition to the background of all teachers, but especially of those who work with the severely disturbed.

BEHAVIOR MODIFICATION

Just as objective teaching requires an initial statement of the specific academic behavior to be learned by the student, the use of behavior modification techniques requires a precise definition of the deviant behavior to be changed.

Both, of course, require a baserate to measure degree of change. Practitioners of behavior modification, then, tend to avoid referring to a pattern of behavior as a syndrome or disease, as is common in traditional approaches. Instead, they attend to those specific deviant behaviors which are most relevant to a child's functioning and attempt to modify them through systematic techniques. This should not suggest a totally atomistic view of the individual (although, of course, this sometimes occurs) as the relationships that exist among various interactions with the environment are of great importance. Furthermore, there is emerging a growing recognition that while we are observing behavior, the individual that is behaving must not be disregarded as an experiencing human being. We believe that the precise modification of behavior does not require a mechanistic view of man, that it can be conducted within an ethical humanistic framework.

CHILDHOOD AUTISM

The pattern of deviant behavior known as childhood autism was first discussed by Leo Kanner in 1943, and constitutes an important area of potential work in behavior modification. According to Kanner, the grossly deviant actions of autistic children are due to constitutional predispositions and inadequate parent-child relationships, both contributing to deficiencies in "ego" development. Children termed autistic may display a wide range of bizarre behaviors, but generally reports tend to indicate the following characteristics:

1 *desire for sameness of environment* (narrow range of behavior) and tantrums, screaming, etc., when changes are instituted (related to this is a tendency toward "insulation" from others)
2 *gross language deficiencies* (including cases of total failure to develop language or idiosyncratic use of language)
3 *self-destructive, disruptive, or other dangerous behavior*

Kanner's view of childhood autism is rather traditional. That is, he acknowledges the role of environmental factors, but employs an inferential concept of faulty ego development, possibly constitutional in nature. As of yet there has been no significant evidence of a constitutional (e.g., genetic) influence and while it is possible that such a factor may eventually be discovered, experimental evidence supports the strong influence of environmental variables.

RANGE OF BEHAVIOR

Ferster and DeMyer (1962) examined the autistic child within an experimental framework and noted the initial narrow range of behavior. Patrick, one of the children studied, was 3½-years-old but had been hospitalized for 14 months. He would not respond to his name and had severe temper tantrums when his routine was changed. He and two other children were placed in a room containing an array of interesting devices, including a pinball machine, a candy vending machine, and an electric train. The machines could be operated by either coins or keys and were used as reinforcing consequences for the children. Each child remained in the room alone for several sessions and the pieces of apparatus, recording equipment, etc., were completely automated. Since the children were deprived of food between meals, candy and food served as powerful reinforcers as the study began. At first, a press of a key obtained a coin which operated all of the reinforcing apparatus in the room. High rates of key pressing were recorded and records were kept to determine how the coins were used by the children. It was clear that the children had a narrow range of behavior and tended to focus on the food dispensing machines. The experimenters then widened the children's repertoire of responses by activating the machines systematically. In other words, coins only worked for certain machines at certain times but were wasted if put in a machine whose coin slot was not lighted. The vending machine was also used to permit discriminations by the children as the candy supply in each of eight slots was varied. Match to sample tasks were also introduced and the children had to match a figure (e.g., a colored dot) to a sample figure (another dot) to obtain a coin reinforcement. When a child matched two figures incorrectly, the machine stopped for a short time. More and more difficult matches were required before the children received reinforcement.

The results clearly support the usefulness of reinforcement in widening the range of behavior in these children. The children were required to do not only more but also more complex tasks in order to obtain reinforcement. A similar procedure might well improve the repertoire of responses of autistic children at home. The high rates of initial interfering behaviors such as tantrums decreased gradually throughout the sessions. More desirable behavior patterns were apparently impeding the undesirable behaviors—a pleasant turn of events.

GROSS LANGUAGE DEFICIENCY

The central role that verbal communication plays in a complex society places severe limitations on those who fail to adequately acquire the ability to speak. Poor language development is an immediate handicap in both academic and social learning, affecting the total life of the individual. Verbal behavior is a function of learning and thus is as amenable to improvement as most other behaviors. On the other hand, language development is extremely complex when compared to many motor skills and requires a particularly systematic approach employing a great deal of modeling and positive reinforcement at carefully programmed steps.

While inadequate language development is itself a serious problem, certain children may not only present a language problem but may also have a number of markedly deviant responses. In some cases, deviant behavior may follow poor language development, but the frequency with which deviant behavior precedes or accompanies language deficiency tends to suggest a competing or interfering function in many cases. Consequently, it is necessary to modify deviant behavior in conjunction with a course of language development and unless this is recognized, many hours will be spent without result. If a child is moving hyperactively about the room, he will not attend to the teacher or therapist; if he is not looking at your mouth and listening to the sounds you emit, he will not be able to imitate.

The work of Lovaas (1966) in developing speech in previously nonspeaking autistic children represents a remarkable achievement in behavior modification. Lovaas worked with a group of so-called psychotic children at U.C.L.A., all of whom had major speech defects ranging from total mutism to echolalia (the tendency to imitate words or phrases). Many of these children had undergone traditional psychotherapeutic treatment to no avail, and the severely deviant behavior which accompanied their speech deficiences presented an enormous challenge to those who worked with them. The children did not, at first, respond to social reinforcement. Since speech development is usually dependent upon such reinforcement, it was necessary to build up social reinforcers through pairing them with primary or tangible reinforcers. For some of the children, however, edibles were heavily used throughout much of the training.

The program consisted of two parts, the establishment of verbal imitation and the development of appropriate language usage. The latter, of course, was dependent on the former as it was necessary for the children to acquire a vocabulary before conversational language could be attempted. Primary reinforcement in the way of the children's meals was given for correct responding, and incorrect responding resulted in temporary withdrawal of reinforcement or, in some cases, punishment.[1]

---

[1]While punishment is generally inadvisable for several reasons (see Chapter 5), it is sometimes required in cases of severely deviant behavior which totally interferes with a child's functioning or which is destructive. For example, certain institutionalized children may bang their heads against hard or sharp objects causing hematomas, while others damage their eyes unless continually physically restrained. In another paper (Lovaas et al., 1965), dangerous self-destructive behavior was successfully suppressed via mild electric shock, which, though unpleasant, was harmless. The alternatives to this technique (heavy drug use, years of physical restraint, etc.) tend to be far worse than the brief discomfort resulting from aversive techniques. Humane use of aversive stimulation to overcome dangerous or damaging behavior in children should not be confused with capricious expressions of anger. When employed, aversive stimulation (punishment) should be used in such a manner as to avoid excessive handling of or struggling with the youngster which sometimes leads to inadvertent bruising or other minor injury. Baserates are obtained and data are carefully collected to observe the effects of the aversive stimulus upon the dangerous behavior.

Lovaas described the verbal imitation program as consisting of four operations:

1   The reinforcement of all vocal sounds emitted by the child in an effort to increase the rate and repertoire of verbal responses. In this early period of training, the child is reinforced when a verbal response occurs at least once in 5 seconds and when the child attends to the teacher's mouth for at least half the time.

2   This step is basically an attempt to get vocal sounds under stimulus control, the stimulus being a sound or word spoken by the teacher. The given word or sound is emitted by the adult about every 10 seconds and the child must make some vocal sound in response within 6 seconds to obtain reinforcement. In this case, it is not necessary that the child replicate the teacher's sound. Any sound will do if it follows the teacher's within 6 seconds. This sets the stage for more accurate imitation to follow.

3   At this point, more accurate imitation is required for reinforcement. The teacher makes selected vocal sounds and may help the child imitate by manually shaping the child's lips. This is gradually faded out and the child must repeat the sound on his own. It is helpful if the words and sounds selected have a high degree of visibility. That is, the child must be able to repeat the sound by imitating the teacher's mouth movement.

4   This is a recycling of the prior step with a new vocal sound.

There are great initial variations both among the performances of the various children and within the performance of the individual child from session to session. It is clear, however, that this approach results in an acceleration of the rate of learning. While it takes a great deal of time and effort for the children to learn to imitate the first few words, later words seem to come more quickly and more easily. It may very well be that successful imitation sometimes involves a reinforcing component in itself.

The second part of the overall program, the development of proper language usage or what Lovaas called an "appropriate context for speech," was divided into three parts: (1) correct verbalization about common objects including the child himself and his activities, (2) the use of abstract terms including positional phrases (e.g., on top of, inside of, etc.), relative terms, and pronouns, and (3) spontaneous and conversational speech. Various interesting techniques were employed to achieve these more complex aspects of language development, some of which may even prove to be of value in the average early elementary classroom.

In teaching the children to correctly identify common objects and activities, positive reinforcement (sometimes the object itself) was at first contingent upon correct labeling or description. Discrimination tasks were then introduced requiring the child to correctly identify the given object from among various others.

Fading was employed, enabling the child to take over more and more of the identification task himself with the teacher gradually moving into the background. All of the children developed labeling ability via these procedures.

The use of abstract terms was accomplished by setting up various positional discrimination tasks utilizing a wide range of familiar objects. The children might be asked to put the block "on top of" the paper or "in" the box. Prompts were used extensively and were systematically faded out. The child was also introduced to pronouns and had to describe what "he" was doing and what was meant by "I." Combinations of pronouns and prepositions were presented in building up the child's use of complex terminology. Attempts to teach the children time concepts so that they could accurately describe past events and make future projections were also undertaken with some of the children.

Getting the children who were only beginning to grasp linguistic concepts to use their newly acquired speech skills in a spontaneous manner was an especially difficult challenge. First the children were required to make verbal demands, often very simple ones such as "milk," before they were permitted the desired object or activity. Through prompting, the teacher introduced more complex sentences and then faded out gradually. A particularly innovative approach the teachers employed was one in which the children gave orders to the teachers (e.g., clap your hands). The teachers' compliance with such requests apparently had strong reinforcing qualities for the children. The children were encouraged to ask questions. In certain cases, rather than answering, the teacher responded that he did not know and directed the child elsewhere to obtain an answer.

Though time consuming and costly, Lovaas' project has clearly shown that even totally mute children can enter the world of verbal communication. As the techniques become refined it may be possible to fully train parents or other lay persons to employ similar methods of language training in the school or community. Furthermore, when one considers the effectiveness of behavior modification in teaching even severely deviant mute children to speak, it becomes clear that the systematic use of these concepts offers vast promise for the less seriously speech deficient child in the classroom.

LANGUAGE TRAINING IN THE CLASSROOM

Johnston (1968) has applied procedures similar to those described by Lovaas to a small classroom situation. Reporting on the case of a 7-year-old boy bearing the double burden of the labels "mentally retarded" and "emotionally disturbed," she described how she successfully employed behavior modification principles to increase his speech and concurrently reduce his tendency to mimic. While imitation is an important step in language development, excessive imitation prevented this child from breaking away from prompts. In other words, he becomes so dependent upon his teacher's cues that he was unable to speak spontaneously. Consistency is of great importance when working with such children, and the teachers carefully planned their daily activities. Basically, three kinds of procedures were employed:

1 Teaching the child to expand the complexity of his requests (technically called "mands"). As the child learned to imitate one-word requests (e.g., "water") and to use them, the teachers began to require more complex sentences (e.g., "I want water.").

2 A similar procedure was used to get the child to answer questions. Prompting and gradual fading out of answers were employed. The teachers required increasingly lengthy answers to questions.

3 Perseverative language usage (i.e., continuous repetition of a word or phrase) was extinguished and the child was reinforced for new non-repetitive speech. Rather than responding to the child's perserverative speech, the teachers provided a cue for another vocal response which they then reinforced. Furthermore, a program was instituted geared to reduce the automatic, mechanical quality of the boy's speech. Attempts were made to ensure that the answers required of the child were appropriate to the particular kind of question. Thus the phrase, "say yes," originally learned by the youngster by imitating the teacher, was corrected to simply "yes."

Various additional classroom procedures were used. Teachers asked the child to convey messages among them or among the children and conversations were heavily reinforced. The results of this comprehensive program of speech and language development were striking. From an initial baserate of about 42 verbalizations per 90 minute class period, his output increased to 180. This increase occurred in about three academic quarters or approximately eight months. Furthermore, while more than 50% of his early verbalizations consisted of imitations, his speech at the end of the project was only about 30% echoic. About 85% of his answers were correct and he often corrected himself without further prompting by the teachers. This reflects a marked overall improvement in the quality of the youngster's speech and provides still further support for the efficacy of the approach employed.

SELF-DESTRUCTIVE AND DISRUPTIVE BEHAVIOR

In addition to their narrow range of behavior and language deficiencies, children who have been labeled autistic, psychotic, or emotionally disturbed may show a wide variety of bizarre behaviors. Though these behaviors are typically learned in a home or institutional setting, they are often so unusual as to attract immediate notice. In fact, the behavior patterns are so removed from the responses of normal children that an underlying emotional disturbance is usually inferred. It is argued that this extremely odd behavior must occur because the child is experiencing an intensely disquieting emotional or psychological state. The only way to really change the behavior, according to this view, is to somehow modify the inferred disturbing state. While there have been literally hundreds and perhaps thousands of suggestions as to how to accomplish this, a frequent recommendation is a high dosage of tender, loving care (TLC). The prescription may further require that the TLC be administered by a person who has established a particularly warm relationship with the child, one who has tendencies toward nurturance and affection. This overly simplified approach quite clearly reflects a failure to recognize the major advances that have occurred in our knowledge of human behavior, advances which form the basis of objective teaching and behavior modification. For example, displays of affection immediately following deviant behavior will tend to strengthen that behavior.

On the other hand, however, it is naive to suggest, as some overly zealous advocates of pure "environmentalism" have asserted, that human life itself consists of little more than conditioned responses. Certainly there exists a whole range of personal experience not amenable to objective analysis. It is essential to recognize that what you see is to a great extent influenced by what you look for, and merely because one has not found a way to observe private inner processes does not negate their influence on us. Like practically anything else, there are infinite ways of explaining human existence, and it is unlikely that any single point of view has cornered the market on wisdom. What is crucial, however, is that one recognize the degree to which his own concepts of human life influence his actions toward others.

In the case of the severely deviant child, a mentalistic viewpoint, such as the one above, fails to take into account the immediate availability of a scientifically sound approach to reduce human suffering by modifying grossly disruptive behavior. On the other hand, to assume that by modifying behavior you have fully understood the human being that is behaving (environmentalistic approach) is erroneous. While systematic modification can surely improve behavior patterns which otherwise result in direct harm to the child and those around him, this just sets the stage for the development of more adaptive learning, self-direction and, hopefully, personal happiness.

A group of researchers shed considerable light on the analysis and modification of severely deviant behavior in the autistic child (Wolf et al., 1964). Since the subject, a 3½-year-old hospitalized autistic boy named Dicky, had a wide range of deviant behavior, a comprehensive examination of the study provides a picture of the modification of a variety of autistic behaviors through reinforcement procedures.

Dicky's parents consulted the researchers after their son underwent cataract surgery which necessitated the wearing of glasses if the child's eyesight was to be preserved. The child, previously diagnosed as retarded, brain damaged, and psychotic, had severe temper tantrums during which he showed self-destructive behavior including face slapping, head banging, and face scratching. Furthermore, he refused to go to sleep at bedtime, seriously interfering with household routine and keeping his parents up late at night. His severely deviant behavior clearly interfered with his wearing glasses, and behavior modification was implemented to overcome this problem. The psychologists recommended that the child re-enter the hospital before treatment was undertaken so that they could obtain better control of his total environment and thereby intercept the inadvertent reinforcement of this deviant behavior which was occurring at home.

The research team initiated careful record-keeping procedures to obtain baserates before modification began. Temper tantrums, responsible for so much of Dicky's self-destructive behavior, received highest priority for immediate treatment. The researchers employed a time-out from positive reinforcement procedure. The child was placed in his room and the door was closed following any episode of tantrum behavior. When the tantrum ceased, the door was opened. Dicky's parents participated in the treatment procedure, visiting the hospital and trying out the new methods under the supervision of the researchers. As the treatment progressed, the child was very gradually reintroduced into his home but his parents maintained the temper tantrum program and other procedures with continued assistance. After about 10 weeks the severe self-destructive behavior was substantially reduced, setting the stage for the modification of other deviant behaviors and for Dicky to learn to wear the required glasses.

They approached bedtime problems in a manner similar to that of the temper tantrum. The child was bathed, fondled, and put to bed. If he got out of bed, he was returned to his room and the door was closed. If he returned to bed, the door was left open. This simple procedure resulted in a rapid decrease in bedtime problems as Dicky began to go to sleep when told after only about 6 days.

The major challenge to the researchers was to try to get Dicky to wear glasses to prevent visual deterioration. This required a systematic shaping procedure using candy and food reinforcement. At first, the child was reinforced (with a "click" followed by tangible reinforcement) for merely touching or handling one of the several eyeglass frames left around the room. There was apparent difficulty with this procedure. The candy and other goodies were not sufficiently reinforcing to Dicky to promote motivation. Consequently, Dicky's breakfast and later other meals were given as reinforcement for responses approximating the wearing of glasses. This stronger reinforcement made the difference as glass wearing was gradually shaped and maintained. Activities such as walks, play, snacks, and car rides were also made contingent upon eyeglass wearing, an application of the Premack principle. When Dicky began throwing his eyeglasses, a relatively infrequent but expensive act, a time-out procedure was again employed with good success.

The success of these techniques encouraged the experimenters to use additional behavior modification approaches to increase speech and language ability and to eliminate disruptive eating behavior. As a result, much of Dicky's food throwing and food snatching was eliminated and imitative skills and verbal labeling were improved. The researchers note, with a well-deserved feeling of accomplishment, "According to a report from the mother six months after the child's return home, Dicky continues to wear his glasses, does not have tantrums, has no sleeping problems, is becoming increasingly verbal, and is a new source of joy to the members of his family."

Self-destructive behavior is far more common among children than is generally recognized. It is a significant problem in institutions for the emotionally disturbed and retarded, and creates profound anxiety in both parents and institutional staff. Lovaas et al. (1965) presented substantial further evidence that self-destructive behavior is a learned response pattern. Presenting carefully recorded data, he showed that such behavior tends to be reduced when a competing response (musical activity) is reinforced, but returns when the competing response is no longer reinforced. Much self-destructive behavior is maintained by social reinforcement. Attempts to talk the child out of hitting himself, since they involve attention, tend to increase the very behavior they are supposed to reduce. This is supported by Lovaas' findings in regard to a 9-year-old "schizophrenic" girl. The girl was told, on the advice of traditionally minded professionals, "I do not think you are bad," whenever she hit herself. Rather than a drop in such behavior, her self-hitting rate climbed dramatically.

Self-destructive behavior may be learned not only as an attention-getting device but as a means of escaping or avoiding unpleasant requests as well. Since it strikes instant fear into the hearts of most adults, such behavior has a high probability of obtaining reinforcement for the child and, as most learned responses, it increases. Furthermore, there is a tendency for the behavior to progress to more violent forms of self-abuse as a still stronger bid for reinforcement (attention or escape). It is highly advisable to ignore self-destructive behavior which is weak (and which, of course, is not associated with physical problems such as inner ear infections). This, unfortunately, is not usually the way such behavior is treated by inadequately trained institutional staff or anxious parents, and the behavior may gradually move from mild face slapping to self-mutilation. Lovaas has administered mild shock to the skin surface as an aversive outcome for dangerous, self-destructive behavior with marked success, suppressing it for almost a year. Suppression occurred within just moments after using carefully programmed shock. This is far better than to restrain a child in bed for months or years, adding to an already deteriorated condition. While it is clearly best to prevent the development of self-destructive behavior in children through education of parents and institutional staff, it is also clear that failure to use established and humane methods of treatment is questionable from a humanitarian viewpoint.

NEGATIVISM

Those who have had extensive experience working with children with severely deviant behavior will frequently point out a general tendency among many such children to be extremely resistive to requests. So intense is the resistance that at times it becomes quite clear that the child is not merely failing to comply, but is doing precisely the opposite of that which is desired of him. This pattern, while present in the behavior of normal children to a mild degree, may be so severe as to seriously handicap learning in a wide range of areas. Such behavior is regarded as negativistic, hence the term *negativism* to describe the pattern clinically. Negativism might be regarded as somewhat the opposite of imitation as discussed earlier. Of course, this is an imperfect contrast in that frequently the child who is negativistic does not merely fail to imitate a model, but also opposes direct verbal instruction such as "sit down." Furthermore, echolalia, in which the child tends to mimic words and phrases, may itself be regarded as a kind of negativism when it impedes language development and resists modification. In traditional terms, negativism has been regarded as an aggressive withdrawal or as a primitive form of regression. From a behavior modification standpoint, however, it would appear more fruitful to examine negativism as a pattern of responding which is somehow maintained through reinforcement. Certainly the child who refuses to comply with parental requests, for example, may sometimes avoid having to obey them at all. This is particularly the case when one or both parents are inconsistent in their requests, sometimes demanding compliance and sometimes not. It may also occur in situations in which a parent, usually the mother, is very anxious in regard to her child's behavior and yields when the child opposes her requests through crying or other behavior. Perhaps the most familiar form of negativism is the severe temper tantrum of the young child who may actually hold his breath (turning blue) to assert his refusal to comply.

In institutional settings for retarded or emotionally disturbed children, negativism may serve the additional function of obtaining adult attention. The exceedingly poor ratio of staff to children which exists in many institutional settings results in various bids for the attention of the staff by the children, and usually the behavior which is most bizarre or which causes the greatest amount of difficulty for the staff tends to get reinforced. Thus, children (or even adults) may refuse to feed themselves though they are perfectly capable of doing so or may resist every request made of them by the staff because of the extra attention they receive as a consequence. Similar behavior, usually far less severe, is not uncommon in the classroom, and task avoidance or attention are usually found to be the reinforcers. Negativism, however, is a broad general tendency to refuse to comply with most requests, or actually to do the opposite of what is requested. It should not be confused with the child's refusal to comply with a few specific requests, which, after all, might well be a legitimate act of asserting personal integrity.

Some interesting research in this area was done by Cowan, Hoddinott, and Wright (1965) who investigated negativism among 12 autistic children. The children, all of whom had severe speech and language deficits, were requested to do various discrimination problems such as picking tiles with particular shapes and colors. The experimental design permitted the researchers to determine whether or not a child actually knew the solution so that they could differentiate failure to comply based on inability from failure to comply rooted in negativism. Of the 12 children, 10 not only selected tiles incorrectly, but did so below the level of accuracy which could be expected by chance alone. In other words, these children were not merely guessing, but were purposely selecting tiles which were contrary to adult instructions. The researchers employed reinforcement techniques, using popcorn as a reinforcer, in an effort to counteract resistance. Interestingly, in this way they managed to modify the pattern in some of the children, getting them to comply with directions. There were six "compliers" and six "resisters" at the end of the project, with some indications that the compliers might be functioning at a somewhat higher level in terms of general ability. The researchers argued that there was no question of perceptual distortion or thought process disturbance affecting the low number of correct responses by the children. Furthermore, the children would often pick a large number of single tiles without choosing the one requested. For example, "When asked for red, they did choose squares; that is, they did not avoid a particular shape *unless this shape had been requested by E.*" This high degree of negativism may partly explain the great difficulty in language development of autistic children. Since the learning of a language is so dependent on early imitative skills, children who refuse to imitate (or who refuse to do anything but imitate) can hardly be expected to develop a large verbal repertoire. The importance of imitation in language is further demonstrated in the work of Baer et al. (1967), and in the work of Lovaas, among others cited earlier. You will recall that imitation was an early step in these programs and provided the verbal content which was systematically extended into usable language. In addition to their rather clear isolation of negativism as a salient factor in many cases of autism, the researchers' finding that negativism is itself amenable to behavior modification is certainly worthy of further exploration. A positive approach to negativism via direct reinforcement may prove to be an important step in improving the general development of the resistive autistic child.

Still further light was shed on the applicability of reinforcement to the negativistic child by the work of Davison (1964). The child, a pretty 9-year-old autistic girl, was very talkative though basically incapable of appropriate use of language. Furthermore, she was extremely disobedient, refusing to comply with most adult requests. The purpose of the study was to devise a reinforcement program to overcome some of the youngster's basic social deficiencies. Since the child spent about 25 hours per week in a day care center, Davison decided to work with her in that setting. He employed the services of two graduate students and spent approximately four 1-hour sessions training them in reinforcement principles and application. Despite this meager training, the student-therapists were quite successful. At first, the child obeyed only one of the 17 requests made by therapist A and two of the 17 made by therapist B. Adequate controls for familiarity of the requests were made. The therapists embarked on a reinforcement program using M & M candies as the reinforcer for a correct response to a request. Though their combined time with the child was only 8 hours per week for 7 weeks, the therapists managed not only to substantially increase the girl's rate of compliance with their requests but also affected overall changes in behavior. The child began to respond according to instruction even without tangible reinforcement, and by the end of the study there was evidence that this increased rate of compliance was beginning to generalize to other adults. For example, another graduate student obtained a score of 14 compliances out of 17 requests from the youngster, a far cry from the child's earlier record.

A fundamental goal in behavioral change is to promote self direction by enabling an individual to gain greater control over his own behavior. While external controls may be initially predominant, they should be gradually superceded by methods which encourage self direction. Kaufman and O'Leary (1972) have reaffirmed the effectiveness of permitting youngsters to evaluate their own behavior and to reinforce themselves accordingly. Sixteen students in a psychiatric hospital school were assigned to either a "cost" class, in which earned tokens could be taken back as a penalty for disruptive behavior, or a reward class involving no such penalties. The classes were concerned with reading. While the researchers, as expected, found the token system effective both in reducing undesirable behavior and in increasing reading skills, they found no significant differences in respect to improvement between the reward class and the class which received both contingent reward and contingent penalty costs. But of particular importance was the finding that a self-evaluative method, one in which students rated their own behavior and received reinforcements on the basis of their own ratings instead of their teacher's, was also effective in producing positive change in behavior.

PARENTS AS BEHAVIOR THERAPISTS

In recent years public information about objective teaching and behavior modification has resulted in growing parental interest in these methods. In response to this, educators and psychologists are beginning to provide parents with specific methods of improving their children's severely deviant behavior at home, avoiding institutionalization and prolonged periods of expensive therapy.

This approach offers enormous promise as it allows parents to deal with their children far more consistently. Furthermore, it enables them to overcome problems of severely deviant behavior which can best be handled in the home, thus overcoming the necessity to reintroduce the child into the home after his behavior has been modified in a specialized setting. But behavior problems need not be severe to benefit from these methods. On the contrary, parents are finding it an effective means of dealing with even rather minor behavior difficulties such as getting children to accept their bedtimes without a fuss or motivating them to complete their household chores or their homework.

All of this is not to suggest that the teacher must take full responsibility for helping parents set up reinforcement programs at home. Frequently there are other factors besides the deviant behavior which can best be handled by other professionals. However, the teacher may certainly provide parents with broad guidelines in dealing with behavior problems and, with additional training in behavior modification, the teacher may develop sufficient expertise to give specific instructions to parents regarding the handling of their child's behavior at home. It is well to remember that certain deviant behavior is stimulus specific; that is, it may occur in only one environment but not in others. The child who shows deviant behavior at home may not display this pattern in school and vice versa. Very severely deviant behavior, however, appears less likely to fit into this category, though even it occasionally does. Generally, the teacher must know the limitations of his competency in behavior modification so that he does not allow his enthusiasm to overwhelm his judgment. Consultation is highly advisable before embarking on a course of parental instruction.

Since much severely deviant behavior which occurs at home is a direct outcome of inadvertent reinforcement by parents, it is necessary to instruct the parents in the selective withholding of reinforcement to produce extinction of the deviant behavior. Of course, they should be taught to record data properly and, perhaps most important, they should be tutored in the proper dispensing of reinforcement. Parents of children with deviant behavior usually fail to reinforce desirable behavior at a high enough frequency and, consequently, it remains weak. This appears to be a function of their attending only to the undesirable portions of their children's behavior repertoire. Attention in the form of verbal praise and other affectional interactions is heavily sought by most children (and adults), but it may be necessary to employ tangible items or activities as well when these are insufficient as reinforcers.

Allen & Harris (1966) reported the successful elimination of excessive self-scratching by a 5-year-old girl by training the mother in behavior modification. The youngster had displayed such behavior for about a year and her face, neck, and other areas of her body were covered with an assortment of sores and lacerations. The researchers worked closely with the mother, providing her with general information about reinforcement and specific instruction as to how to apply it to the child. Reinforcement was systematically held back by the mother whenever the child displayed self-scratching, but was heavily dispensed for desirable behavior. The researchers also instructed the mother to thin the schedule of reinforcement, moving from continuous to intermittent reinforcement as the project progressed. In just 6 weeks the child's body and face were free of sores. A follow-up indicated that 4 months later the behavior did not recur.

While here we have been dealing largely with individual cases of deviant behavior, it frequently occurs that an entire pattern of severely deviant interactions exists in the relationships among children in a family. This is not merely the typical arguing and occasional fighting that goes on among brothers and/or sisters, but is far more disruptive and in some cases dangerous. Deviant sibling interactions are amenable to modification through the systematic rearrangement of the home environment by the parents. O'Leary and his colleagues (1967) described such an approach. The problem involved the relationship between a 6-year-old boy and his 3-year-old brother. These children were continually engaged in serious fighting and various kinds of destructive behavior. Not depending solely on parental reports, the researchers entered the home, observed the deviant behavior in its natural setting, assessed the resources, and set up a plan by which the mother gradually assumed the role of behavior therapist. A token reinforcement system was actually established in the home with the therapist, and later the mother, reinforcing for desirable, nondeviant behavior but using time-out (removal) for assaultive or destructive behavior. This procedure not only proved effective in improving the boys' behavior at home, but also had a positive effect in other situations. Both parent and teacher reports indicated marked improvement in overall behavior.

One of the more difficult problems sometimes encountered in setting up a behavior modification program in a home environment is that of inconsistency. It will be recalled from Risley's Juniper Gardens Project described earlier that parents tend to interact differently with their own children than with others, even in highly structured learning situations. In other words, the parent-child relationship is so influenced by subjective, emotional factors that it is often extremely difficult to get parents to view their children's behavior in the objective manner required for modification. This makes it necessary for the behavior modification expert to observe interactional patterns quite closely and provide very explicit instructions to the parents as to just what to do under a variety of conditions. Very careful recordings must be made to ensure that subjective reporting of behavior change is kept to a minimum. At first, the expert may spend a considerable amount of time in the home, gradually fading out and letting the parents take over. However, it is advisable that he do frequent "quality control" checks, making sure that the parents are reinforcing appropriate behavior heavily enough and extinguishing severely deviant behavior in the prescribed way.

Another hazard encountered in setting up a modification program in the home is that of enlisting the aid of older brothers and sisters. Since teenagers may not be home much, they may not be too affected by the deviant behavior of their younger sibs. They often find themselves unable to deal with their younger brothers or sisters according to instruction and may give in to them, unwittingly reinforcing the very behavior the parents may be trying to eliminate. This inconsistency is not easily overcome and unless it appears feasible to obtain the cooperation of the entire household, behavior modification may fail due to lack of proper implementation.

To deal with the problem of inconsistency, there have been increasing efforts to set up small family apartments within hospitals or other behavior modification facilities in which the parents and children can be observed over a short period of time (perhaps a week) by a professional staff. Interaction patterns are assessed and parents may be given an opportunity to view films or videotapes of themselves and their children. Finally, a program is established with very specific behavioral goals and the parents are carefully tutored in carrying out reinforcement and other procedures. The constant feedback enables the parents to pick up the subtle errors in their own reactions that have led to the development of the deviant behavior in the first place. The techniques learned in the special apartment setting are then hopefully generalized into the home.

More recently, a number of projects have been undertaken which involve the more intensive training of parents in behavior change methods. Ora and Wagner (1970) have reported such a program designed to teach parents to deal more effectively with "oppositional" children who show destructive and hard to control patterns of behavior. In this approach, parents of children four and below were observed by behavioral specialists as they interacted with their children in 20 minute sessions of structured play. Then, once these parents developed some expertise in improving their own children's behavior, they themselves trained other parents of oppositional children in behavior change methods. This pyramid approach deserves considerable attention as it greatly increases the number of behavioral "experts" available to work with parents and children in the community.

Herbert (1970) reported on a relatively simple technique which enabled two mothers to modify the undesirable behavior of their children. In addition to regular training, these mothers were also instructed to both observe and record the number of appropriate responses by their children to which they attended. This focus on the parents' own behavior promoted both improved parental responding and a reduction in their children's inappropriate behavior.

Hall et al. (1972) describe a number of cases in which parents have successfully altered their children's troublesome behaviors. Four of the researchers were the parents themselves, reporting on their work with their own children. In one case a couple significantly reduced their 4-year-old's rate of whining and shouting by simply turning around and ignoring his behavior completely whenever he displayed the undesirable pattern. As a result, the undesirable behavior declined from a daily rate of 10.2 whines or shouts to a rate of 2.8. Perhaps the most interesting of these studies was one involving a 5-year-old girl who was an extremely slow dresser, requiring an average of 3 hours, 10 minutes. The parents made T.V. watching contingent upon completion of dressing within a half hour. This resulted in a dramatically reduced average dressing time of only 23 minutes. A reversal, that is a return to the usual noncontingent situation, produced an immediate increase in dressing time to 1 hour, 26 minutes. Fortunately, returning to the T.V. contingency resulted in a rapid decrease again, this time the dressing averaging 20 minutes. What is most striking in these cases is that they required little parental training and very simple procedures. With consistent use objective behavioral techniques produce rapid progress in improving undesirable behavior which has frequently defied more costly and extensive psychotherapeutic measures.

PREVENTION OF DEVIANT BEHAVIOR

Whether in school or at home, it is far easier to prevent the development of severely deviant behavior than to attempt to eliminate it once it is occurring at a high rate. Much deviant behavior may be considered "designed" to disrupt the environment and is maintained by such reinforcers as adult attention, escape or avoidance of unpleasant assignments and, in some cases, the sheer chaos which is created. Once the pattern is well established, it impinges upon the entire environment, the family or the class as a whole, and many more factors have to be taken into consideration at this point than would have been necessary if the behavior had been dealt with earlier. Self-destructive behavior is an example of this. When a child first begins to slap himself or bang his head, usually as part of a tantrum, simple extinction through complete withdrawal of attention can be fairly safely implemented because the child does not actually do much damage at these early stages. Usually, such an early pattern can be eliminated in just a few sessions of nonreinforcement. Once the pattern has progressed, however, and the severity of the damage during even one episode is so great as to necessitate immediate intervention for the safety of the child, more serious treatment may be required. This, of course, is true in other such patterns as well. Early modification is far superior to later efforts simply because as the behavior becomes more heavily and/or more inconsistently reinforced (intermittent), it is difficult to extinguish and treatment may involve several family members or classmates as well.

Another problem that must be dealt with once a deviant pattern becomes well established is that of expectation. The adults and children who come in contact with a youngster displaying severely deviant behavior begin to think of him in terms of his behavior. Thus, he may be regarded as the "screamer," the "head banger," or the "trouble maker" rather than as a total human being with some deviant behavior. Once a child gets a reputation such as this, adults and children tend to approach him with the expectation that he will behave in his usual way. In effect, they set him up to behave in just this way through subtle cues, prompts, and other setting events. As an example, one of the authors was told by a child's special teacher, while in the child's presence, to be careful because the youngster was a "biter." "He is now," responded the author. We must remember, after all, that it is often highly reinforcing to have one's expectations about another confirmed and when a child behaves according to one's expectations, this behavior may be maintained to some degree through the subtle expressions of pleasure by those around him. By preventing the development of such a pattern of deviant behavior, the parent or teacher helps the child avoid a bad reputation which might influence the behavior of others toward him in an adverse way.

Negative expectations directed toward the child with deviant behavior also reduce the probability of his receiving reinforcement for behavior which is clearly desirable. Since the undesirable behavior frequently turns the teacher or family away, positive reinforcement, especially social reinforcement, becomes extremely scarce. An imbalance of reinforcement begins to develop in which undesirable behavior is inadvertently reinforced while desirable behavior, so vital to the welfare of the child, goes virtually unnoticed. As this process continues, the child develops higher rates of undesirable behavior and, in an effort to secure more reinforcement, may extend his repertoire of undesirable behavior through learning. This leaves him with few, and sometimes no avenues of desirable behavior for which to obtain positive reinforcement. When the deviant behavior pattern has progressed to this point, only a comprehensive broadening of the child's repertoire of desirable behavior by means of modeling and contingent reinforcement may prove effective.

The prevention of severely deviant behavior, then, requires a consistent approach at home and in school. By defining or setting reasonable limits, as described in Chapter 5—that is, by establishing clearly what is acceptable and what is not—you can immediately view the child's behavior much more objectively. If the parent or teacher is unsure as to what a child should be permitted to do and what he shouldn't, is there any doubt that the youngster will be uncertain too? Desirable behavior must also be defined according to the child's present response capability and the behavioral goals which he is required to meet. Such behavior must be shaped, or modeled so that it will be easy for the child to behave appropriately at first. Only gradually should increasing behavioral requirements be set for the child, and each step should progress naturally as the step before is mastered by the youngster. Insufficient reinforcement is often the problem at these early periods in learning, and the parent or teacher should be generous in reinforcing desirable behavior, especially if it is weak, new, and competing with predominantly undesirable patterns.

Basically, the prevention of undesirable behavior is best accomplished by the encouragement of desirable behavior. By establishing an environment in which high rates of adaptive learning can occur through modeling and reinforcement, the chance of undesirable behavior developing is automatically reduced. However, extinction of undesirable responses at the earliest possible moment can prevent endless heartaches later. Good overall planning in the home and classroom which develops from a personal sense of ethics and a real concern for children as people raises the quality of learning and the quality of life for any child.

SUMMARY

The same procedures which have been so effective in improving classroom behavior are also being used with increasing frequency in the treatment of more severe behavior disturbances at home and in institutions for emotionally disturbed children. While we propose more objectively sound and more precise methods of promoting desirable behavior, we feel that such an approach need not be overly mechanistic. Severely deviant behavior can be changed within a humanistic framework. A systematic analysis of the environment in which a child lives, especially the pattern of reinforced responses, sheds valuable light on the development and treatment of severely deviant behavior.

Using the concept of childhood autism as a general framework, we examined severely deviant behavior within three basic categories: (1) range of behavior, (2) gross language deficiency, and (3) self-destructive behavior.

An increasing number of projects have been reported recently which apply objective teaching and behavior modification techniques to the autistic child. The narrow range of behavior which characterizes such children has been extended through the innovative use of desirable objects and machines which dispense reinforcers. Several projects report highly successful use of reinforcement in increasing the imitative responses which are prerequisite for language development. Self-instituted reinforcement, based on a student's own assessment and reinforcement of his behavior, has been effective in improving behavior and fostering greater self-direction. Programming has successfully handled increasingly complex speech and language training. Generally, abstract use of language is built upon simple use of words to identify objects. Self-destructive and disruptive behaviors are readily amenable to modification through a well planned reinforcement program. Often these behaviors are learned through inadvertent social reinforcement such as parental attention, and modification requires a redistribution of reinforcement in favor of desirable behavior. Negativism frequently contributes to other deviant behavior but evidence indicates that it, too, can be reduced.

There is now a rapidly increasing trend toward training parents to be behavior therapists for their own children. We cited recent studies which strongly support the effectiveness of parents acting as behavior specialists for their children. The professional instructs the parents and gradually fades out of the picture as the parents learn to reinforce desirable behavior and extinguish undesirable behavior properly. The teacher may provide general guidelines in behavior modification to parents or, with additional training and use of consultation, may actually supervise a parent who is acting as a behavior therapist for his child.

In some cases parents who develop enough expertise can train other parents to employ behavior change methods with their children.

Finally, we discussed the prevention of deviant behavior through good planning, consistency, and real regard for children as people.

REFERENCES

Allen, K. E., & Harris, F. R. Elimination of a child's excessive scratching by training the mother in reinforcement procedures. *Behavior Research and Therapy*, 1966, **4**, 79.

Cowan, P. H., Hoddinott, B. A., & Wright, B. A. Compliance and resistance in the conditioning of autistic children. *Child Development*, 1965, **36**, 912–923.

Davison, C. G. A social learning therapy programme with an autistic child. *Behavior Research and Therapy*, 1964, **2**, 149–159.

Ferster, C., & DeMyer, M. A method for the experimental analysis of the behavior of autistic children. *American Journal of Orthopsychiatry*, 1962, **32**, 89–98.

Hall, R. V., Axelrod, S., Tyler, L., Grief, E., Jones, F. C., & Robertson, R. Modification of behavior problems in the home with a parent as observer and experimenter. *Journal of Applied Behavior Analysis*, 1972, **5**, (1), 53–66.

Hawkins, R. P. Behavior therapy in the home: Amelioration of problem parent-child relations with a parent in a therapeutic role. *Journal of Experimental Child Psychology*, 1967, **4**, 99–107.

Herbert, E. W. *Parent programs—bringing it all back home*. Paper presented at the annual meeting of the American Psychological Association, Miami Beach, Florida, 1970.

Johnston, M. K. Echolalia and automatism in speech: a case report. In *Operant procedures in remedial speech and language training* (H. H. Sloane, Jr. and B. MacAulay, eds.). Boston: Houghton Mifflin Co., 1968.

Kanner, L. Autistic disturbances of affective contact. *Nervous Child*, 1943, **2**, 217–250.

Kaufman, K. A., & O'Leary, K. D. Reward cost and self-evaluation procedures for disruptive adolescents in a psychiatric hospital school. *Journal of Applied Behavior Analysis*, 1972, **5** (3), 293–309.

Lovaas, OI. A program for the establishment of speech in psychotic children. In *Childhood autism* (J. W. King, ed.). Oxford: Pergamon Press, 1966.

Lovass, I., Gilbert, F., Gold, V., & Kassorla, I. Experimental studies in childhood schizophrenia 1: Analysis of self-destructive behavior. *Journal of Experimental Child Psychology*, 1965, **2**, 67–84.

O'Leary, K. D. Modification of a deviant sibling interaction pattern in the home. *Behavior Research and Therapy*, 1967, **5**, 113–120.

Ora, J. P., & Wagner, L. I. Contextual variables in oppositional child training. Paper presented at the annual meeting of the Southeastern Psychological Association, Louisville, Kentucky, 1970.

Russo, S. Adaptations in behavioral therapy with children. *Behavior Research and Therapy*, 1964, **2**, 43–47.

Wahler, G., Winkel, G. H., Peterson, R. F., & Morrison, D. C. Mothers as behavior therapists for their own children. *Behavior Research and Therapy*, 1965, **3**, 113–124.

Wolf, M. M., Risley, T., & Mees, H. Application of operant conditioning procedures to the behavior problems of an autistic child. *Behavior Research and Therapy*, 1964, **1**, 305–312.

SUGGESTED READINGS

Bernal, M. E. Training parents in child management. In *Behavioral modification of learning disabilities* (R. H. Bradfield, ed.). San Rafael, California: Academic Therapy Publications, 1971.

Holland, C. J. An interview guide for behavioural counseling with parents. *Behavior Therapy*, 1970, **1**, 70–79.

Kroth, R. L., Whelan, R. J., & Stables, J. M. Teacher application of behavior principles in home and classroom environments. *Focus on Exceptional Children*, 1970, **1**, 1–12.

Mira, M. Results of a behavior modification training program for parents and teachers. *Behaviour Research and Therapy*, 1970, **8**, 309–311.

Straughan, J. H. Treatment with child and mother in the playroom. *Behavior Research and Therapy*, 1964, **2**, 37–41.

Walder, L. O., Cohen, S. I., Breiter, D. W., Warman, F. C., Orme-Johnson, D., & Pavey, S. Parents as change agents. In *Handbook of community psychology* (S. E. Colann and C. Eisdorfer, eds.). New York: Appleton-Century-Crofts, 1971.

Williams, C. D. The elimination of tantrum behavior by extinction procedures. *Journal of Abnormal and Social Psychology*, 1959, **59**, 269.

Common Classroom Problems

The following is a listing of problems and questions which frequently concern teachers. The column at the right is an aid in locating some of the key sections or pages[1] of the book in which the problem is discussed.

[1]The pages given frequently indicate the point at which the discussion begins.

Glossary

Autism: A pattern of behavior, especially in young children, characterized by a narrow range of behavior, gross language deficiencies and bizarre responding.

Backward chaining: A programmed sequence of responses requiring the learner to complete the very last step in a complex task first, then the next-to-last step, and so on until he can complete the entire task.

Baserate: The initial rate of behavior before modification, often called the "baseline."

Behaviorism: The branch of psychology dealing with the objective study of behavior, especially as a function of conditioning.

Contingent: Dependent upon another event. In objective teaching reinforcement is contingent upon the student's behavior.

Contract: A mutual agreement between student and teacher establishing the specific behavior required by the student if he is to obtain reinforcement.

Cue: That aspect of the environment that provides an individual with information about what he is to do if he is to receive reinforcement.

Echolalia: Excessive mimicking of another's words or phrases.

Environmentalism: The tendency by some behaviorists to dismiss the richness of personal experience in their zeal for environmental control.

Error rate: The objectively recorded rate at which errors are emitted.

Extinction: The diminution of a response through nonreinforcement.

Fading: Gradual removal of cues and prompts in the learning of responses.

Imitation (generalized): A repeated imitative response which does not lead to external reinforcement but which has been learned in conjunction with other imitative responses that have been reinforced.

Interfering behavior: Undesirable behavior which occurs at a high rate, impeding desirable behavior.

Mentalism: The rejection of scientific analysis of behavior in favor of various hypothetical constructs of mind.

Model: A person whose behavior is imitated by others.

Modeling: The systematic presentation of behavior (usually by the teacher) which the student is required to imitate for the purpose of learning.

Negativism: A pattern of behavior in which a child (or adult) not only refuses to comply but actually does the opposite of whatever is requested.

Operant conditioning: The conditioning of behavior through reinforcement.

Premack principle: Behavior that occurs at a high frequency can be used as a reinforcer for behavior which occurs at a low frequency.

Programming

　Branching: Adjustment in the level of difficulty of the material as a function of error rate, or the use of a multiple choice format so the student, upon making a wrong response, can learn why he was wrong and try again.

　Frame: The material presented at each step in a program.

　Linear: The arrangement of the materials to be learned in a step-by-step progression.

Prompt: A very specific cue often used to speed up the rate of emission of learned responses.

Punishment: The presentation of an aversive stimulus which decreases the rate of the response which it follows.

Random: Occurring by chance.

Reinforcement

　Positive: Presentation of a stimulus (event or object) which increases the rate of the response which it follows.

　Negative: Removal of an aversive stimulus which increases the rate of response.

Reinforcement schedules

　Fixed interval (FI): Reinforcement is given for the first response following a fixed period of time.

　Fixed ratio (FR): Reinforcement is contingent on a specific number of responses.

　Variable interval (VI): Reinforcement is given for the first response following a systematically varied period of time.

　Variable ratio (VR): The number of responses required for reinforcement is systematically varied.

Reinforcer: An event or object (stimulus) which strengthens the response which it follows. Primary reinforcers are basically edible objects. Secondary reinforcers may be social (e.g., praise) or tangible (e.g., tokens).

Response: A single completed action which has a clearly observable beginning and end.

Setting event: "An antecedent environmental change that alters the probability of a large number of subsequent responses." (Peterson & Whitehurst, 1971).

Stimulus: In Pavlovian conditioning, sensory input which elicits a response ($S \rightarrow R$). In operant conditioning and objective teaching, there are two basic kinds: a discriminative stimulus (see "cue" above) and an outcome stimulus such as a reinforcer or a punisher. In this latter sense, the stimulus does not necessarily set off a response but is an environmental event which affects the individual, even if it follows a response.

Time out: The momentary isolation of a disruptive student.

Token: An object (e.g., a poker chip) which acquires value because of its cash-in properties. Tokens serve essentially the same purpose as money.

Variables

> *Dependent variable:* The condition in an experiment which varies as a function of the independent variable or treatment. It is the outcome variable.
>
> *Independent variable:* The condition which is manipulated by the experimenter. In objective teaching this is teacher behavior or environmental modification which is intended to influence student behavior.

Author Index

Davison, C. G., 218, *226*
Day, R. G., 198, *205*
deBaca, P. C., *62*
Deci, E. L., 48, *61*
DeMyer, M., 208, *226*
Devine, J. V., *62*
Dill, N., 110, *116*
Doubros, S. G., *80*
Dulaney, S., 75, *80*
Dunham, R. M., 182, *190*
Dunlap, A., 188, *189*

E

Edlund, C. V., 183, *189*
Esveldt, K. C., *95*
Everett, P. M., *80*

F

Ferster, C., 208, *226*
Fine, M. J., *80*
Friesen, W., 24, *176*

G

Gall, R. S., 47, *61*
Gallimore, R., 73, *79*, 196, *206*
Galloway, C., *190*
Galloway, K. C., *190*
Ganzer, V. J., 88, *94*, 193, *206*
Garcia, E., 17, *24*
Gilbert, F., 210, 216, *226*
Gilmore, L., 123, *127*
Glaser, R., *116*
Glynn, E. L., *62*, 123, *127*
Gold, V., 210, 216, *226*
Goodall, K., *10*, 203, *205*
Gotts, E. E., 110, *116*
Grief, E., 222, *226*
Grieger, R.. M., *175*
Griffiths, M. T., *62*
Griffiths, W. J., *62*
Gruen, G., 195, *206*
Guess, D., 17, *24*
Gump, P. V., 65, *79*

H

Hall, R. V., 52, *61*, 70, 78, *79*, 188, *189*, 222, *226*

Haring, N., 32, *34*, 51, *61*, *80*, *95*, *116*, 184, 185, *190*
Harris, F. R., 104, *116*, 179, *189*, 220, *226*
Harsh, R. J., 26, 27, *34*
Hart, B. M., 70, *79*, 104, *116*
Hartley, C., *62*
Hawkins, R. P., 77, *80*, *226*
Hayden, A., 51, *61*
Henke, L. B., 179, *189*
Herbert, E. W., 222, *226*
Hoddinott, B. A., 218, *226*
Holland, C. J., *227*
Holz, W., 160, 161, *175*
Homme, L., *62*, 124, *127*, 188, *190*, 196, *206*
Houser, J. E., 75, *80*

J

Jackson, D., 52, *61*, 70, *79*
Jacobson, J. M., 199, *206*
Jacobson, L., 180, *190*
Jensen, A. R., 201, 202, *206*
Johnson, S. M., *175*
Johnston, M. K., 212, *226*
Jones, F. C., 222, *226*
Jones, R., *190*

K

Kanfer, F., 14, *24*, 122, *127*
Kanner, L., 208, *226*
Kassorla, I., 210, 216, *226*
Kaufman, K. A., 219, *226*
Kidder, J., *116*
Kidder, J. D., 187, *189*
Kinzelmann, H., *116*
Kirby, F. D., *176*
Kounin, J. S., 65, *79*
Krasner, L., *10*, 161, *175*
Krishnamurti, J., *10*, 120, *127*
Kroth, R. L., *227*
Kunzlemann, H. P., 32, *34*, *80*, 185, *190*

L

Levinsky, D., 187, *190*
Lindsley, O. R., 18, *24*
Linke, K., *176*
Linley, J., *176*
Lindsley, O. R., *34*

Subject Index

U

V